EXPLORING MYSTICISM

A Methodological Essay

EXPLORING MYSTICISM

A Methodological Essay

FRITS STAAL

MOTILAL BANARSIDASS PUBLISHERS
PRIVATE LIMITED • DELHI

First Indian Edition : Delhi, 2013
Earlier published by University of California Press

ISBN: 978-81-208-3556-6

MOTILAL BANARSIDASS
41 U.A. Bungalow Road, Jawahar Nagar, Delhi 110 007
8 Mahalaxmi Chamber, 22 Bhulabhai Desai Road, Mumbai 400 026
203 Royapettah High Road, Mylapore, Chennai 600 004
236, 9th Main III Block, Jayanagar, Bengaluru 560 011
Sanas Plaza, 1302 Baji Rao Road, Pune 411 002
8 Camac Street, Kolkata 700 017
Ashok Rajpath, Patna 800 004
Chowk, Varanasi 221 001

Printed in India

By RP Jain at NAB Printing Unit,
A-44, Naraina, Phase-I, New Delhi 110 028
and Published by JP Jain for
Motilal Banarsidass Publishers (P) Ltd, 40-41 U.A.
Bungalow Road, Jawahar Nagar, Delhi 110 007

Contents

Description of Illustrations

King Jayavarman VII in meditation (frontispiece). The reign of Jayavarman VII (1181–1218 A.D.) marks an increase of Buddhist influence in the Khmer empire of Cambodia. Inscriptions of that period stress Buddhist virtues such as charity, nonviolence and compassion toward the entire world. The Ta Prohm inscription of Jayavarman VII relates to the establishment of a great institution of learning, providing board and lodging for 439 professors and 970 scholars studying with them (see Staal 1970c). Jayavarman VII adapted the traditional cult of divine kingship to his Buddhist faith, and many statues portray him as the bodhisattva Lokeśvara. As the Bayon style, which is typical of his reign, develops, the sculptures, which often represent the king in meditation, increasingly seem to portray a real person (see Coedès 1967, 108–109).—Khmer, sandstone, Museum Phnom Penh.

Śrī yantra or śrī cakra (on title page). This is an object for meditation. It may be built from a variety of materials, engraved on a metal plate, drawn on a piece of paper or on the floor in front of the *yogin*. It is constructed from triangles, some with the base toward him (*vahni* "fire"), the others with the base away from him (*śakti* "power"). The former are connected with male deities like Śiva, the latter with female deities like Pārvatī. The nine triangles, which together form 43 small triangles, are surrounded by eight lotus petals, then sixteen lotus petals, circles, and a pattern of straight lines (called *bhūpura*). The construction of the *yantra* starts in the middle: the sides of the small triangles are meticulously produced. Such diagrams are also constructed at the outset of many rituals. Meditation on the *yantra* starts from the outer lines and proceeds to the center. (See Zimmer 1926, plate 36; Pott 1966, figure 7; Avalon 1948, and other works of Avalon or Sir John Woodroffe.)

PLATES
Following page 74

1. VIṢṆU ASLEEP BETWEEN CREATIONS. At the end of each world period, when society has fully disintegrated, all traces of truth and goodness are lost, and sages and saints are no longer found, the creator Viṣṇu reabsorbs the universe. First Viṣṇu becomes the sun and his scorching rays turn the world into dust. Then, as fire, he burns the earth. Finally, as rain, he floods the earth, which dissolves into the cosmic ocean together with the sun, the moon and the stars. In that ocean Viṣṇu sleeps, alone and unperceived, until through meditation he manifests a new creation (see Zimmer 1946, pp. 35–53).—Khmer, limestone, early twelfth century (Rijksmuseum, Amsterdam).

2. THE FORCE OF TAPAS: DESCENT OF THE GANGES. At a time of excessive drought and widespread famine, when there was not enough water even to perform the ancestral rites, the royal sage Bhagīratha attempts to move the Gods into releasing the river Ganges which flows in heaven. For a thousand years he performs ascetic exercises and builds up ascetic energy (*tapas*), keeping his arms constantly raised and frying himself sitting under the midday sun and between four fires. Impressed by his *tapas*, God Brahmā appears and hears his request. But Brahmā opines that the release of the Ganges would cause such ferocious downpours of water, that the earth would be split. Only Śiva is strong enough to withstand such force. So Bhagīratha goes to the Himalayas and engages upon a second round of *tapas*, standing on one foot with his arms raised and living on water and air. At last Śiva responds and grants his request: the waters come pouring down. With his head Śiva catches the mighty stream and causes the water to meander through the labyrinth of his long matted hair. Thus the river Ganges descends from the Himalayas (see Zimmer 1946, pp. 109–121).—The large relief at Māmallapuram near Madras (Pallava, early seventh century A.D.) depicts these events (though another interpretation is possible: Krishnaswami Aiyangar 1917). At the bottom, Bhagīratha does penance at Gokarṇa; on the right a pig, beneath the tusk, imitates him. Above, he intensifies his *tapas* until Śiva appears with his retinue of forest dwarfs. Through the vertical cleft the Ganges pours down, its presence marked by serpentine water goddesses.—Photograph by Robert Gardner, Cambridge.

3. ŚIVA, THE DIVINE YOGIN. Śiva as wandering ascetic (*bhikṣāṭanamūrti*), a drum in his right upper hand and a begging bowl, made from a human skull, in his left lower hand. His headgear and the matted hair of the ascetic are adorned with a skull, a cobra, a crescent moon, and are studded with the flowers of the hallucinogenic Dātura plant. His

third eye clearly visible, he wears a male and a female earring, and another cobra around his waist. A young deer tries to reach the fingers of his lower right hand.—Early Chola bronze, from 1048 A.D., Tiruveṅgādu, Tanjore District, South India (now in the Madras Government Museum; a different photograph in Sivaramamurti 1963, plate 87).

4. Śiva's dance of destruction *(gajasaṃhāramūrti).* When evil assumes the shape of a wild elephant, Śiva compels the dangerous monster to dance, and goes on until his victim falls dead. He flays him, and with the two uppermost hands of his eight arms, stretches the skin. The next two hands carry an elephant's hook and a noose. The next pair a drum and the elephant's tusk. The lower hands carry the trident and an alms bowl made of a skull, Śiva's attributes as a wandering ascetic.—Recent South Indian bronze from a private collection.

5. Śiva, the divine preceptor *(vyākhyāna-dakṣiṇāmūrti).* Śiva as *guru* is called *dakṣiṇāmūrti* because he faces south (*dakṣiṇā*). He faces south since the traditional teachings come from the north. His images occur on the southern outer walls of the four gateways (*gopura*) of each of the great South Indian temples. There are three forms: *jñāna-dakṣiṇāmūrti, yoga-dakṣiṇāmūrti* and *vyākhyāna-dakṣiṇāmūrti.* In the form depicted here Śiva expounds a commentary (*vyākhyāna*) and holds a book in his left hand, while he expounds knowledge with his right. The rear right hand holds a rosary, with a snake curling above it; the left hand holds fire. Behind him stands a stylized tree. The audience consists of a bull and several bearded sages. Under his foot lies the dwarf demon "forgetfulness," which is also trampled by Śiva as Naṭarāja "king of the dance."—Stone sculpture from the eastern gateway of the Chidambaram temple, late Chola (photograph by J. C. Harle, also published in Harle 1963, plate 109).

6. Karman: Ritual activity in a Vedic sacrifice. While *karman* has come to denote any activity, it referred originally to Vedic ritual. These Vedic rituals originated in their present form more than two and a half thousand years ago; they are still being performed, albeit rarely and in a few inaccessible places. Here South Indian brahmans perform such a ceremony in Tanjore District, Madras State. The Yajurveda priest in the foreground makes an oblation into the fire. The priest behind him chants the Sāmaveda with folded hands.—From a collection of photographs presented to the author by one of the participating priests.

7. Prapatti: Surrender to God. The philosopher Rāmānuja (born A.D. 1018), founder of the philosophic system *Viśiṣṭādvaita* ("non-dualism of the qualified absolute") which stresses loving devotion and surrender to a personal God. This is the traditional representation of

Rāmānuja, as a brahman with a sacred thread, with Viṣṇu's symbols on his forehead, the staff of a wandering ascetic (*saṃnyāsin*) and his hands folded in devotion.—Recent South Indian bronze from a private collection.

8. PRAJÑĀ: SPIRITUAL WISDOM. The Buddhist mystical notion of *prajñā* corresponds to a large extent to the notion of *jñāna* found in the Upaniṣads and the Vedānta. The Buddha is here portrayed with the traditional protruberance on his head (*uṣṇīṣa*) and with a circle of white hair (*ūrṇā*) between the eyebrows. These have been related to the turbans and jewels, respectively, found on earlier statues (Lamotte 1958, p. 739). In accordance with canonic texts, curls on the Buddha's head and the *ūrṇā* turn clockwise (*pradakṣiṇāvartakeśa*).—Buddha head from Plaosan, Central Java, ninth century A.D. (Rijksmuseum voor Volkenkunde, Leiden).

Following page 138

9. BHAKTI: LOVING DEVOTION (THE SAINT SUNDARAMŪRTI). Sundaramūrti (eighth century A.D.) was "born of poor Brahmin parents but his beauty as a child was such that he attracted the attention of the local chieftain Narasinga Munaiyadaraiyan who, with the consent of the parents, brought him up. When his marriage with a girl of his own caste was about to take place it was stopped by the mysterious intervention of Śiva who claimed him as his slave. A little later Sundara fell in love with two women, one a dancing girl of Tiruvālūr and the other a *śūdra* girl of Tiruvoṟṟiyūr. Their jealousies, it is said, could only be resolved by Śiva himself acting as a messenger to one of them. . . . Sundara is also credited with many miracles and the contemporary Chera ruler, Cheramān Perumāl, was his friend. They visited each other regularly and made their last journey to the abode of Śiva in Mount Kailāsa together, Sundara on a white elephant and Cheramān Perumāl on a horse. Sundara's devotion to Śiva was that of an intimate friend so that he was given the title *Tambirān-Tōḻan* ('Friend of God')" (Nilakanta Sastri 1955, p. 407).—Chola bronze, thirteenth century (collection James D. Baldwin, Fairview, Pennsylvania).

10a. HORNED DEITY WITH ANIMALS FROM HARAPPĀ. This famous Harappā seal, made of the soft stone called steatite and possibly 4,000 years old, represents a horned deity surrounded by animals. This personage, also depicted on two other seals, has buffalo horns and is adorned with bangles and what appear to be necklaces. Ithyphallic, cross-legged and possibly three-faced, he is here surrounded by a rhinoceros, a buffalo, an elephant and a tiger. Beneath his stool are two antelopes or goats, which have been compared to the deer in representations of the Buddha preaching his first sermon in the Deer-park at Banaras (Basham 1954, p. 23). Sir John Marshall called this God "Proto-Śiva"; Siva, after all, is sometimes called Paśupati "Lord of Beasts." The figure has often been considered a yogin, but without much justification.

10b. THE SIX CAKRAS IN KUṆḌALINĪ YOGA. The six *cakras* or nerve centers through which the kuṇḍalinī rises during yogic meditation, correspond to specific regions of the spinal column (here drawn on the left) and to specific deities and their consorts (here drawn on the right): *mūlādhāra* (between anus and genitals) to Gaṇapati, *svādhiṣṭhāna* (above genitals) to Brahmā, *maṇipūra* (around the navel) to Viṣṇu, *anāhata* (around the heart) to Rudra, *viśuddha* (around the throat) to Maheśvara, and *ājñā* (between the eyebrows) to Sadāśiva. The corresponding mantras are: Lang, Vang, Rang, Yang, Hang and Oṃ (cf. Pott 1966, which discusses also Buddhist parallels).—Ink and color on paper, Tanjore, nineteenth century (collection Ajit Mookerjee, now in the Tantra Museum, London; also reproduced in Rawson 1973, plate 55).

11a. YANTRA OR MAṆḌALA: AERIAL VIEW OF BOROBUDUR ON JAVA. The *yantra* diagrams or *maṇḍala* circles which are constructed for meditation and at the outset of many rituals, well known from Tibetan scrolls, also occur in the groundplans of many temples and religious monuments in the countries where Indian civilization has spread. The groundplan of Borobudur (Central Java, ninth century), here seen from the air, enables pilgrims to perform a circumambulatory meditation, starting from the outer terraces which depict scenes from the life of the Buddha and proceeding inward towards the Buddha statues inside the numerous circular stūpas.—Prusahaan National Aerial Survey, Jakarta; Fontein, Soekmono and Suleiman 1971, plate 8.

11b. RITUAL PREPARATION OF A MAṆḌALA. Many religious ceremonies begin with a consecration in the form of a *maṇḍala* prepared on the floor. Here a preparatory rite for a buffalo sacrifice is the drawing of a *maṇḍala* by Brahmins in the Himalayan village of Sirkanda, Garhwal District, Uttar Pradesh.—Photograph by G. D. Berreman, Berkeley; cf. Berreman 1972, p. 391.

12. MUHAMMAD'S HEAVENLY ASCENT. A verse of the Koran (17:1): "Glory to him who made his servant go from the mosque al-Ḥarām to the mosque al-Akṣā" refers to Muhammad's nocturnal trip from the Kaᶜba in Mecca to a mosque either in Jerusalem or in heaven. This journey (*isrā'*) is generally interpreted as a mystic ascent to heaven (*miᶜrāj*). The prophet, his face veiled to prevent the direct vision of God, is seated on Burāḳ, a mare with a woman's face, guided by Gabriel and surrounded by other angels. The mystical character of this journey

is corroborated by later traditions. One of these relates how Muhammad, after 70,000 conversations with God, returned to find his bed still warm and the water from a jug, kicked over when he hurriedly left, not yet fully spilt (Wensinck and Kramers 1941, pp. 227–228, 509–511).—Persian miniature painting, sixteenth century, from a manuscript of a work by the poet Nizāmī entitled *Makhzan al-asrār* "The treasury of mysteries" (Patris 1948, p. 51).

13. CHUANG TZU'S DREAM OF THE BUTTERFLY. "Once Chuang-tzu dreamed that he was a butterfly, a butterfly gaily fluttering (was he showing himself what it would please him to be?), and did not know that he was Chuang-tzu. Suddenly he awoke, and all at once he was Chuang-tzu. He does not know whether he is Chuang-tzu who dreamed that he was a butterfly or a butterfly dreaming that he is Chuang-tzu. Between Chuang-tzu and the butterfly certainly there was a dividing; this is all that is meant by the transformations of things" (from the second chapter of Chuang Tzu's work: Graham 1969, p. 159; see also Watson 1964, p. 45).—A painting by the Japanese artist Nakayama Kōyō (1717–1780) of the Nanga school (see Cahill 1972, pp. 11, 24). In a private collection, Japan.

14a. KALMU IN 1958 WITH HIS GOAT HERD. Kalmu, son of a blacksmith, in the Himalayan village of Sirkanda, Garhwal District, Uttar Pradesh. Kalma was then thirteen years old, a third-grade dropout from the village school, "uninterested in learning from his father his hereditary trade" and "not particularly interested in or challenged by life" (Berreman 1972, p. 381), but perchance photographed by Berreman (1972, plate 32). Note that according to Chadwick, because of "solitude and quiet," "a large proportion of seers have been drawn from the shepherd class all over Europe and Asia" (Chadwick 1942, p. 59). They are the precursors of the "wanderers" (*parivrājaka*) of the ascetic tradition.

14b. KALMU IN 1968 AS DEVATĀ (GOD) IN FRONT OF HIS TEMPLE. When Berreman visited Sirkanda again in 1968, Kalmu had become a mystic or shaman. At 18, he had been married to an attractive Kholi (weaver) girl of Taal village. Within two years, two children were born. "Then tragedy struck, in the form of an illness which afflicted all four members of the young family, and from which only Kalmu survived. Grief-stricken, he tried to immolate himself on his wife's funeral pyre but was prevented from doing so by bystanders. He brooded for some time thereafter, drifting aimlessly from place to place and spending considerable time in worship and meditation on other-worldly matters. Then one day, while meditating and worshipping in his father's house, and in the company of several other people, there was a sudden commotion in the semi-darkness, and a silver coin, a brass coin, and a small smooth, oblong stone (described as a "*bindī*" and regarded as a Shiva lingam) dropped from nowhere into a brass tray he had been holding. He then grasped a pumpkin from nearby, stood up, and as he held it over his head, an unseen being ate half of it before the onlookers' amazed eyes. Then Kalmu began to be 'played upon' or possessed by a supernatural being" (Berreman 1972, pp. 381–395; plate 33).

15. Hanumān, the Monkey God, in meditation. Hanumān (litt. "with the large jaws") as danced in Kathakali, the sacred dance-drama of Kerala. The artist is Ramankutty Nair. Hanumān belongs to a class of beings whose facial make-up is classified in the Kathakali tradition as "white beard." In addition to his white beard, he has a white *cuṭṭi,* made from rice paste and lime (nowadays sometimes paper), attached to his cheeks and reaching to the ends of his eyebrows. The face is painted in black, red, green, and white. The head-gear resembles a Chinese hat (cf. Bharatha Iyer 1955, p. 48; also plate XXI, figure 2). The hand gestures (*mudra*) for meditation displayed here are called *mudrākhya.* The scene comes from the beginning of the drama *Kalyāṇa Saugandhika*, derived from the epic *Mahābhārata.* The actors do not speak; the story is chanted in Malayalam verse. It relates how Bhīma, the great hero and Hanumān's brother, searched the jungle for a flower for his wife "like the sweetly perfumed one which a wind from Paradise had wafted to her feet." "Hanuman is seated in meditation in the forest, his eyes rolled up, his right arm raised, his left hand pointing inwards to his navel. The approach of Bhima penetrates his yogic trance; three times he stirs from it but returns again to his absorption. At last he starts into full consciousness and begins to reconstruct the scene and to picture the possible intruder" (de Zoete 1953, pp. 100–102; cf. plate 14d).—Photograph from Kerala Kalamandalam, Cheruthuruthy, through the American Society for Eastern Arts, Berkeley.

16. Jñāna: Śrī Ramaṇa Maharṣi at age 21. Śrī Ramaṇa Maharṣi (1879–1950), whose original name was Venkataraman, was born in a small village in South India and went to the sacred hill of Aruṇācala "the hill of dawn" when he was seventeen years old. At the foot of Aruṇācala lies Tiruvannamalai, a small town with a large Śiva temple and now with an *āśrama* called after Śrī Ramaṇa. Before he left, Venkataraman was struck by the fear of death: "I felt: 'Now I must die.' " He did not consider calling a doctor, a relative or even a stranger. "I felt that I had to solve this problem by myself, here and now, immediately." He enacted his own death: he stretched out stiff like a corpse,

closed his eyes and held his breath. Then he said to himself: "All right, this body is dead. But am I dead? Is this body 'I'?" Ever since, Śrī Ramaṇa Maharṣi asked only one question: "Who am I?" He spoke little and wrote less. His few teachings, mostly taken down by pupils and visitors, are expressed with rare intensity and directness. Though they hardly refer to the traditional scriptures, these teachings constitute the closest contemporary parallel to many passages in the Upaniṣads (see Zimmer 1944).—Photograph from Sri Ramanasramam, Tiruvannamalai

Preface

As the title indicates, this essay deals primarily with the exploration of mysticism, not with mysticism itself. It reviews the methods by which mysticism is generally studied, and it explores methods by which it can be studied more fruitfully. In doing so, it is also concerned with mysticism itself, but my results in this area are haphazard and probably premature. In the discussion of methods I have attempted to be more systematic and comprehensive, so that future explorations may have a firmer foundation.

In the study of mysticism, a common drawback is lack of experience. However, prejudices prove to be the most persistent obstacles, especially to professional students of religion, but also to those who approach it from other angles. I have tried to present a case for a rational point of departure, and have indicated in which directions one might go from there. This has taken me into mystic domains which are widely regarded as beyond the pale of critical investigation. I argue that they are not, though I do not wish to be understood as meaning that we should try to reduce them to common sense.

One conviction which underlies my approach is that the present situation in the study of man, and of mysticism as a special case, is profoundly unsatisfactory. I believe that the two main approaches have failed: the attempt to assimilate the humanities to what the natural sciences are imagined to be (as we find, for example, in positivism, in behaviorism, and often in the social sciences); and the attempt to exalt the humanities to something very special that requires a unique approach (as we find, for example, in existentialism, in phenomenology, and often in Western religion). Because of these failures, we understand surprisingly little of the human mind —one of the reasons, incidentally, that mankind is in such a bad shape.

Insofar as the study of mysticism is a study in the humanities, my essay may be regarded as an essay in the methodology of the humanities. But mystical experiences affect the body as well as the mind, and therefore pose problems which are within the purview of the natural sciences (e.g., physiology and neurology). Mystics, moreover, are members of society, even if they are drop-outs, so that the social sciences can also contribute to the investigation. This variety of approaches is not confined to the study of mysticism, but characterizes the study of man in many other respects. So much so that one wonders whether such departmentalization is anything more than mere division of labor.

To the extent that philosophy analyzes different approaches to the study of man, my essay may be called a philosophical essay. I have already indicated that it does not fit in the traditions of positivism, behaviorism, existentialism, or phenomenology. It is less antagonistic to what is sometimes vaguely referred to as analytical philosophy, but here some clarification is in order. Modern analytical philosophy is rightly criticized for confining the use of excellent tools to the miniature arena of conceptual analysis. The better practitioners try to extend this region. Since I believe that the mind is still largely unexplored, I am working further away, in a hazier area. This has its own charms, and its own pitfalls.

From a logical point of view I have used only light equipment, in particular a theorem that may be regarded as the foundation of rationalism: the theorem that self-contradictions are false. This principle does a lot of work in logic and a good job in philosophy, Eastern as well as Western. When applied to the study of mysticism its impact is devastating. Not that it affects mysticism itself. On the contrary, it shatters the glittering edifices constructed by scholars and research workers, only to show glimpses of their true object, which now begins to glow and reveal aspects of the mind we are not accustomed or trained to perceive or describe, let alone explain.

If I had to choose a single label to distinguish my approach from those that have been mentioned, I would settle for "rationalism." This term stresses, to say the least, the need for rational explanations. Past studies and fieldwork in India on several occasions, and my own experience of so-called altered states of consciousness may have added substance to what otherwise might have remained idle speculation. But my demonstrations do not depend on these experiences.

The use of Indian materials calls for a word of caution, as readers of a different background may come across unfamiliar terms and concepts. Such readers are advised to read, and occasionally return to, the section on "Sources of the Indian Tradition" at the end of the Introduction. There is also a Glossary that may be of assistance.

Though I have made use of existing translations, the translations from the Sanskrit, unless specified otherwise, are my own. Where the Sanskrit originals are lost and only their translations into Chinese are extant (as in the case of Mādhyamika texts), my quotations are based upon Lamotte's French translations.

In its present form, this essay has grown out of reflections, readings, conversations, discussions, and lectures, at Berkeley and elsewhere, on the significance and possible relevance of Indian and other forms of mysticism. Its main approach, as applied to the study of Yoga, has been the subject of lectures at Oslo, Copenhagen, Berkeley, San Diego, Tokyo, Koyasan, and Kyoto. In each of these places, excellent audiences have helped me to add precision to my thoughts and develop them further.

A great many students, colleagues, and other friends have commented, orally or in writing, on earlier drafts of this essay or on selected portions. I should like to thank here Arne Naess (Oslo); R. F. Beerling (Leiden); Edward Conze (Sherborne); Björn Merker (Connecticut); A. K. Ramanujan (Chicago); Willard Johnson (Long Beach); Gananath Obeyesekere (San Diego); Julian Boyd, Zev Brinner, Paul Bucharest, Frank Cioffii, George Dales, Bert Dreyfus, James Ebin, Peter Eggenberger, David Flattery, Robert Goldman, Warren Ilchman, Padmanabh Jaini, Lewis Lancaster, Leonard Nathan, Graham Parkes, Martin Schwarz, John Searle, Hans Sluga (Berkeley); Carl Bielefeldt, Minoru Hara, Sengaku Mayeda (Tokyo); Musashi Tachikawa (Nagoya); Yuichi Kajiyama and Yutaka Ojihara (Kyoto). I am particularly thankful to Muneo Tokunaga (Kyoto), who has checked the quotations and translations from the Sanskrit. I owe a special debt to Richard Olsen (Kathmandu) for extensive and constructive criticism of an earlier draft of the section on Buddhist irrationalism, which remains one of the most difficult parts of this essay.

I am grateful for much clerical assistance from a variety of sources. At Berkeley, my secretary, Ellen Moy, has typed almost three complete versions with such speed and accuracy that she appears endowed with some of the Yogic powers referred to in this essay. At Kyoto, Toru Yagi has retyped one tricky chapter. The staffs of the International House of Japan, Tokyo, the Centro Culturale Italo-Giapponese, Kyoto, and the Department of South and Southeast Asian Studies, Berkeley, have assisted me with typing as well as with typewriters.

In connection with the illustrations I have also received considerable help from friends, colleagues, art collectors, museum curators and others who know or have access to the materials here reproduced. I want to thank in particular: James D. Baldwin (Fairview, Pennsylvania), Gerald D. Berreman (Berkeley), Woodbridge Bingham (Berkeley), James Cahill (Berkeley), Joseph Campbell (New York), Lokesh Chandra (New Delhi), George Dales (Berkeley), Nalin and Marina Fernando (San Jose), Virginia Fields (New York), Jan Fontein (Boston), M. M. van der Gaag (New Delhi), Robert Gardner (Cambridge), J. C. Harle (Oxford), J. C. Heesterman (Leiden), J. E. van Lohuizen-de Leeuw (Amsterdam), T. M. P. Mahadevan (Madras), David Mandelbaum, Roger S. Monroe (Berkeley), Ajit Mookerjee (New Delhi), V. Raghavan (Madras), R. Ramachandran (Chidambaram), Howard Rogers (Berkeley), S. T. Satyamurti (Madras), Laurence Sickmann (Kansas City), C. Sivaramamurti (New Delhi), E. Gene Smith (New Delhi), Graeme van der Stoel (Berkeley), T. N. Venkataraman (Tiruvannamalai), F. Vos (Leiden), Joanna Williams (Berkeley), and my wife Saraswathy Panikker.

Acknowledgments are further due to John Murray (London) for permission to quote from A. C. Graham, *The Book of Lieh-Tzu*; to Basic Books, Inc. (New York), by arrangement with George Allen & Unwin, Ltd. and the Hogarth Press, Ltd., to quote from S. Freud, *The Interpretation of Dreams*, ed. J. Strachey; and to the following institutions which have helped me to find or permitted me to use illustrations: Archaeological Survey of India (New Delhi), Government Museum (Madras), Kerala Kalamandalam (Cheruthuruthy), Prusahaan Nasional Aerial Survey (Jakarta), Tantra Museum (London), Rijsksmuseum (Amsterdam), Rijksmuseum voor Volkenkunde (Leiden), Royal Netherlands Embassy (New

Delhi), Netherlands Consulate General (Bombay), Netherlands Consulate (Madras), McGraw-Hill Book Company (New York), Thames and Hudson, Ltd. (London), and the American Society for Eastern Arts (Berkeley).

Though I have benefited enormously from help, criticism, and advice, I remain obstinate on a few points. My approach combines the mystical with the rational. But in most circles where it is fashionable to be rational, it is not fashionable to be mystical; and in most circles where it is fashionable to be mystical, it is not fashionable to be rational. I am grateful to the publisher for his willingness to accept a work which is therefore at most only half fashionable. The text which is published here is a slightly revised and expanded version of a text published simultaneously as a Pelican book.

Western irrationalism, which is one of the dogs running through this essay, is not confined to knowledge alone. While some Westerners devote themselves to the study of Asian civilization, others are at the same time bent upon its massive destruction. As a reminder of this tragedy, and as a tribute to a great and fast-disappearing culture, I have selected an illustration from the Khmer art of Cambodia for the frontispiece and the jacket. It pictures King Jayavarman VII, plunged in meditation. I am grateful for the use of this photograph to Luc Ionesco-TOP, Paris.

FRITS STAAL

Kyoto and Berkeley

Preface to the Second Printing

When *Exploring Mysticism* was published first in English and subsequently in Swedish, Dutch, Italian, and Japanese translations, it was heralded as a plea for taking drugs, enriched by information on their uses as accessories in the mystical traditions of Asia—Vedic, Hindu, and Buddhist, as well as Taoist. As the subtitle of the American edition indicated, however, the book's aim had been different: this "essay on method" claimed that the student of mysticism should, among other things, engage in meditation and experiment with drugs just as any investigator of vision would freely use an innate ability to see together with any available technical improvements. To refuse to do so would be tantamount to adopting the attitude of the women of the imperial court who objected to the spectacles prescribed for the last emperor of China.

Exploring Mysticism is reprinted without change not because it was perfect but because it led to a new approach in the human sciences that I have tried to develop in subsequent publications. The methodology adopted in these later writings is the same as that of *Exploring Mysticism,* but it has become more explicit and is now, I like to think, better founded. I still maintain that the rationalism advocated in Part I of *Exploring Mysticism* is the only adequate foundation for any investigation in philosophy or science. The thesis that such rationalism is characteristically Asian has been more fully developed in another book, *Universals* (University of Chicago, 1988). This is relevant if we accept that the human sciences of the future will be not merely Western but universal.

Underlying Parts II and III of *Exploring Mysticism* is the assumption that there exists no basic difference between the human, physical, and social sciences. Arguments in support of this view are given in *Rules without Meaning* (Peter Lang, 1988) and are exemplified by its analysis of ritual and mantras, based upon *Agni: The Vedic Ritual of the Fire Altar* (Asian Humanities Press, 1983). *Rules without Meaning* also tries to explain and overcome the remarkable convergence, discussed in Chapters 3 and 4 of *Exploring Mysticism,* between behaviorism, Ludwig Wittgenstein's ordinary language philosophy, phenomenology, hermeneutics, and other recent developments, to which deconstructionist approaches may now be added. In all these respects, *Exploring Mysticism* paved the way.

Viewing this book from the vantage point of later research, I can now clarify with greater precision than would have been possible in 1975 what *Exploring Mysticism* did and did not achieve. At present, I cannot reread the book without feeling that its apparent meanderings are segments of a chain of reasoning that leads to a definite conclusion. To draw this conclusion, however, we have to look beyond the study of religion to anthropology, linguistics, and logic.

A useful point of departure is Emile Durkheim's study of religion in terms of beliefs and rites. Because of his positivistic bias, Durkheim ignored mystical experience although it is as intrinsic a part of what is traditionally regarded as religion as are beliefs and rites. Mystical experience, moreover, corresponds to ordinary experience (e.g., vision) just as belief and ritual correspond to thought and activity, respectively, as Durkheim had noted. Positivism is not the only feature of Durkheim's prejudice. Christianity is another, although it is much less obvious, at least to a Western reader. Durkheim assumed, without proof or investigation, that rites depend on beliefs. This assumption was questioned in *Exploring Mysticism*—which studied superstructures as interpretations—but only *Rules without Meaning* established beyond reasonable doubt that, if there is any priority at all, rites must come first. In Asia, where *orthopraxy* (insistence on right activity) takes the place of *orthodoxy* (insistence on correct doctrine), ritual precedes belief. The predominance of belief over ritual is confined to the monotheisms of the West: it is found in Judaism, widespread in Islam, and a special characteristic of Christianity.

Rules without Meaning tries to show that ritual and mantras are independent not only of belief, but of religion in general, of society, and even of language. This view takes up where Kautsa, an Indian ritualist discussed in the first chapter of *Exploring Mysticism,* left off more than two thousand years ago. The criticism of Durkheim's sociology of religion thereby turns into a general critique of anthropology. Here *Exploring Mysticism* paved the way by showing, in scattered sections, that mysticism is sui generis and independent. To what extent religious beliefs and in particular mythology are also independent of religious doctrines and society, but not of language, will be studied in *Kailasa: Center of Asia* (University of Chicago, 1989).

Many books succeed in showing what is wrong with others but are less successful in establishing a thesis of their own. This unflattering description applies to some extent to *Exploring Mysticism.* It is easy to agree with most of its negative comments contained in "How Not to Study Mysticism." But in "How to Study Mysticism" we are provided with a series of remarks and observations rather than a single comprehensive theory. What contribution does it make?

The main conclusion of *Exploring Mysticism,* hidden in contexts that are various and therefore sometimes misleading, is that the altered states of mystical consciousness constitute a return to a state of the human mind that existed before the emergence or origination of language. This theory explains many of the book's observations, for example, the observation that mysticism belongs to a Golden Age, that it goes "beyond language," and that reciting or meditating on mantras leads to mystical states. That mantras are not utterances of language but belong to a prelinguistic state of biological evolution is supported by a wealth of data discussed in *Rules without Meaning.* The reader of *Exploring Mysticism* is prepared for this startling conclusion by the demonstration that mysticism as a whole represents a prelinguistic state of development.

Several points remain with respect to which subsequent research has confirmed, disconfirmed, or otherwise moved beyond *Exploring Mysticism.* The most glaring error I committed—as did others during the 1970s—is that I paid serious attention to the best-selling books of Carlos Castaneda. Though Castaneda continues to have his defenders, not excluding serious anthropologists (e.g., Mary Douglas), it is now known that he was a perhaps genial imposter who took his data from anywhere and elaborated on them artfully. Castaneda's unreliability does not affect any thesis defended in *Exploring Mysticism,* but it shows that much of his evidence derived from data already known from humanity's mystical traditions.

On another specific issue progress can be reported. In *Exploring Mysticism,* I endorsed Gordon Wasson's brilliantly defended theory that the ancient Indian Soma was the same as the hallucinogenic mushroom *Amanita muscaria* because, as the Appendix put it, "there is at present no other theory which offers another candidate for the identity of the *Soma* with the same amount of seriousness and detail as does Wasson's theory." At present, there are two such rival theories, already published or about to be published: one due to David Flattery and Martin Schwartz, the other due to Harry Falk.

Exploring Mysticism may be looked upon, at least in part, as a study in Asian, particularly Indian, philosophy. In this area of research, several of its conclusions have been corroborated and others rearrived at independently. The December 1987 issue of *The Journal of Indian Philosophy* contains illustrations of both. In this issue Georg Feuerstein studies the concept of God in the Yoga system as a special kind of accessory assisting in the Yogic search for isolation. Frank J. Hoffman shows that *saddhā,* the Pali equivalent of the Sanskrit *śraddhā,* signifies confidence in the Buddha's teachings and is therefore different from the Christian notion of faith. Yu-Kwan Ng aligns himself with existing rational interpretations of Nāgārjuna by Robinson, Nakamura, and Kajiyama. Other recent publications by Kamaleshwar Bhattacharya and Musashi Tachikawa have gone even further in establishing the logical nature of Nāgārjuna's *Mādhyamaka* philosophy.

Regarding the understanding of mysticism itself, there have not been, to the best of my knowledge, any recent breakthroughs. Documentation increases, but the experimental and scientific approaches advocated in *Exploring Mysticism* need to cover much wider ground before we may expect any substantial deepening of our insight. Discovering that mysticism is prelinguistic sheds light on the place of language in biological evolution and on the Aristotelian definition of man as *ζῶον λόγον ἔχον*, freely interpreted by Martin Heidegger as "the being that possesses the capacity for language." That discovery does not answer such questions as whether mysticism is a divine gift or a pathological regression. Nor does it facilitate the technique of passing from one state of awareness to another that may be effected by meditation, mantras, or drugs, including the common sleeping pill. What does it do?

The abiding interest of the study of mysticism lies in its peculiar position within the human sciences. If mystic means prelinguistic, the return to what we are pleased to call our normal state of consciousness is an ontogenetic *principium individuationis* equivalent to the phylogenetic origin of the human as the animal that talks. Paradoxically, therefore, not getting high but coming down illuminates our human condition.

F. S. January 1988

Chuang Tzu and Hui Tzu were strolling along the dam of the Hao River when Chuang Tzu said, "See how the minnows come out and dart around where they please. That's what fish really enjoy."

Hui Tzu said, "You're not a fish—how do you know what fish enjoy?"

Chuang Tzu said, "You're not I, so how do you know I don't know what fish enjoy?"

Hui Tzu said, "I'm not you, so I certainly don't know what you know. On the other hand, you're certainly not a fish—so that still proves you don't know what fish enjoy."

Chuang Tzu said, "Let's go back to your original question. You asked me *how* I know what fish enjoy—so you already knew I knew it when you asked the question. I know it by standing here beside the Hao."

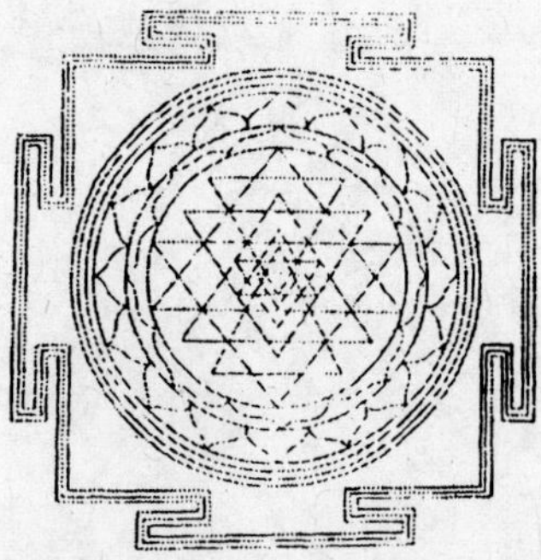

EXPLORING MYSTICISM

This volume is sponsored by the
CENTER FOR SOUTH AND SOUTHEAST ASIA STUDIES
University of California, Berkeley

Introduction

parokṣapriyā devāḥ • The gods love what is out of sight.
Śatapathabrāhmaṇa

φύσις κρύπτεσθαι φιλεῖ • Nature loves to hide itself.
Heraclitus

The chemical sense of a thing leaves no room for any other wider or deeper sense. It is the sense of the whole. It is the last word. That sense is never understood; that word is never uttered. Both go always beyond us. The ultimate sense is a mystery, which again and again reveals itself and yet remains always hidden.

This quotation is not taken from a chemistry textbook, not even from a manual of alchemy. It is the result of substituting the word "chemical" for the word "religious" in a translation of a passage in which the study of religion is characterized by G. van der Leeuw, the founder of the phenomenology of religion.[1]

In this essay I propose to analyze and criticize the notion that religious phenomena are ultimately mysterious, cannot be "rationally" studied—as if they could be studied irrationally—and therefore cannot be adequately understood or explained. This notion has kept the study of religion on a level with alchemy,[2] has prevented significant discoveries in that domain, and is, as I shall argue, noth-

1. "Le sens religieux de la chose est celui auquel ne peut succeder aucun autre sens plus large ou plus profond. C'est le sens du tout. C'est le dernier mot. Or, ce sens n'est jamais compris; ce mot n'est jamais prononcé. L'un et l'autre nous dépassent toujours. Le sens dernier est un mystère, qui se revèle toujours a nouveau et cependant reste toujours caché." Van der Leeuw, 1955, p. 663, quoted in Waardenburg, 1961, p. 318, n. 3.

2. I refer here to alchemy, old-fashionedly, as a prelude to chemistry (Read 1966), not as a process of psychological self-realization (Jung 1944) or as a spiritual art (Burckhardt 1971).

ing but the outcome of a bundle of prejudices. There are historical causes for these prejudices. I shall try to establish that an irrational approach is also unproductive when applied to mysticism. It does not follow from the thesis that this approach is unproductive in the realm of religion, for I hope to show that mysticism need not necessarily be regarded as a part of religion.

To claim that rational explanations can be given in these areas does not imply that reason is our only faculty, or even our best. I believe that we can do better things than study. But studying is a rational activity, and if we decide to engage in studying something then there is no point in the next moment saying that it cannot really be done because the domain is irrational. The objects of our inquiry need not, of course, be rational. Trees and rocks cannot be meaningfully called rational, but it does not follow that they are therefore unintelligible or cannot be studied rationally. There is no need to assume that there is a threshold beyond which things are unintelligible, unless we can show that there is such a threshold. It is not enough to point at certain things that are difficult to understand or that appear or happen to be unintelligible; we have to establish that they will always remain, or are in principle, unintelligible. As long as that is not done we have only two options as far as understanding is concerned: either to try to understand, or to admit that we do not wish to—a perfectly legitimate move.

The question arises whether we can ever show anything to be unintelligible. The answer is in the affirmative. First, there are certain metaphysical theories that can be said to be unintelligible in the sense that they try to point at what cannot be understood. Understanding requires duality, for example, if not multiplicity. Accordingly, in such philosophies as the Advaita Vedānta, according to which reality is nondual, reality cannot be understood. *Taittirīyopaniṣad* 2.4 (and elsewhere) refers to this situation paradoxically by saying that the absolute is "that from which all words return—having failed to reach it with the mind" (*yáto vāco nívartante áprāpya mánasā sahá*).

Unintelligibility can also be established in a less metaphysical realm. Theories which incorporate falsehoods as if they were true are unintelligible. This principle applies to inconsistent theories, or theories which incorporate a contradiction, as when two statements are both presented as true but one is the negation of the other, in the same respect. In logic, there are theories of which the inconsistency can be established by a precise proof; as soon as we show that two contradictory statements can be derived in a given theory, we have thereby shown that the theory is inconsistent. Since contradictions are false, theories which accept contradictions as true are unintelligible.

The earliest formulations of the principle of noncontradiction in Western philosophy are due to Aristotle. Examples are: "the same cannot belong and not belong to the same under the same respect"; "contradictory statements are not true together"; and "it is not possible to assert and deny the same" (Bocheński 1951, pp. 38–39). The added phrase "under the same respect" confines the principle to real contradictions, and excludes apparent ones. There is no contradiction, falsehood, or unintelligibility in a position which affirms that a statement holds in certain respects but not in others; for example, that people are in some respects ugly, in others, not. Only the affirmation of a statement and at the same time the negation of exactly that same statement is inconsistent and unintelligible. For example, it makes no sense to claim that people are always and in all respects ugly, and also that they are not always and in all respects ugly.

Mostly what people call contradictions are only apparent contradictions, in philosophical and religious contexts as well as in politics and in everyday life. A typical example is the position taken by the late Prime Minister of India, Jawaharlal Nehru, at a press conference in 1960, when the conflict between India and China was beginning to develop.

> . . . when Nehru in his letter to Chou En-lai had seemed to rule out a summit meeting, a journalist followed up the Prime Minister's remarks about his willingness to negotiate with the question: "Is it still the Indian stand that our frontiers are not negotiable?" "That is our stand," Nehru replied; "at the same time there is nothing that is not negotiable." He caught himself up on this paradox and explained: "It seems to be contradictory. But there is no question of negotiation or bargaining about the matter (of the boundaries). But it is a somewhat different matter in dealing with them in letters and talks. One cannot refuse to talk to another country" (Maxwell 1972, p. 141).

Even Marxist politicians, who adopt versions of Hegel's view, according to which the principle of noncontradiction is not valid, do not in fact accept that two statements which contradict each other can both be true in all respects. In a well-known essay, Mao Tse-tung distinguished two types of contradictions: contradictions "among the people," which are "nonantagonistic," and contradictions "between the enemy and ourselves," which are "antagonistic" (Schurmann 1968, p. 53). Neither type is inconsistent with the law of noncontradiction. On the contrary, it is clearly implied that two contradictory positions cannot both be true. For Mao maintains that such contradictions are to be "solved," whether by discussion or by war; if they are maintained as possible views, they can be maintained only temporarily. In fact, two such positions are only maintained or tolerated in the sense that the majority position is for the time being accepted: "the minority opinions must be preserved against the possibility that they may eventually prove correct" (*ibid.*, p. 55).

Armchair philosophers may produce an utterance, which seems to assert that two contradictory statements can both be true, but which in fact does not convey any meaning and is merely a sequence of sound. In reality, nobody can effectively talk or act without assuming, at least implicitly, the validity of the law of noncontradiction, which asserts that two contradictory statements cannot both be true in the same respect.

Even this mere sketch of an analysis has definite implications in the present context. If the search for rational explanations means that we should not rest content when we come across things that appear unintelligible, we should also not rest content with contradictions, when we find them, or assign them explanatory value. To accept as true contradictions which are false is to accept defeat. Though we can repeat it and make variations on it, we have no means of accepting as true a contradiction, that is, the simultaneous affirmation and denial of the same statement. The notion "understanding" implies that we are successful in understanding to the extent we have been successful in removing unintelligibility and contradictions. And so I shall reject as irrational, at any rate, any alleged account of mysticism which contains and rests content with contradictions. The reason is simply that such an "account" would not be an account at all.

To claim that understanding can be obtained, that rational explanations can be given in these areas, does not mean that any given rational explanation is final. Actually, such a claim would be irrational, for it would exclude in advance that a given explanation might be contradicted by future evidence or future insight. This state of affairs does not obtain anywhere in the realm of knowledge; in fact, rational inquiry implies that no theory is immune to revision.

When I advocate a rational approach to this kind of study, I do not imply that I believe that all the phenomena we deal with are simple, plain, or ordinary. On the contrary, in the domain of mysticism, many events appear to be not merely complex, subtle, and bewildering, but quite extraordinary. I do not claim to be in a position to provide adequate theories which explain all such events. My only concern is to show that the search for rational explanations and theories, here as elsewhere, is meaningful, fruitful, and necessary (Part I).

Many philosophers and students of religion or mysticism would not share van der Leeuw's conviction. Plato, Śaṅkara, or Spinoza, for example, would not agree with it. But the idea that religion cannot be rationally understood is at the background of most recent academic approaches to the study of religion and of mysticism, and consequently all such studies are inadequate and unsatisfactory. In order to support this statement, I shall review the four principal kinds of approach to the study of religion and of mysticism: dogmatic approaches (in chap. 5); philological and historical approaches (chap. 6); phenomenological and sociological approaches (chap. 7); and physiological and psychological approaches (chap. 8). I am aware that this division is abstract and to some extent arbitrary. Some of these categories overlap or contain further subdivisions, and some features and students of religion resist classification.

The inadequacy of these four approaches becomes evident as soon as we analyze, even superficially, the notion of rational explanation itself. A rational explanation of a phenomenon requires the formulation of a theory which purports to explain that phenomenon. In the case of mysticism, some mystics have themselves already formulated such a theory, or something like a theory (e.g., that mysticism is divinely inspired), in which case we should seek to determine whether that theory is correct or, at least, likely to be correct. But in order to do this, we must first ascertain what it is that we—and they—wish to explain. This question is basic, but has been strangely neglected. It forces itself to our attention once we realize that a person is called a mystic because he has had certain experiences—mystical experiences—and that these experiences purport to be experiences of something. The investigator of mysticism, first of all, has to determine whether these experiences are the experiencs which, in each case, they purport to be. The study of mysticism, then falls naturally into two parts, of which the first and more fundamental is the study of mystical experiences and their validity; the second is the study of the interpretations mystics and others have offered to account for these experiences.

The question of the validity of mystical experiences, which from a methodological point of view is of the most elementary sort, is concerned with the primary interpretation of the data. Such interpretations, when given, are subject to revision if and when necessary (in the light of new data, within the framework of better theories, etc.). If such preliminaries are not considered, mysticism cannot even be said to have been taken seriously, let alone have been made an object of rational inquiry. But when evaluated in these terms, the four approaches mentioned before collapse dramatically. The dogmatic approach is characterized by the fact that its adherents have already adopted an explanation before even considering the data. The advocates of the other three approaches simply disregard the question of whether the mystical experiences are valid. They treat them as uninterpreted or uninterpretable phenomena and relate them, sometimes in a very superficial manner, to each other and to other phenomena and other theories (Part II).

The study of mysticism, to the extent that it has so far been undertaken, resembles the sketching of a territory that is never visited and only described from hearsay. It has, accordingly, tended to deteriorate into enumerations and classifications of a variety of narratives, without any attempt at a critical evaluation. We have no means for distinguishing, for instance, a real mystic from a phony one, not only in practice but also in principle. Not surprisingly, the territory itself appears increasingly hazy and tends to disappear in a maze of research and scholarship. When pressed, the investigators produce generalities purporting to show that the territory cannot be visited by scholars. And as if to confirm these prejudices, some of the visitors who have gone there seem not to have returned or to have ceased to be investigators. I shall argue that this entire failure of the critical spirit of rational inquiry is due to misconceptions; that a rational, theoretical, as well as experimental, approach to this area is not only possible but necessary if mysticism is ever to become a serious subject of investigation; and that there are, in fact, indications that a theory of mysticism, based in part upon such critical investigations, is promising. In the last part of this essay, some such indications will be explored (Part III).

Underlying my approach to the study of mysticism is not only a certain methodology, but also some intuitive notions of what mysticism is like. These notions never become explicit, and I think this is as it should be. One might wish to be provided with a definition. But that would be premature. Since we do not have a theory of mysticism, we do not precisely know what mysticism is and we are not in a position to provide a definition. At this stage it is better to explore an area, use the term "mysticism" where it seems intuitively appropriate, and let the entire exploration serve for the time being as a rough and contextual outline of the concept.

While definitions come at the end, intuitions come at the beginning. Apart from having intuitive notions of what is and what is not mystical, I am also familiar with borderline cases, to which I do not quite know whether I should apply the term "mysticism" (e.g., the cases discussed by Deikman in the last section of chap. 8). Such intuitions, however, tend to change, are sometimes proved wrong, and are different for different people. For these and other reasons, I do not think it would be helpful to analyze my intuitions and extract a definition from them. Rather, let us explore the area of mysticism, even if it seems for the time being a hazy notion. Russell said, quite rightly, "Instinct, intuition, or insight is what first leads to the beliefs which subsequent reason confirms or confutes" (Russell 1953, p. 19). The present essay is concerned with methods of exploration. It may pave the way, but it does not arrive at a theory.

Though the three parts of this essay are concerned with the study of notions of mysticism that appear to be more or less universal and that are selected for analysis because of this apparent universality, the materials drawn upon also reflect particular interests and a particular area of knowledge. Because I am primarily familiar with Indian material, I quote Indian sources more often than others (e.g., Chinese, Japanese, Muslim, or Christian sources). Since the names of Indian sources are unfamiliar to readers of a different background, I have attached to this introduction a brief and simplified sketch of the main sources of the Indian tradition, mentioning some Sanskrit concepts and terms which will be relevant to our exploration.

Sources of the Indian Tradition

The history of Indian civilization may be divided into five periods: Harappā, Vedic, classical, medieval, and modern. I shall mostly be concerned with the second and the third periods. Our knowledge of the Harappā civilization (before 1500 B.C.) derives mainly from archeological evidence. The Vedic period begins with the introduction of Indo-European speech into the Indian subcontinent, some centuries before 1000 B.C., and ends around 500 B.C. The oldest documents are the four Vedas, the *Ṛgveda* (consisting of hymns), the *Yajurveda* (consisting of sacrificial formulas, poetry, and prose), the *Sāmaveda* (consisting of chants), and the *Atharvaveda* (consisting of hymns and magical spells). Each of the Vedas has several branches; for example, the *Taittirīya* is a branch of the *Kṛṣṇa* (Black) *Yajurveda*. To each of these branches were appended *Brāhmaṇas*, which interpret them; *Āraṇyakas*, which were transmitted in the seclusion of the forest (*araṇya*); and *Upaniṣads*, which purport to expound the inner meaning of the Veda. Although the earlier speculation centers on ritual activity, called *karman* (plate 6), which may lead to *svarga* "heaven," the Upaniṣads are often skeptical about the efficacy of *karman*, and concentrate on *jñāna* "knowledge, insight" (plate 16), which leads to, and in fact, constitutes *mokṣa* "liberation." Though the Upaniṣads are regarded as part of the Vedic heritage, some are ancient and venerable (e.g., the *Chāndogyopaniṣad* or the *Bṛhadāraṇyakopaniṣad*), many are later (e.g., the *Śvetāśvataropaniṣad*, the *Kaṭhopaniṣad*, the *Taittirīyopaniṣad*, or the *Māṇḍukyopaniṣad*), and the latest Upaniṣads were written during the medieval period.

During the early Upaniṣadic period many other traditions, some undoubtedly of non-Vedic origin, made their appearance. Increasing emphasis was laid on the notions of *saṃsāra* "transmigration" and of *saṃnyāsa* "renunciation" (by *saṃnyāsins* "renouncers") of *saṃsāra* and of the world of Vedic authority, ritual, and caste. Ascetics, hermits, and yogins of various persuasions began to propagate their ideas, already hinted at in the *Ṛgveda*, in a more systematic fashion. New sects were born, and even new religions (e.g., Jainism). The Buddha (sixth century B.C.) established a non-Vedic religion, which is related to some of the Upaniṣadic teachings. He referred to liberation as *nirvāṇa* "extinction." From now on we witness the development of two main traditions in Indian philosophy: the Hindu schools, allegedly based upon the Veda, but in fact often very different (the term "Hindu" itself being of foreign and much more recent origin); and the Buddhist schools.

The civilization of the classical period reflects the spread of Sanskrit culture, incorporating Vedic as well as indigenous elements, over most of the subcontinent. During this period the epics were composed. Though the *Bhagavad Gītā* was later called an Upaniṣad, it is part of the great *Mahābhārata* epic. In the *Gītā*, theistic elements are found which correspond to similar notions in some of the later Upaniṣads. This long poem attempts to arrive at a synthesis of *karman* and *jñāna* with *bhakti* "loving devotion" to the Hindu God Kṛṣṇa.

During the classical period the six Hindu schools of philosophy (*darśana*) were established. Each of these is based upon a fundamental text, called a *sūtra*, formulated in a brief and terse style. Among the six schools, I shall refer only occasionally to the logical system of the Nyāya. But three others are relevant in the following context.

(1) The Mīmāṃsā, based upon the *Mīmāṃsāsūtra* of Jaimini (perhaps second century B.C.), a philosophy of Vedic injunctions and ritual which goes back to the *Brāhmaṇas* and to *sūtra* texts dealing with ritual technicalities, which were appended to each of the branches of the Veda.

(2) The Vedānta, "end of the Veda," based upon the *Vedāntasūtra* or *Brahmasūtra* of Bādarāyaṇa (early in the Christian era), which goes back to the Upaniṣads and falls later into several competing schools: the Advaita Vedānta of Śaṅkara (A.D. 700–750?); the Viśiṣṭādvaita Vedānta of Rāmānuja (around A.D. 1100) (Plate 7); and the Dvaita Vedānta of Madhva (thirteenth century). The

latter two reflect the theistic trends of medieval Hinduism and develop theologies of the Hindu God Viṣṇu. The Advaita Vedānta teaches the nondual reality of the absolute *brahman*; the Viśiṣṭādvaita Vedānta teaches a nondualism of the qualified absolute; and the Dvaita Vedānta a pluralism.

(3) The Yoga, based upon the *Yogasūtra* of Patañjali (of uncertain date), which is fairly independent of the Vedic tradition and incorporates age-old practices of meditation and other spiritual and physical exercises. In most of these schools, later philosophers expound their theories, which may be quite original, in commentaries and subcommentaries upon the basic *sūtra* text. For example, Śaṅkara's main work is the *Vedānta-* (or *Brahma-*)*sūtra-bhāṣya* "the commentary (*bhāṣya*) upon the *Vedānta-* (or *Brahma-*)*sūtra*."

Alongside these so-called Vedic or "orthodox" Hindu systems, several schools developed within Buddhism, in the Theravāda (Doctrine of the Elders), early established in Ceylon, as well as in the Mahāyāna (Great Vehicle). The Theravāda doctrines are contained in the Pāli Canon, which transmits the Buddha's teaching in a Middle Indic language, Pāli, and not in the Sanskrit in which most philosophical works in India are composed. I shall quote the *Dhammapada*, the *Dīgha-nikāya*, and the *Majjhima-nikāya* from this canon. But soon philosophers began to clarify this tradition by writing in Sanskrit. One of the basic works in Buddhist philosophy is the *Abhidharmakośa* of Vasubandhu (fourth century A.D.?). Among the Mahāyāna schools, I shall refer to the Mādhyamika or Mādhyamaka (Middle School), of which the foremost representative was Nāgārjuna (around A.D. 200). Among his works are the *Mūlamadhyamakakārikā* and possibly the *Mahāprajñāpāramitāśāstra* "Treatise on the Perfection of Wisdom," of which the Sanskrit original has been lost but a Chinese translation has been preserved. Nāgārjuna's teachings emphasize the void (*śūnyatā*) and wisdom (*prajñā*; plate 8), which corresponds to the notion of *jñāna* in Advaita Vedānta.

After the first millenium A.D., Buddhism, a world religion, disappeared from Indian soil. By that time it had established itself in Southeast Asia, where it was sometimes combined with Hinduism, as also in Nepal; in central Asia, in Tibet, and in Bhutan; and in the Far East, where it often merged with local traditions (e.g., Taoism in China and Shintoism in Japan). The Hindu schools developed further in India and incorporated on the one hand more logic, on the other hand more theistic notions such as *bhakti*, taken, for instance, from Śaivism (the religion of the Hindu God Śiva; plate 9) or Vaiṣṇavism (the religion of Viṣṇu).

In present-day India, the Mīmāṃsā, though rarely studied as a system of philosophy, remains the implicit ideology of the orthodox. Forms of the Vedānta are widespread among the educated; the teachings have been transmitted through teacher-pupil lineages, for example (in the case of the Advaita Vedānta), in the traditional centers of the Śaṅkarācārya at Śṛṅgeri and of the Śaṅkarācārya at Kanchipuram. While the Yoga is no longer transmitted as a system of philosophy, yogic ideas and practices continue to be widespread.

In the present essay I shall mainly be concerned with material from the mystical traditions of the Vedānta, of Buddhism, and especially of the Yoga, the latter both as expounded systematically in Patañjali's *Yogasūtra* and as a tradition of practice. I shall refer only rarely to the later systematizations of the *rājayoga*, the *haṭhayoga*, or the *kuṇḍalinīyoga* (e.g., plate 10b). While there is ample justification to regard Buddhism as a reaction against Vedic orthodoxy, the same may be said of the Yoga and indeed of several features of the Vedānta itself. But such characterizations are of course merely negative and refer more to Vedic ritualism than to the Vedas themselves. T. R. V. Murti (1955) has characterized Indian philosophy by its contrast between the *ātmavāda* "doctrine of the self" of the Vedāntic and Hindu trends, and the *anātmavāda* "doctrine of the non-self" of the Buddhists. From a different perspective one might say that with the establishment of Buddhism as an organized religion, it is the Yoga which retained its independence and individualism to the largest extent, whereas both the Vedānta and Buddhism developed into orthodoxies. The Buddha had adopted Upaniṣadic notions, and the Advaita school of the Vedānta in turn incorporated notions from the Buddhist Mādhyamika school. One of the intermediaries was Gauḍapāda (fifth century A.D.?), whom some regard as an early Advaitin, others as a Buddhist. And so there is a similarity which is not at all fortuitous between Nāgārjuna the Buddhist and Śaṅkara the Vedāntin.

While the Yoga as a system of philosophy developed theories distinct from those of the Vedānta (though not always from Śaṅkara himself), and sometimes closer to Buddhist doctrines, the practice of Yoga has long been widespread and has been incorporated to some extent into the mystical practice of most of the schools. With regard to the later periods, the same might be said of Tantric practices, which in Hinduism are claimed to be based upon the Vedānta and in Buddhism upon the Mādhyamika but which are probably of earlier and more popular origin. Some may be traced back to the *Atharvaveda*.

The divisions and subdivisions of the Indian religious tradition manifest extraordinary variety and incorporate in some form or other almost all the features found in the other religions of mankind. However, in the context of the present essay, the similarities are even more striking, and we shall see how many different doctrines and practices are in fact closely related.

A Note on the Pronunciation of Sanskrit

The Sanskrit vowels, pronounced as in Italian or Japanese, are short (*a, i, u, ṛ, ḷ*) or long, that is, twice as long as the short ones (*ā, ī, ū, ṝ, e, o, ai, au*). The consonant *r* is pronounced as in Italian, while the vowels *ṛ* and *ḷ* contain a vocalic element similar to the short *i* in the third syllable of English *ability*. Among the consonants, there is a series of dentals (*t, th, d, dh, n, s*) and a corresponding series of retroflexes or cerebrals (*ṭ, ṭh, ḍ, ḍh, ṇ, ṣ*). The former are produced when the tip of the tongue touches the teeth (as in French), the latter when the tongue is bent backward and touches the palate (the English pronunciation of *t, d, n*, and *s* is more or less in between). In the Sanskrit *s* and *ṣ*, the tongue points in the same respective directions, but the breath passes over it. The palatals are pronounced when the tongue touches the front of the palate: *c* as in English *chair*; *j* as in *jar*; *ñ* as in Spanish; and *ś* as in *sheet*. The aspirates (*kh, gh, ch, jh, ṭh, ḍh, th, dh, ph, bh*) are pronounced with a clearly audible release of breath following the consonant: *th* as in *anthill*; *dh* as in *bald-head*, etc. The *ṃ* expresses nasalization of the preceding vowel, and the *ḥ* sounds like an *h* followed by a short echo of the preceding vowel (*agniḥ* as *agnih*ⁱ). The *ṅ* is pronounced as *ng*. The other consonants are pronounced as in English.

Unlike English, Sanskrit differentiates between the stem of a noun (e.g., *dhyāna-*, *dhīti-*, *karman-*) and the nominative case, which is used when the noun functions syntactically as the subject of the sentence (e.g., *dhyānam*, *dhītiḥ*, *karma*). I generally refer to nouns by their stem form, but some of the sources I quote use the nominative case form.

PART I

The Alleged Irrationality of Mysticism

Our intellect occupies in the order of intelligible things the same rank as our body in the expanse of nature.

PASCAL

A common Western prejudice has it that the West is rational and the East, irrational.[1] Since it is unlikely that the term "rational," whatever its precise meaning, can without straining be applied to a civilization which spends its greatest efforts on destruction and war, this rationality is held to be inherent in another feature of Western civilization, that is, science. The irrationality of the East, in contrast, is thought of as being especially appropriate in the

1. Strictly speaking the prejudice is that everything which is not Western is irrational. See, for example, the opening sentences of *Time*'s report on Castaneda (March 5, 1973, p. 36): "The Mexican border is the great divide. Below it, the accumulated structures of Western 'rationality' waver and plunge. . . ."

area of religion. This supposition supports and is supported by another prejudice which is the product of a particular development within Western civilization—that religion, and mysticism, are irrational. Christianity possessed from the earliest times an irrationalist tendency, which has been on the increase in recent centuries.

As a result, the contemporary West is unhappily divided between a major rationalist trend, linked with science, and a minor irrationalist trend, linked with religion. The same person who during weekdays cultivates, at least in principle, a certain critical, skeptical, and rational outlook, accepts on Sundays the most awesome irrationalities with blind faith. Since people tend to approach Oriental philosophies in a religious spirit, they generally regard both Oriental philosophies and religions as falling squarely within the realm of the irrational.[2] The resulting picture is comforting to birds of many feathers: to those in the West (and now in the East) who boast of science and progress, and decry the backwardness of the East; and to those in the East (and now in the West) who boast of spirituality and decry the materialism of the West.

When we consider the evidence more dispassionately, the situation appears less simple and straightforward. First of all, science is not confined to the West. With regard to China, the volumes of Needham's *Science and Civilization in China* speak for themselves. With regard to India, it is beginning to be realized that the study of Sanskrit grammar, seemingly an unimportant area of specialization, developed into linguistics as a rational discipline, and was regarded as the ideal and model science, just as mathematics was in Europe. What the Greek mathematician Euclid is to the West, the Sanskrit linguist Pāṇini is to India, and just as the form of Western thought is often mathematical, the form of Indian thought is often linguistic (cf. Staal 1965). Whatever the differences between scien-

2. Cf. Eliot (1954, III, pp. 223–224) on the alleged irrationality of the Chinese mind: "But Europeans are prone to exaggerate the mysterious, topsy-turvy character of the Chinese mind. Such epithets are based upon the assumption that human thought and conduct normally conform to reason and logic, and that when such conformity is wanting the result must be strange and hardly human, or at least such as no respectable European could expect or approve. But the assumption is wrong. In no country with which I am acquainted are logic and coordination of ideas more wanting than in the British Isles. . . ."

tific, mathematical, and linguistic modes of thought, they are certainly all rationalistic.

In the area of religion, many more qualifications are necessary. At no time in the history of mankind has there been a large-scale, systematic search for a rational explanation of religion. But while the Western monotheistic religions and especially Christianity regard the subject as taboo, mysticism has, in India and China, been considered a worthy object of rational inquiry and experimentation. It would be no exaggeration to say that in the realm of religion the situation is the exact opposite of what the common bias suggests: In general, the East is rational; the West, irrational.

This has far-reaching implications for the study of the humanities in general. In the West, reason was generally confined to the study of nature. In a limited way it expanded into other studies, such as philology, but in severely restricted forms (in particular, without proceeding to theory formation), and so it did not much benefit the humanities at large. The human soul was the subject of religion, and the humanities developed, to the extent that they did develop, in that hazy area where irrationalism is well thought of. The "positive" sciences did not often touch man's soul or his mind, and when they made the attempt, they used a "positivistic" methodology resulting from an impoverished notion of what the natural sciences were imagined to do. That linguistics is an area of rational investigation, for example, is a relatively recent discovery in Western civilization. The general thesis I am about to defend—that mysticism can and should be explored rationally—implies *a fortiori* that the humanities are a field of inquiry amenable to rational methods of analysis. For if the apparently most irrational, most extraordinary, and least accessible manifestations of the soul, that is, its mystical properties, are amenable to rational analysis, the same will certainly hold for its more ordinary features.

The view that religion and mysticism are irrational is a myth, which has stifled the progress of our understanding and which should be abandoned, modified, or at least scrutinized. In order to see clearly to what extent this is possible, it is instructive to look more closely at its historical background, and contrast it with other approaches.

1

Christian Irrationalism

Among the religions of mankind, the Western monotheistic religions are alone in putting severe restrictions on the acquistion of knowledge. This was first expressed in the Old Testament in the legend of the tree of knowledge (Genesis 2 and 3). In Paradise there were two special trees, the tree of knowledge of good and evil and the tree of life. God forbade Adam to eat the fruit of the tree of knowledge of good and evil, warning him that he would thereby become mortal. But a snake told Eve that if she ate of the fruit she would not die, but would become like gods, knowing good and evil. They then ate the fruit, learned good and evil, felt ashamed, and put on aprons of fig leaves. God cursed the snake, told Eve he would multiply her sorrows, and condemned Adam to a life of hard labor. God acknowledged that Adam and Eve had now become "like one of us," and expelled them from Paradise lest they should eat the fruit of the tree of life and again become immortal, but now endowed with knowledge. So the tree of knowledge of good and evil seems to symbolize at least three things: (1) knowledge of good and evil; (2) becoming like gods; and (3) loss of immortality.

The close association between knowledge, evil, death, and becoming like gods runs through the history of the Western monotheistic religions. Disobedience to the divine command adds a special element of rebellion and pride, which is also characteristic of Satan himself. This applies to Christianity as well as to Islam, where Satan is the angel who fell because he said of Adam to God:

"I am better than he is" (Koran 7:12). In Christian civilization, the association between knowledge, evil, and pride is widespread, for example, in the Faust legend from the middle ages, developing via Marlowe, Goethe, and Thomas Mann. The Christian view has led to further extremes, such as the conviction that all knowledge is evil.

It would not be correct to say that, in the Christian view, knowledge is bad. God, after all, possesses knowledge. But for man it is sinful, because knowing is becoming like gods and acting against the divine command. Thereby it caused the fall of man. In the New Testament, a new element is added: irrationalism. This view that truth is not marred by contradictions or inconsistencies was advocated by Paul, according to whom Christ was both fully god and fully man. Hence we meet with such statements are: "We preach Christ crucified, to the Jews a scandal, and to the Greeks foolishness" (I Corinthians 1:23). It is not farfetched to suppose that the early Christians, not unlike modern irrationalists, stressed irrationalism not only because of their ardent faith, but also because they knew that in the realm of reason it would be difficult to compete with the Greek philosophers.

In the development of Christianity we come across other avowedly irrational articles of faith, such as the doctrine of the Trinity. An early father of the church, Tertullian, made a desperate attempt to combine rational argument with this trend of irrationalism in Christianity. He argued that such articles of faith must be right, since no one could have thought up anything so absurd: *credo quia absurdum* ("I believe because it is absurd") and *certum est quia impossible est* ("It is certain because it is impossible").

Such colorful ingenuities, however, were soon left behind, and the importance of reason began to be acknowledged. The history of the Christian philosophy of the middle ages, which can be described as a result of the interaction of Christianity and Greek philosophy, is to a large extent the history of analysis of the relationships between faith and reason. Faith was bound to be the victor in this unequal struggle, since a medieval philosopher would have ceased to be a Christian if he had subordinated faith to reason. But even so, the Christian articles of faith were approached more rationally during the middle ages than at any other time. In this sense, Christianity can be said at least then to have been taken very seriously. Until

Nicholas of Cues (1401–1464), says Gilson (1955, p. 536), "All the mediaeval philosophies and theologies had been swayed by the Aristotelian principle of contradiction." It is true that the early rationalism of Anselm (1033–1109) or Peter Abelard (ca. 1079–1142)—whom Bernard of Clairvaux regarded as an agent of Satan—was rejected by the great philosophers of the thirteenth century, Albertus Magnus and Thomas Aquinas. But they still assigned to reason a relatively respectable task, namely to constitute the foundation "if not of faith, at least of the preambles of faith" (Gilson 1952, pp. 756–757).

Gilson observed in this context that the transition from the almost unhampered rationalism of Anselm and Peter Abelard to the more limited rationalism of Albertus Magnus and Thomas Aquinas was partly due to the discovery of inadequacies and limitations in Aristotle's *Physics* and *Metaphysics,* works which had become known in the meantime. Since reason was identified with Aristotle, what Aristotle had taught, or was believed to have taught, was taken to delineate the domain of what can be known; and what he had not taught was taken as the domain of what cannot be known and must therefore be believed. Thus in noting the limitations of Aristotle, it was imagined that the limits of reason had been discovered. By the same token the existence of a domain of faith, which is beyond reason, was taken to have been established (Gilson 1952, p. 756).

Alongside these philosophical developments, in which reason was assigned at least a certain place, the more outspokenly irrationalist trend of Christianity, which stressed faith to the exclusion of reason, continued to exist throughout the middle ages. With Nicholas of Cues, irrationalism was given a philosophical lift, and with the Reformation it received a new lease on life. It soon became rampant in the domain of religion, and also spread to other areas where it had never before been taken seriously. This gradually led to the modern view, that one of the characteristics of the religious is that it is irrational—so much so that nowadays there is hardly a person who regards himself as religious and also as a rationalist.

I can mention only a few steps in this spectacular evolution. Pascal contrasted the rational God of the philosophers with the irrational God of Abraham, Isaac, and Jacob, preferring the latter (e.g., *Thoughts,* no. 556). Kant carved out a large area where reason proper does not belong. Later the so-called rationalism of Hegel provided a repertory for the most awesome irrationalities and inconsistencies. Other dialectical philosophers contributed their share; so did Kierkegaard; and later Protestant theologians used dialectics to emphasize the irrationality of Christian beliefs. Karl Barth, for example, denounced both philosophy and mysticism in the name of the irrationalism of faith. Lastly, with existentialism which developed, despite its obvious Christian antecedents, both Christian and atheistic forms, we reach an outright adoration of the absurd.

This entire development may be summarized in the following terms: Among the great religions of mankind, Christianity stresses faith and irrationalism to an extent that the others (including Islam) never even considered. During the middle ages, Christian philosophers produced valiant attempts to give a rational account of the Christian articles of faith. But on the whole, in the area of Western religion, irrationalism prevailed. And so the modern Western opinion with regard to religion, whether friendly or unfriendly, is that it squarely falls within the domain of the irrational.

It is time to return to the study of mysticism. Mystical experiences, like any other experiences, may be valid or invalid (in particular cases, or in general), but it makes no sense to say that they are rational or irrational. The expressions used by mystics to describe their experiences sometimes seem irrational, but to evaluate their expressions without first evaluating the experiences themselves is bound to be fruitless. The doctrines and theories of many mystics, lastly, may be correct or incorrect, but they are often rational. It is precisely for this reason that they were rejected in many dogmatic forms of Christian irrationalism. The best early example is Augustine, who converted to Christianity from Manicheism. Manicheism was a very ascetic, mystical, and rational world religion, which disappeared after more than a thousand years of development and which covered, at the time of its largest expansion, an area from Spain in the West to China in the East. Manicheism taught (like earlier Gnostic sects) that man attains salvation through spiritual insight alone. It accordingly emphasized empiricism, right knowledge and reason, and had no room for blind faith. In one of its texts, the *Kephalaion* (142), for example, it is stated that "man should not believe what he has not seen with his own eyes" (quoted in Puech 1949, p. 157, n. 281). According to Puech, the young Augustine was attracted by Manicheism mainly because of these scientific and rational tendencies (Puech 1949, p. 72). But Augustine subsequently rejected its rationalism as sinful pride, and substituted Christian humility and irrationalism for it. In the *Confessions* (3.6.10), for example, he referred to the Manicheans when he addressed the Christian God as follows: *etiam vera dicentes philosophos transgredi debui prae amore tuo* ("For the sake of your love I had to go beyond the philosophers even when they spoke the truth").

Discussions on faith and reason were not confined to Christianity. What is perhaps the most glaring example of the incompatibility of both in Western monotheistic religion occurs in the work of the Muslim philosopher Ibn Ru*sh*d (or Averroës) (1126–1198). Though Ibn Ru*sh*d felt strongly about the contradictions between the claims of reason and those of faith, he was unable to give up either. He did not really hold the doctrine of double truth, though he was much criticized for doing so, but he did not shrink from making such statements as: "On account of reason I conclude with necessity, that the intellect is one in number; but notwithstanding that I firmly hold the opposite on account of faith."[1] This is of course unintelligible. What the Arab philosopher really thought remains, in Gilson's words, "hidden in his most secret conscience" (Gilson 1955, p. 219; cf. Gilson 1952, p. 360; Gauthier 1948, pp. 277–279, claims to understand it).

Though Averroës' anxiety may seem to suggest the opposite, Islam is as a matter of fact less irrational than Christianity. Instead of the Trinity, it teaches an unmitigated form of monotheism. Jesus is not regarded as the son of God, but merely as a prophet, just like Muhammad, who is fully human and has no power to work miracles. Pascal, who attacked Islam in numerous passages, blamed Muhammad precisely for not having performed miracles, unlike Jesus, he says (*Thoughts*, p. 600). The only mystery the Koran recognizes is its own revelation: the smaller units of its sūras, or chapters, are called *āyāt*, which means "signs, miracles."

Irrational expressions generally come from the pens of theolo-

1. *per rationem concludo de necessitate, quod intellectus est unus numero, firmiter tamen teneo oppositum per fidem* (Gilson 1952, p. 360).

gians and philosophers, not from mystics. The mystics' own statements have been called irrational, but more often by theologians and philosophers than by the mystics themselves. Similarly, irrationalism as a doctrine has been seriously advocated mostly by theologians and philosophers. Mystics are not interested in doctrines. When mystics use language that may be interpreted in irrationalistic terms—for instance, when they claim that God is both distant and close or, better yet, is both distant and not distant[2]—we are certainly entitled to ask whether such use of language is metaphorical,[3] imprecise, incomplete, or combinations of these, before we resort to an irrationalist interpretation. To ask and try to answer these questions is preferable from a methodological point of view, for the meaning of the irrationalist interpretation is quite unclear and questionable; and mysteries should not be multiplied beyond necessity. But if we tried to discover what is really meant, we might find that the above statement conveys that God is in some respects distant, in others, close. This would not violate the law of noncontradiction, which Aristotle had sensibly formulated as "the same attribute cannot at the same time belong and not belong to the same subject and *in the same respect*": κατὰ τὸ αὐτό (*Metaphysica* Γ 3, 1005b, 19–20). Accordingly, the same statement might mean, more specifically, that God is distant in ordinary experience, but

2. Here is an example from Angelus Silesius' *Cherubinischer Wandermann*: *Gott is ein Geist, ein Feur, ein Wesen und ein Licht. Und ist doch wiederum auch dieses alles nicht* ("God is a spirit, a fire, a being and a light; and also none of these things is right").

3. As Lewis Lancaster pointed out to me, if a mystic states that he has seen a blue light, the expression "blue light" is not metaphorical in the sense in which "the light of reason" or "blue despair" are metaphorical. Of course, there may be a metaphorical sense of "seeing," in which sense he *saw* a blue light, even if there was no blue light in front of his eyes. This may be because a part of his brain was affected in the same way in which it would be affected by an impression of blue light received from his retina, without there being such a light. Similarly, when someone states that he has dreamed of an ocean, the word "ocean" is not used metaphorically, even though there may not have been an ocean which the sleeper could have perceived had he been awake, and even if his bed was wet (which might have been the *cause* of his dream). That the blueness perceived in a mystical vision is not "blue" in any straightforward metaphorical sense is confirmed by Buddhist descriptions which compare the blue of a visionary experience to the color of a flax flower, or an excellent Banaras silk—and similarly for other colors (Lamotte 1970, p. 1285).

close in mystical experience. Of course, none of these expressions can be properly evaluated unless we are prepared to look at what they purport to refer to.

Theologians have gladly embraced the allegedly irrational statements of mystics as literal statements, or even accepted them as dogmatic assertions. Why? Because such statements seem to provide further evidence for an irrationalist position which is not easily defended on other grounds. Many religious doctrines and beliefs are not acceptable to men, who are supposedly rational beings, unless they are placed in a realm which is "beyond reason"; hence the continuing concern with the establishment of such a realm. The medieval Christian philosophers derived its existence not only from faith but also from the study of Aristotle, as we have seen. Other philosophers have taken care to exploit the irrationalist interpretation of mystical statements for similar reasons, as weapons in a general crusade against rationalism. They have also used them to show that man is an unfathomable mystery, instead of facing up to the truth that he is largely unknown. In the last resort, theologians have exploited mystical statements to buttress their unwillingness to answer the arguments of opponents. Such irrationalism is sometimes motivated by the genuine desire for humility which we found, for example, in Augustine. But scholars seek insight more than virtue. Had Descartes been humble, he might have been a nicer man, but we might not possess his "Discourse on Method." Anyway, irrationalism, be it humble or not, leads to a measure of ignorance which borders on blindness and which is only welcomed by those who believe that all knowledge is indeed sinful pride.

Contemporary philosophers in the analytic tradition have not had such heavy axes to grind as the irrationalists in the Christian tradition. With few exceptions (e.g., Danto 1972; cf. Staal 1974) they have merely neglected mysticism or subordinated it to other concerns. Following Wittgenstein, they have used mysticism as an excuse for discussions on the possibility of a "private language." (It is sometimes suggested that Wittgenstein, who stressed the limitation of language, was also a mystic; that seems justifiable only in that very vague sense of the term in which it is sometimes applied to certain poets or composers). Logicians have referred to mysticism when asking themselves whether languages, in which the principle of noncontradiction does not hold, can be meaningful.

All these reactions have little to do with mysticism. The mystical experience stands unaffected, and irrational approaches, by definition, throw no light on it. But also many mystical expressions, which seem to express a doctrine, remain unaffected. The reason is that one feature of such apparently irrational statements is that they are not statements at all, but instruments of therapy, intended to bring about a change in mental state. Since this is especially apparent in Oriental religions, I shall make a detour to consider some of the Oriental evidence.

The therapeutic value of linguistic expressions occurs in Vedic mantras, in the "great sentences" (*mahāvākya*) of the Upaniṣads, such as *tat tvam asi* "you are that (*brahman*)," in sayings used in some Buddhist sects, and in the *kōans* of Zen Buddhism. These may have an effect on adepts who have an intense desire for spiritual liberation, who have undergone a period of intensive training, and who are in a state of mental and physical exhaustion (cf. Vos and Zürcher 1964, p. 31). Though these expressions may seem to exude irrational fragrances, they have as little to do with irrationalism as with literature. Since such therapeutic utterances are not statements, they cannot be taken literally, let alone be regarded as dogmas.

The case of mantras is particularly instructive in this regard. In Indian religions, mantras are now mainly regarded as aids or means to meditation or concentration. There are other similar aids, such as *yantras* (diagrams; see title page and plates 11 a-b), which are objects of contemplation, representations, or images of deities used as objects of worship. In Vedic times, the Vedic mantras came to be regarded as effective when properly recited at the proper time and place during the elaborate ritual—not when interpreted or provided with meaning, a more transient, academic, and individualistic pastime. The person who adopted that view in its most radical form was an ancient ritualist, Kautsa, whose thesis was that "the mantras are meaningless" (*anarthakā mantrāḥ*). Renou has drawn attention to the fact that one of the phonetic and phonological treatises attached to the *Atharvaveda* is attributed to the same Kautsa (Renou 1960, p. 68). Now treatises on phonetics and phonology traditionally exclude meaning by definition. The *Atharvaveda*, moreover, is largely a repository of magical practices. It is not surprising, therefore, that those ritualists who treated the mantras as charms were hardly in a position to regard them at the same time as linguistically meaningful utterances (cf. Staal 1967, p. 24).

The *Nirukta*, an ancient (sixth century B.C.?) treatise on etymology, rejected Kautsa's view, which was also criticized in the ritual philosophy of the Mīmāṃsā. The basic text of this system, the *Mīmāṃsāsūtra* of Jaimini, lists some of the reasons which the followers of Kautsa had adduced in support of their theory: often the mantras are simply absurd; they speak of things that do not exist (e.g., something with four horns, three feet, two heads, and seven hands); they address inanimate objects (e.g., herbs and stones); they are self-contradictory or redundant; there is a tradition of learning them by heart, but no corresponding teaching of their meaning; and so on (cf. Renou 1960, pp. 68 ff.; Staal 1967, p. 45).

Kautsa was a rational ritualist. To him, the mantras appeared irrational, and so he declared them devoid of meaning. The *Mīmāṃsā*, on the other hand, proceeded to provide rational interpretations for such mantras, and hence disagreed on rational grounds with the equally rational position of Kautsa.

In later times, mantras are used as instruments that may bring about almost anything. At the same time they assume sounds and shapes so different from anything found in natural Indian languages that their literal meaninglessness is apparent. This tendency culminates in Tantrism, where we meet with such mantras as *Oṃ a oṃ āḥ hūṃ phaṭ svāhā* (Snellgrove 1959, I, p. 50). Their precursors in the Vedic period were the so-called *stobhas* of the *Sāmaveda*, whose function was partly melodic, though they were also used to conceal the real meaning (e.g., *Hābu hābu hābu hā ū hā ū hā ū / Kāhvāhvāhvāhvā kāhvāhvāhvāhvā kāhvāhvāhvāhvā*, etc.; hear Levy and Staal 1968). Though it would be correct to say that the Tantric mantras are literally meaningless, it is of course always possible to provide them with symbolic interpretations. The *Māṇḍukyopaniṣad* and other Upaniṣads had already done this for the sound constituents of the famous mantra OM (see p. 151 below). The main function of such mantras, however, has nothing to do with the expressive function of a natural language. They are instruments bringing about a change in mental state and are used, for example, as aids in meditation. To insist that mantras are irrationalistic is therefore to miss the point. And what holds for mantras holds for many other religious statements. The therapeutic value of such statements does not support irrationalism.

Scholars looking for meaning are understandably repelled by the meaninglessness of much religious discourse. Kosambi (1965, p. 114) enumerates the inconsistencies in the character of the Hindu God Kṛṣṇa and comments: "The whole Krishna saga is a magnificent example of what a true believer can manage to swallow." Brough, commenting on the *Dharmapada*, writes:

> The resulting vast accumulations of insipid mediocrity which piety preserves are by no means peculiar to Buddhism. It is even probable that religions in general have an inherent tendency to conserve indiscriminately the dreary and the insufferable, which, because of the virtuous intentions of their authors, are accorded no less reverence than great religious art and literature (Brough 1962, p. xvii).

It is sometimes claimed that some philosophical mystics have expressed a kind of irrationalism since they have described their experiences as going "beyond reason." This claim may be trivial, since there are many things that cannot be meaningfully called rational, as I mentioned before. So we may try to make their claim more interesting by resorting to a more specific interpretation of the phrase "beyond reason." If it were to mean that such descriptions could not be arrived at by logical inference (like a conclusion inferred from generally accepted premises), that is also obvious, for of no experiences can the descriptions be derived that way. But a more clearly irrationalist interpretation, such as that these descriptions are contradictory within themselves or inconsistent with each other or with others accepted as valid, is rarely claimed and is never clearly warranted by descriptions of experiences. Often what is stressed is merely the distinctiveness of the attitude of the mystic and his independence from the rules and conventions that govern the activities of most other men.

This, for example, and not irrationalism or the acceptance of contradictions or inconsistencies, is expressed in chapter XX of the *Tao Tê Ching* (Waley, n.d., pp. 168–169):

> I droop and drift, as though I belonged nowhere.
> All men have enough and to spare;
> I alone seem to have lost everything.

Mine is indeed the mind of a very idiot,
So dull am I.
The world is full of people that shine;
I alone am dark.
They look lively and self-assured;
I alone, depressed.
I seem unsettled as the ocean;
Blown adrift, never brought to a stop.
All men can be put to some use;
I alone am intractable and boorish.

Let us return to Christianity. Many Christian theologians defend Christianity not only because it emphasizes the irrational but also the personal, the historical, and the unique; and they reject mysticism because of its emphasis not only on rationality but also on what is impersonal, eternal, and general. In Christianity, God has become man only once, God has created the world out of nothing only once, and man lives only once (see, e.g., Cullmann 1948; Puech 1951, and the references listed there). But in many forms of mysticism, uniqueness is rejected in favor of repeatability, commonality, and generality, just as the personality of God is often rejected in favor of an all-pervading impersonal divine absolute. In Indian religions, where mysticism is very common, Gods are conceived of as continuously or repeatedly creating and destroying, or manifesting and absorbing universes (cf. plate 1); Gods are believed to descend repeatedly to earth, and men to have many lives. These are rationalistic moves, whether right or wrong. If they take the form of justifications we don't agree with, we call them rationalizations (e.g., the theory of *karman* interpreted as a theory which explains human suffering). Mystics tend more generally to reject the irrational need for faith and dogmatism. The God mystics claim to have found through personal experience is no more irrational than the God philosophers have postulated to explain the universe. Christian theologians accordingly tend to reject some philosophers' idea of God because it is rational and, in the final resort, mystical.

The views of Emil Brunner, foreshadowed by Augustine, Pascal, and others, express this attitude very well. For him, each "system" is pantheistic, monistic, and ultimately mystical, because the thinker "who stays with himself, is confined to his own thought" and does not reach God (Brunner 1930, p. 10). According to Brunner, God as creator cannot be expressed by any category of thought. He can only be known through his revelations as the Lord, and when thus known he is known as an unintelligible mystery (Brunner 1930, p. 17). The existentialist philosopher Karl Jaspers, though defending a "philosophical faith" against such theological presumptions, agrees with Brunner on the basic assumption, which he expresses with uncharacteristic brevity: *Ein bewiesener Gott ist kein Gott* (Jaspers 1948, p. 33: "A proven God is no God").

I am aware of the fact that this irrational trend in Western religion has not only been evolved as a cover for lack of argument. Its roots may be metaphysical (as apparently in Genesis 2 and 3), or it may have a noble inspiration, such as the desire to extol the divine beyond all man's qualities, including his reason. Only some such attitude can motivate the sincerity of the extreme belief that all knowledge is bad. But whatever its motivation, this particular development within Western religion has had for its result that rationalism and religion have in the West become opposite and competing trends. Since mysticism is generally, though I think erroneously, regarded as part of religion (despite the uneasiness most mystics have felt in the Christian and Muslim traditions), there is therefore a widespread prejudice that mysticism too is not susceptible to rational, objective analysis.

We shall often have to distinguish between experiences and doctrines or interpretations. Experiences are always approached in terms of interpretations. That mystical experiences are amenable to rational analysis, without being themselves rational or irrational, is itself a rational doctrine. Such a rationalist conviction is implicit in most of Buddhism, Yoga, Advaita Vedānta, and Taoism. It is significant that many of these Oriental doctrines stress the value of knowledge. But in Western religion, the opposite attitude prevails. Therefore Westerners tend to regard Oriental mystical doctrines as irrational, whether they criticize them or whether they adopt them. In fact, Oriental mysticism attracts many Western adepts because of this alleged irrationalism. Those who have had enough of science and rationality, and also of the Christian establishment, look at exotic repositories of the irrational; the Oriental religions and cults seem to meet such a description very well. Only if we look more closely do we find something different.

2

Buddhist Irrationalism

It would not be difficult to show that many Oriental mystical doctrines, whether true or false, are basically rational, especially in comparison with Christianity. Early Buddhism, in particular, appealed to an earlier generation of Westerners, scholars as well as seekers of truth, mainly on account of its alleged rationalism and empiricism. The present generation, mainly on account of the Christian irrationalism inherent in existentialism and similar philosophies, and for political reasons (for no person in his right mind can fail to be struck by the irrationalism of allegedly rational political and social institutions and behavior) is less inclined toward rationalism. And so it turns to forms of Buddhism which appear to be more irrational, like certain features of the Mahāyāna.

Buddhist scholars from Theravāda countries such as Ceylon continue to stress the rational features of Buddhism, and this is not surprising. But since Mahāyāna is the only form of Buddhism now existing in the Far East, it is instructive to read the authoritative statement of a leading Japanese Buddhist scholar, which is by no means irrational:

The relationship between faith and reason is an important consideration in comparing Christianity and Buddhism. There is a strong emphasis on reason within the traditions of Buddhism. The relationship between faith and reason is more problematical in Christianity. Gotama is often pictured as instructing his disciples in a Socratic manner. Jesus is not. His teachings are more picturesque than argumentative. Many strains within Christianity downgrade reason as an appropriate approach to salvation. However, there is a tradition of Christian thought which holds reason in high regard. The tradition has been influenced by the contact between Christianity and Greek philosophy (Nakamura 1973, p. 30).

This statement supports my earlier claims, and provides a transition to the present section. But in order to support the claim that not only certain traditions in Buddhism, but Oriental mystical doctrines in general are rational, we should look at what appear to be the exceptions. Since the most blatant examples of irrationalism are cases where the principle of noncontradiction is violated, these would be the most relevant. Before considering them, I shall briefly refer to statements of that principle itself.

This entire section will necessitate some technical detail, and will refer to a variety of texts. The reader may at this point wish to consult once more the survey of the Indian tradition (pages 10–14).

The principle of noncontradiction was formulated not only by Aristotle and not only in the West. In India, for example, it was formulated in the system of logic or Nyāya in terms of *virodhī* "contradicting" or *viruddha* "contradicted": a *hetu* "reason" is called *viruddha* (and is hence fallacious) if it is contradicted by the *sādhya*, "inferendum," the entity which is sought to be inferred from the "reason." An example is provided by the inference: "Sound is eternal because it is produced." This is considered fallacious because the reason, "being produced," is held to be contradicted by the inferendum, "eternity."

The principle of noncontradiction is implicitly accepted, and sometimes explicitly formulated, in most of the Nyāya, in the traditional system of Sanskrit grammar (*vyākaraṇa*), the supreme science in ancient India, and also in such systems of Hindu philosophy as the orthodox ritualistic system of the Mīmāṃsā and the nondualism of Śaṅkara's Advaita Vedānta (see Staal 1962a). The principle was also accepted by Buddhist philosophers, including the Mādhyamika, which is sometimes regarded as the central philosophy of Buddhism (e.g., by T. R. V. Murti and by Edward Conze) and which is the Indian source from which many Buddhist philosophies in Tibet, China, and Japan developed.

The main philosopher of the Mādhyamika is Nāgārjuna, one of India's great philosophers, who lived around A.D. 200. As the father of the Mādhyamika, the grandfather of Ch'an, and the great-grandfather of Zen, he is often regarded as a typical proponent of

Buddhist irrationalism. However, according to Robinson (1957, p. 295), the principle of noncontradiction is "invoked constantly" in Nāgārjuna's *Mūlamadhyamakakārikā*, where it is "stated in general form in two places." The first of these is: *ekatve na hi bhāvaś ca nābhāvaś copapadyate* (7.30b), which Robinson translates as follows: "for being and non-being cannot occur in the same thing." Actually, the *Prasannapadā* commentary of Candrakīrti seems to interpret this phrase to mean that in case of a contradiction, there is neither being nor nonbeing. This is not a statement of the principle of noncontradiction, and may be interpreted in algebraic terms as: "If $a = -a$, then $a = 0$ and $-a = 0$." It may mean that a thing cannot at the same time exist and not exist.

The second statement of Nāgārjuna quoted by Robinson can indeed be regarded as a statement of the principle of noncontradiction: *parasparaviruddhaṃ hi sac cāsac caikataḥ kutaḥ* (8.7b) "for how could the real and the non-real, being mutually contradictory, occur at the same time?"

In his book on the early Mādhyamika in India and China, Robinson has listed several other passages where Nāgārjuna invokes other logical principles which presuppose the principle of noncontradiction (Robinson 1967, pp. 50–51). Nakamura (1958, p. 388) has drawn attention to a similar statement by Candrakīrti, the main commentator on Nāgārjuna: "since being and non-being are mutually contradictory, they cannot both exist in the same place in Nirvāṇa" (*bhāvābhāvayor parasparaviruddhayor ekatra nirvāṇe nāsti sambhava iti*) (*Madhyamikavṛtti* [1903–1913], ed. de la Vallée Poussin, p. 532).

There are, however, areas of Indian thought where the principle of noncontradiction appears to be violated or rejected. The doctrine sometimes evoked in this context, also due to Nāgārjuna, and adopted by Śaṅkara, is that which distinguishes between two levels of truth, called *paramārtha-satya* and *saṃvṛti-satya* in the Mādhyamika, and *pāramārthika* and *vyāvahārika* in the Advaita Vedānta. These two levels may be roughly characterized by saying that the lower level is the empirical level of everyday experience, while the higher level is reserved for the Absolute, that is, *śūnyatā* "emptiness" in the case of the Mādhyamika and *brahman* in that of the Advaita Vedānta. It is clear that truths on these two levels often contradict each other. For example, the world-appearance or *māyā* may be regarded as "not real" from the perspective of the Absolute, though in everyday life one would certainly assume it to be real. Here then, it seems, the principle of noncontradiction is violated, and we seem to have a case similar to the doctrine of double truth attributed to the Averroists in the Western middle ages (see page 24).

However, this is misleading, and in fact, not the case. The situation is similar to that of the *prātibhāsika* level. This is a level postulated to account for errors or false appearances within the *vyāvahārika* level of everyday experience. For example, in a case of erroneous perception, we think we see a snake when in fact there is only a rope. But the contradiction between the two is only apparent: there *is* no snake. Similarly, for the two truths on the *paramārtha* and the *saṃvṛti* levels: they are not meant to be equally valid. True, the "higher" truth may refer to nonordinary reality, while the "lower" truth may have some positive significance and be of assistance in attaining the "higher" truth (cf. Streng 1971). But most Buddhist and Advaitin authors who care to elucidate the logical significance of the distinction are quite unambiguous: ultimately, the *paramārtha-satya* is true, and the *saṃvṛti-satya* is false. The Advaita philosopher Vidyāraṇya, for example, says in his *Pañcadaśī* in a verse (6.130) quoted by Mahadevan (1957, 231):

tucchā'nirvacanīyā ca vāstavī cety asau tridhā
jñeyā māyā tribhir bodhaiḥ śrautayauktikikaiḥ

"Māyā is understood in three ways: by the man in the street as real, by the logician as undeterminable, by the follower of the scripture as nonexistent."

It is obvious here that the follower of the scripture is taken to be right, and the man in the street is not. Murti (1955, p. 252) is correct with respect to the Mādhyamika and the Advaita Vedānta both when he says: "Saṃvṛti is totally false; and nothing of it is taken up in forming the paramārtha."

The most striking case of an Indian doctrine that seems to directly violate the principle of noncontradiction is the Buddhist *catuṣkoṭi* or "tetralemma." Though its earliest formulation seems to be due to the skeptic Sañjaya, whose followers were ridiculed by the Buddhists as "eel-wrigglers" (Raju 1954, pp. 694–697), the principle reemerges in the Pāli Canon itself. The *Majjhima-nikāya* (sutta 63) describes how a peculiar consideration presented itself to the mind of the venerable Mālunkyāputta, when "in seclusion and plunged in meditation." Māluṅkyāputta wondered why the Buddha had not elucidated such questions as "that the saint exists after death, that the saint does not exist after death, that the saint both exists and does not exist after death, that the saint neither exists nor does not exist after death" (translation Warren 1947, pp. 117–122). These musings of the venerable Māluṅkyāputta were destined to have a great future in the history of Buddhism. By the time we arrive at Nāgārjuna, we find the central teaching of the Buddha formulated as follows:

sarvaṃ tathyaṃ na vā tathyaṃ tathyaṃ cātathyam eva ca/
naivatathyaṃ naiva tathyam etad buddhānuśāsanam//

"Everything is such as it is, not such as it is, both such as it is and not such as it is, and neither such as it is nor such as it is not. That is the Buddha's teaching" (*Mūlamadhyamakakārikā* 18.8).

The alternatives of the *catuṣkoṭi*, formulated variously in a large number of works, especially in the Mādhyamika school, usually appear in the following form: (1) *x* exists, (2) *x* does not exist, (3) *x* exists and does not exist, (4) *x* neither exists nor does not exist. Conze comments: "The third and fourth members of the tetralemma may seem to us to be rather contradictory and absurd, and to violate essential logical law, and their interpretation requires further research" (Conze 1692, p. 219). It would appear that the third clause of this principles does indeed conflict with the law of noncontradiction, and the fourth with the law of the excluded middle (as emphasized by Murti 1955, pp. 146–148, and Kajiyama 1957, p. 293); but the latter law, unlike the law of noncontradiction, is not a prerequisite for rationality. Several scholars have been puzzled by this. "Many European commentators," Conze continues (1962, p. 220), "convinced that the Aristotelian principle of contradiction is everywhere the unvarying law of all valid thought, have misinterpreted Buddhist ontology through sheer inability to grasp its fundamental principle."

The difficulty is not, however, that Aristotle's principle is a law of thought, which might be thrown overboard by anyone who prefers to engage in activities other than thinking. The difficulty is rather that this principle makes explicit the function of the particle "not," of which the occurrence, when used in any other way, makes no sense. Of course, we may avoid using "not" altogether. But if we make use of "not," it is perverse to use it in such a manner as to conflict with its proper function. That is not what words are for. Such precisely is the reason that any violation of the principle of noncontradiction is irrational. One can say "*A* and not-*A*" (or "not-*A* and *A*," which comes to the same), and then try to find out what this could mean. But one soon realizes that saying "not-*A*" means that we do not affirm *A*, and in the face of that it is irrational to persist in affirming *A*. The particle "not" has no other function than to exclude such an affirmation. The principle of noncontradiction prevents us from rejecting and accepting the same statement at the same time. One disconcerting consequence is that one cannot reject the principle of noncontradiction without, in doing so, accepting it. In general, it is just as senseless to expect that the improper use of words establishes the invalidity of logical principles, as to reject screwdrivers because we cannot fry eggs with them.

Several logical interpretations have been offered which seek to make sense of the *catuṣkoṭi*. Raju (1954, pp. 710–713) has proposed to interpret the opposition between *A* and not-*A* in the tetralemma not as an opposition between contradictories (e.g., "all *x* is *F*" vs. "not all *x* is *F*") but as an opposition between contraries (e.g., "all *x* is F" vs. "no *x* is *F*"). He has rightly pointed out that "two contraries can both be negated, but not the contradictories" (p. 710). Unfortunately, the propositions of the *catuṣkoṭi* do not involve quantification, since they do not mention "all," "some," or "no," so that there is no textual support which entitles us to apply the distinction between contradictory and contrary to the Indian material. Robinson has also offered a logical interpretation which makes sense; he has interpreted the four alternatives as: (1) All *x* is *A*, (2) No *x* is *A*, (3) Some *x* is *A*, and some *x* is not *A*, (4) No *x* is *A*, and no *x* is not *A* (Robinson 1957, p. 302; 1967, p. 57). But here again, there is no textual justification.

Matilal (1971, pp. 162–165), reviving an interpretation given in the Svātantrika branch of the Mādhyamika school, has argued that the contradictory character of the *catuṣkoṭi* disappears when we interpret the negations not as *paryudāsa* but as *prasajya-pratiṣedha*. This makes use of a technical distinction between two kinds of negation which was due to the Indian grammarians and ritualists. It may be understood along the following lines. In a *paryudāsa* negation a *term* (which is expressed by a noun or an adjective on the syntactic level) is negated. This can be stated in general as "not-*x* is *F*," where "*x*" is a term and "*F*" is a predicate. An example is "An *in*vertebrate is an animal." Here the prefix "*in*-" negates the term "vertebrate." But in a *prasajya-pratiṣedha* negation the predicate is negated. This can be expressed in general as "*x* is not *F*," where "*x*" again is a term and "*F*" a predicate. An example is "This animal is *not* a vertebrate." Here the particle "*not*" negates the predicate "is a vertebrate." (For further analysis see Staal 1962a, pp. 59–61).

Matilal is certainly right that the negations in the *catuṣkoṭi* have to be interpreted as *prasajya-pratiṣedha*; for, since there is no explicit distinction between terms and predicates in the propositions of the tetralemma, there is no justification whatsoever for a *paryudāsa* interpretation. However, it is not true that contradictions do not arise between *prasajya* negations. On the contrary, the principle of noncontradiction applies only to such negations. It is the *paryudāsa* negation for which it need not hold (see Staal 1962a, p. 61). We can very well say, for example, that vertebrates as well as invertebrates are animals; but it makes no sense to say that there are animals which are vertebrates and also not vertebrates.

Raju's, Robinson's, and Matilal's logical attempts to save the *catuṣkoṭi* from inconsistency are therefore unsatisfactory. The discussions of Raju and Matilal are further marred by their failure to distinguish clearly between the principle of noncontradiction ("not both *A* and not-*A*") on the one hand, and the two principles of the excluded middle ("either *A* or not-*A*") and of double negation ("not-not-*A* implies *A*") on the other (the two latter principles are equivalent). The principle of noncontradiction implies that a vase is not both blue and not blue; that of the excluded middle, that it is either blue or not blue; that of double negation, that, if it is not not-blue, it is blue. The only interpreter of the materials who has clearly distinguished between these principles, Hanson (1970, pp. 70–72), is inconclusive on the main issue and overly optimistic when he expects, quite gratuitously, that it is not "outside the competence of modern symbolic logic to devise a notation and system which would *reconcile*" (italics mine) "the paradox of the Mādhyamika, in particular the principle of 'Four-cornered Negation' " (p. 72).

How then are we to make sense of the *catuṣkoṭi*? If we assume that it was conceived as a scheme for expressing a mutually exclusive and collectively exhaustive set of possible views on any given topic, it is only its third clause ("*A* and not-*A*") which conflicts with the principle of noncontradiction. The fourth clause ("neither *A* nor not-*A*") conflicts with the principle of the excluded middle (or excluded third), that is, "*A* or not-*A*." We can only solve these riddles if we assume, following an observation of Richard Olsen (unpublished), which is in accordance with Nāgārjuna's practice, that the Mādhyamika philosophers, despite passages like *Mūlamadhyamakakārikā* 18.8 quoted above, rejected all the four clauses, which the Buddha had failed to affirm, as invalid or inappropriate.

If this assumption is correct, the case for irrationalism cannot be made. For there is nothing irrational in the Mādhyamika rejection of these clauses. In rejecting the third clause, the denial of the principle of noncontradiction is rejected, not the principle of noncontradiction itself. As regards the fourth clause, it is possible and rational to either accept it or to reject it. In Western logic, the principle of the excluded middle is accepted in so-called classical logic. Classical logic is therefore also called two-valued logic: For every *A*, there are only two possible values, corresponding to *A* and not-*A*; hence, "*A* or not-*A*" is accepted as valid. But the principle is rejected in the intuitionistic logic constructed for the intuitionistic mathematics of L. E. J. Brouwer. According to Brouwer, when we are dealing with sets consisting of infinitely many objects, we may not be in a position to determine whether *A* or not-*A* is valid. Hence in this logic there are more than two values. This system of three-valued logic has been generalized, and we have studies of many-valued logics. In such logics, the principle of the excluded middle is not valid.

If we were to accept the fourth clause of the *catuṣkoṭi*, it would be tantamount to denying the validity of the principle of the excluded middle. As we have just seen, that is not irrational. If we reject the fourth clause, as the Mādhyamika philosophers did, we are free to accept the principle of the excluded middle. But we don't have to, since denying the denial of the excluded middle only implies the excluded middle if we accept the principle of double negation, which is itself equivalent to the excluded middle.

There is no need to get further entangled in these logical principles. As we shall see, the Mādhyamika philosophers, in a different context, do in fact reject the principle of the excluded middle. My only concern has been to show that such a rejection is not irrationalistic. Moreover, there are quite different avenues of interpretation.

A sensible interpretation offered by Robinson, following Candrakīrti's *Middle Treatise* (Robinson 1967, p. 56), would be to regard the *catuṣkoṭi* not as a statement, but as a pedagogical or therapeutic device. As we have seen, many mantras, the *mahāvākyas* of the Upaniṣads, and the *kōans* of Zen Buddhism are precisely this. They are not intended to elucidate, but they may cause a sudden transformation in a person who is suitably prepared and who has an intense desire for spiritual illumination. I shall return to this interpretation.

So far we have seen that the Mādhyamika rejection of the *catuṣkoṭi* is not irrational in that it nowhere contradicts the principle of noncontradiction. But what can be said for the opponents of the Mādhyamika, who apparently accepted as a possible alternative the *catuṣkoṭi* and in particular its third clause, which explicitly denies the principle of noncontradiction?

Since the Mādhyamika claim that they refute everybody, it would be time-consuming to list all the views of their opponents. Rather, we might profitably distinguish between nonphilosophers and philosophers, and among the latter, between non-Buddhists and Buddhists. It is clear that among nonphilosophers there will always be people who are prepared to affirm the possibility of "*A* and not-*A*," opining that they thereby convey sense while in fact they are only uttering sounds. But confining ourselves in the present context to Buddhist philosophers of schools different from the Mādhyamika, we find that some of these thinkers did not regard the apparent contradiction of the third clause as a real contradiction, but interpreted it instead in a rational manner which is quite consistent with Aristotle's principle. They did so by simply observing that the predicate occurring in these alternatives should not in each case be taken as applicable *to the same subject.* This position implies, for example, that Māluṅkyāputta was wondering whether the sage in one sense can be said to exist after death, and in another not to exist after death. Such double questions are often expressed by means of an apparent contradiction, either for rhetorical effect or merely on account of carelessness (cf. page 5).

This rational solution is found in the Vijñānavāda school, not surprisingly, for its adherents were the best logicians in Buddhism. It is also implicit in a controversy between the Vaibhāṣika and Sautrāntika schools on the relation between *dharma* (roughly, "permanently existing element") and *kāritra* (roughly, "impermanent activity" of such an element). The Vaibhāṣika, who propose this solution and refer to the other, similar cases where it is also applicable, held that a *dharma* does not change though its *kāritra* changes, but that the *kāritra* is not independent of the *dharma*. Their Sautrāntika opponents ridiculed this doctrine by misrepresenting it in the following verse:

> *kāritraṃ sarvadā nāsti sadā dharmaś ca varṇyate /*
> *dharmān nānyac ca kāritraṃ vyaktaṃ devaviceṣṭitam //*

"Kāritra does not exist permanently, dharma is characterized as existing permanently; yet kāritra is not different from dharma—indeed a caprice of the deity!" (*Abhidharmakośa* 5.57, translated in Schayer 1938, pp. 25, 73; I have slightly edited this and the following quotation).

To this the Vaibhāṣika philosopher Saṅghabhadra replied as follows:

> This irony is improper. For the Lord Buddha also teaches: "The Tathāgata [i.e., the Buddha] is and is not beyond this world"; "the character of dependent causation is and is not permanent." Should the Lord Buddha also be ridiculed because of that? We accept that *dharma* exists always and, at the same time, we teach that *dharma* is not eternal. But your criticism is unfounded because the terms "eternal" and "not eternal" are used here in two different senses. Therefore one should not deride the Buddha. Is it not so in this case as well? The *dharma* lasts eternally, but the *dharmabhāva* [i.e., the mode of existence of the *dharma*] changes . . . Therefore we teach: the *dharma* is eternal, but the *dharmabhāva* is not eternal. So what remains of your irony in saying that this is a caprice of the deity? (*Nyāyānusāra* 633c, translated in Schayer 1938, p. 26).

Thus, a great Buddhist philosopher regards the irrationalist interpretation of these alleged contradictions in Buddhist doctrine as perfectly ridiculous. Instead, he makes simple sense of them, as any intelligent schoolboy would. In the case of the apparent contradictions, which the Buddha mentioned, he does not even consider the irrationalist interpretation which would regard them as real contradictions. So why should we?

Now let us return to the Mādhyamika. We have already seen that Mādhyamika philosophers like Nāgārjuna and Candrakīrti, as Robinson and Nakamura, respectively, have shown, explicitly accept the principle of noncontradiction. Moreover, the Mādhyamika rely on the principle of noncontradiction whenever they attempt to refute their opponents, for the notion of refutation depends on the correct use of the particle "not" and makes no sense unless that principle is presupposed. The method of *prasaṅga* or *reductio ad absurdum*, which they practice throughout, is effective only to the extent that the derived contradictions are felt to be intolerable, that is, to the extent the principle of noncontradiction is accepted as valid. If the Mādhyamika were willing to harbor contradictions in their own position, they could not claim to have refuted their opponents on the ground that they did the same. Moreover, if the principle of noncontradiction is not accepted as valid, the opponent's views are just as good as the negations of these views, and cannot therefore be shown to be false.

This interpretation is supported by the texts. Bhattacharya's English translation of Nāgārjuna's *Vigrahavyāvartanī* (1971) clearly shows that Nāgārjuna tried to refute the Naiyāyika by using logic and the principle of noncontradiction. Robinson (1957) had shown essentially the same for the *Mūlamadhyamakakārikā*. Bhattacharya (1971, p. 217) concludes that "Nāgārjuna does not disdain logic," which confirms Robinson's assessment that "he makes mistakes in logic, but does not deny any principles of logic" (Robinson 1957, p. 307).

In the Mādhyamika texts there is also direct textual support for a rational interpretation of the third clause of the *catuṣkoṭi*, that is, that the alleged contradictions are not real. In the *Prasannapadā*, Candrakīrti's commentary on Nāgārjuna's *Mūlamadhyamaka-kārikā*, a quotation of an apparent contradiction is provided with a paraphrase which dissolves the contradiction by supplying different missing contexts: "Some have been taught that all of that is such as it is and not such as it is. In that case, all of that is such as it is with respect to ordinary people, but false with respect to the learned . . ."[1] Though this passage ridicules those, who (like Can-

1. *keṣāṃcit sarvam etat tathyaṃ cātathyaṃ ceti deśitam/ tatra bālajanāpekṣayā sarvam etat tathyam/ āryajanāpekṣayā tu sarvam etan mṛṣā* . . . : "A quelques-uns, il a été enseigné

drakīrti himself in other contexts) accept the principle of identity (*A* is *A*), it does not violate the principle of noncontradiction which, as we have seen, applies only when both the affirmative and the negative clause are held to be valid *in the same respect*. So Candrakīrti makes sense of the third clause of the *catuṣkoṭi*, even though he later rejects it.

Another passage of the *Prasannapadā* is even more revealing of the basic character of the *catuṣkoṭi*. It was referred to by Robinson (1967, p. 56) in support of his "therapeutic" interpretation. This passage states that the last clause of the *catuṣkoṭi* is merely used to express that the predicates that occur in it are not applicable—just as we might say that grass is neither intelligent nor unintelligent:

> Some who have for a very long time practised the correct view of reality and who have almost entirely eradicated the root-obstructions, have been taught that that is neither such as it is nor such as it is not. It is in order to root out the last remnants of obstruction that these alternatives are refuted, as in the case of the barren woman's son, when the view that he is white and the view that he is black are both refuted.[2]

This passage shows two things: first, that these alleged contradictions arise when we use semantically ill-formed expressions; second, that these alleged contradictions are not to be taken as statements at all, but serve a function in the process of meditation. The obstructions (*āvaraṇa*) mentioned here are of two kinds: *kleśāvaraṇa* "obstructions which are passions" and *jñeyāvaraṇa* "obstructions which are objects of knowledge" (de Jong 1949, p. 28, n. 75). These obstructions are like the "knots" of *karman* (*karmagranthinaḥ*) of the Upaniṣadic tradition (see pages 110–111). They are dissolved or

---

que tout cela est vrai et non-vrai à la fois. Tout cela est vrai par rapport aux sots, mais faux par rapport aux saints . . ." (de Jong 1949, p. 28).

2. *keṣāṃcit tu aticirābhyastatattvadarśanānāṃ kiṃcinmātrānutkhātāvaraṇatarumūlānāṃ naivātathyaṃ naiva tathyaṃ tad iti deśitam/ tasyāpi kiṃcinmātrasyāvaraṇasya prahāṇārthaṃ vandhyāsutasyāvadātaśyāmatāpratiṣedhavad ubhayam etat pratiṣiddham*: "A quelques-uns qui ont pratiqué pendant un tres long temps la vue de la réalité et qui ont arraché à peu pres entièrement les racines d'arbres nommées les obstructions, il a été enseignè que cela est à la fois ni vrai et ni non-vrai. C'est pour couper ce petit résidu d'obstruction que ces deux alternatives sont réfutées, comme dans le cas du fils d'une femme sterile, on réfute aussi bien la supposition qu'il soit blanc que la supposition qu'il soit noir" (de Jong 1949, p. 28).

removed through meditation. The last clause of the *catuṣkoṭi*, then, is the instrument which is supposed to bring this about. That obstructions are obstacles to enlightenment is in accordance with Candrakīrti's expression of the Mādhyamika doctrine, where the empirical level of *saṃvṛti* is explained as "folly" (*moha*) because "it sets obstacles before true nature" (*svabhāvā-varaṇāt*) (Nagao 1954, p. 553).

It seems likely that these alleged contradictions constitute one of the sources for the tradition of *kōans* (Chinese: *kung-an*) made widely known through the Rinzai branch of Zen. The barren woman's son being black or not-black, in the *Prasannapadā*, is similar to the Zen teacher's questions about the whereabouts of the pupil before his parents were born, or the case of the master whipping his pupils while exclaiming, "If you don't understand—thirty blows! If you understand—also thirty blows!" (see, e.g., Vos and Zürcher 1964, p. 34).

We have seen that the Mādhyamika method of *prasaṅga* or *reductio ad absurdum* presupposes the principle of noncontradiction but rejects the principle of the excluded middle. Jacques May (1959, p. 221, n. 761; cf. Schayer 1931, XXV) has collected the relevant passages. These establish that the use of *prasaṅga* entails negation, but when the Mādhyamika philosopher negates a proposition, it does not follow that he himself accepts the negation of that proposition. Accordingly, there are other alternatives than *A* and not-*A*, and the principle of the excluded middle does not hold. Elsewhere May (1959, p. 136, n. 382) quotes Stcherbatsky and de la Vallée Poussin, who had asserted that the term for such a "simple negation, which does not necessitate any affirmation of the opposite," is *prasajya-pratiṣedha*. This usage is also reported by Kajiyama (1957, pp. 328–329), followed by Martilal (see above, page 37). In a recent article, Kajiyama discusses the specific Mādhyamika function of *prasajya-pratiṣedha* and *paryudāsa*, which the Buddhist logicians distinguished from each other by a technical use of the particle "only" (Kajiyama 1973).

The main characteristic of *prasaṅga*, according to the Mādhyamika philosophers, is that they, by utilizing this method, sought not to propound any propositions (*pratijñā*) themselves (May 1959, p. 221, n. 761). Whether or not this is true, it is ultimately due to the fact that they were interested in talking about what cannot be talked about, namely, the level of the absolute *paramārtha*. This generally leads to paradoxes. According to Nāgārjuna in *Vigrahavyāvartanī*, statements regarding the *paramārtha* are not to be construed as propositions (May 1959, p. 225, n. 773). Said he: "I have no proposition": *nāsti mama pratijñā* (Bhattacharya 1971, p. 237). Unless this statement itself is not a proposition, we have a paradox here. But if Nāgārjuna got caught in paradoxes and contradictions, he is not worse off than most philosophers. What would make him an irrationalist is the desire to be illogical. Here Robinson's and Bhattacharya's views are supported by Kajiyama, who states in even more general terms: "The learned scholarly world of India which had much developed in logic since early ages did not, especially after appearance of Dignāga in the Buddhist world, permit illogical argument even on religious matters" (Kajiyama 1957, p. 297).

Stanislaw Schayer, who was one of the best connoisseurs of the *Prasannapadā*, came very close to drawing the conclusion that there is nothing irrational about the *catuṣkoṭi*, and that it merely expresses the inapplicability of ordinary language to absolute reality: "But that" (i.e., the *catuṣkoṭi*) "means the same as the statement, that nothing that can be a subject of predication is real, that objects in the sense of a pluralistic ontology do not exist, and that absolute reality cannot be captured by judgments" (Schayer 1931, XXVI).

Nāgārjuna therefore adheres to an ancient Indian tradition, expressed, for example, in the *Taittirīyopaniṣad*: "*ydto vắco nívartante dprāpya mánasā sahá*" "(*brahman* is that) from which words return—having failed to reach it with the mind." The first line of the verse preceding Nāgārjuna's verse quoted above uses nearly identical concepts:

nivṛttam abhidhātavyaṃ nivṛtte cittagocare /

"What words can express comes to a stop when the domain of the mind comes to a stop" (*Mūlamadhyamakakārikā* 18.7a). To express the view that one knows that certain things cannot be expressed and cannot be known is paradoxical in at least one sense. The Mādhyamika thinkers felt such difficulties and interpreted their doctrine in different ways (see Kajiyama 1957 and Ruegg 1971). But the view that there are realms of reality where ordinary language is not applicable is not, of course, paradoxical, inconsistent, or contradictory. Such a situation is quite common not only in philosophy but also elsewhere, e.g., in mathematics or engineering, where for that reason artificial languages are constructed. Whenever we have semantically ill-formed expressions, the same situation obtains; for example, it does not make literal sense to say that grass is intelligent, or that it is not. In such cases, where neither *A* nor not-*A* is applicable, the principle of the excluded middle does not hold.

There is one final consideration that may be taken into account if we wish to explain this confounding tendency to use expressions of the form "*A* and not-*A*," which appear to violate the principle of noncontradiction: namely, the structure and character of the Sanskrit language. In Sanskrit it is regarded as stylistically attractive to form a pair of a positive and its negation. Gonda, who has written about this feature, quotes as an example a phrase from the *Atharvaveda*: *akṣitiś ca kṣitiś ca* "indestructibleness and destruction" (Gonda 1959, pp. 116–117). Nominal compounds of the *dvandva* variety very frequently exhibit the same tendency: *gatāgata* "gone (*gata*) and not-gone (*agata*)," *nityānitya* "permanent (*nitya*) and impermanent (*anitya*)," etc. (for further facts, see Renou 1961, sec. 87). These features of Sanskrit have much to do with the tendency in Indian thought to go beyond the "pairs of opposites" (also called *dvandva*) and with expressions such as the *catuṣkoṭi*. They also reinforce an already existing tendency to use negative expressions, to which several scholars have drawn attention (Gonda 1959, p. 95–117; Nakamura 1964, pp. 52–59). Such features go back at least as far as the celebrated hymn of *Ṛgveda* 10.129: "Then there was neither non-existence nor existence" (*nā́sad āsīn nó sád āsīt tadā́nīm*).

Whatever will turn out to be the correct interpretation of the Mādhyamika position, an irrationalist interpretation of Buddhist doctrines by modern scholars is readily explained by the prevailing Western prejudice that religion and oriental philosophy are basically irrational. If we approach Buddhist thought on its own terms, there appears to be little justification, if any, to speak of "Buddhist irrationalism."

3

Modern Irrationalism

The traditional Western prejudice that mysticism—both doctrines and experiences—is irrational and outside the scope of objective analysis has been further shrouded by particular limitations which several contemporary philosophies have imposed upon themselves. Some of these limitations were originally merely methodological; but, as is often the case, they became in due course metaphysical. The Christian emphasis on uniqueness has been incorporated, lock, stock, and barrel, into phenomenology and especially into existentialism, where man has become as personal, unique, and incomprehensible as God was before. Existentialists use man's uniqueness as an argument against rationalism: for how could anything unique ever be an object of rational inquiry? The answer is simple: it can be done. Every tree, every language, every prime number is equally unique; but what rational analysis intends to discover is what these unique phenomena have in common. This aim applies to subjectivity as much as it applies to uniqueness. We are all "subjective" to a certain extent, and this is itself a general and objective fact susceptible of further rational analysis.

Uniqueness appears even more unmanageable and inaccessible to rational analysis if one is in addition convinced that only what appears on the surface counts; for what appears unique may in reality not be unique at all. Here we meet with another self-imposed limitation, which is shared by most contemporary philosophers, whether continental existentialists and phenomenologists, or British ordinary language philosophers: the addiction to surfaces. This irrational attitude is related to positivistic methodologies of science, ranging from operationalisms of various types to behaviorism and stimulus-response theories. Grave doubts have been cast on this institutionalization of superficiality by the development of generative linguistics, due mostly to the work of Noam Chomsky. This development has already had significant implications for the study and methodology of the humanities. Since any addiction to surfaces would render the rational exploration of mysticism impossible, a brief sketch of the "rationalization" that has taken place in linguistics is in order here.

Chomsky would not have been interested in exploring new avenues had he not been dissatisfied with existing ones. The situation which prevailed in linguistics at the time he started to work provides a perfect illustration of the kind of surface addiction I am referring to. Linguists in the first half of the twentieth century, especially (though not exclusively) in the United States, had taken to the study of a multiplicity of languages with an apparently very scientific zeal, itself largely inspired by the positivistic and neopositivistic analysis which philosophers had given of the spectácular achievements of the natural sciences. On closer inspection, the activity of these linguists was rather disastrous, resulting in an artificially impoverished and restricted notion of human language. On the one hand, the ideal of the half-understood and only partially interpreted physical sciences had led linguists to a concentration on sounds and a total neglect of meaning. On the other hand, they fell prey to a positivistic methodology which had been extremely beneficial within philosophy, where it had exposed the meaninglessness of much metaphysical speculation, but which, in so-called empirical and avowedly "scientific" linguistics, had led to a concentration on the surface and on observables together with a total neglect of theory. Linguistics (very unlike physics, but rather like a kind of physics from which theoretical physics has been painfully extracted) confined itself to a classification of elements; language was conceived of as a series of utterances by people (available on tape recorders or in written transcription) without anyone asking how such utterances came about or attempting to explain or account for them in even the vaguest of terms.

It would not do to defend the structural school of linguistics, which embraced this misguided form of empiricism, by arguing that these linguists, and the positivists, behaviorists, operationalists, and phenomenologists who similarly excluded meaning, were simply not interested in meaning and cannot therefore be accused of an addiction to surfaces. The contribution of Chomsky's generative linguistics is not that "meaning" is also relevant, in addition to surfaces; its contribution is that "surfaces" cannot be adequately understood without postulating much more abstract levels of analysis. For example, to account for the phonological structure of a language, one has to take its syntax and, according to many contemporary linguists, also its semantics into account.

Structural linguists failed to reach the goals they set themselves. Structural linguistics, behaviorism, positivism, operationalism, and phenomenology are not merely partial studies of separate areas of reality. The study of language has shown that they are basically inadequate because they cannot fully account for the very features in which they are interested. Generative linguistics, by making stronger and more abstract assumptions about language than its predecessors, can provide a more adequate treatment of the phenomena the structural linguists were interested in (e.g., phonology), and can in addition account for many linguistic phenomena (especially in the area of syntax) which the structural linguists did not even consider. The basic reason for this success is the attention Chomsky and his followers paid to theory formation.

From a methodological point of view, the situation in linguistics may be unique within the humanities, where theory formation is rare, but such a state of affairs is quite common in the natural sciences. In the theory of electromagnetism, for example, classical field theory, which starts with macroscopically measurable quantities, made relatively few theoretical assumptions, but could not explain certain phenomena, such as electrolysis. In order to account for these, more abstract assumptions concerning the corpuscular nature of electromagnetic energy were required. A similar situation obtains in the theory of heat:

> The phenomenological method employs only concepts like temperature, quantity of heat, etc., which are taken from the macroscopic world of observations and which can be measured directly. The laws thus obtained have the advantage of being free from hypothetical assumptions. On the other hand, in the Theory of Heat, e.g., in connexion with the

Law of Entropy, we feel the need of a deeper "explanation." Such an interpretation, deeper because more vivid, is furnished by the atomic, statistical view (Joos 1947, p. 457).

Again, entire sciences like chemistry and astronomy depend on physics for theoretical explanations of many of the phenomena they deal with and which could not be accounted for in terms of their own methods and concepts.

The main technical tool which enabled Chomsky to go beyond the various empiricisms which preceded him is the notion of rule (see especially Chomsky 1961; for a general exposition see Chomsky 1965). Chomsky took this notion from logic and introduced it into linguistics, where it had never been used outside India—the country where Pāṇini and other Sanskrit grammarians had discovered and employed is equivalent, the notion of *'sūtra.'* Chomsky thereupon discovered that the rules he needed for linguistics had to be of very special types. He also found that rules do not simply operate on the observed utterances of a language, or even on the abstract and idealized sentences which are postulated as underlying utterances, but on underlying structures of a much more abstract sort. All resulting insights could be attained only because nonobservables (e.g., rules, structures on which rules operate, ordered sets of rules, etc.) were postulated, and abstract theories were put forward to interpret and explain the data.

Even apart from theoretical considerations, the fruitfulness of the conversion of linguistics from a respectable domain of scholarship into a contemporary, rational, and scientific discipline suggests that the humanities can only develop if they avoid the addiction to observables and surfaces which many of the social sciences have adopted, and which is erroneously attributed (by some philosophers and methodologists) to the natural sciences as well.

The humanities have been in a particularly unfortunate situation. The apparently more manageable parts of the humanities—such as philology, and more generally the study of language—have suffered from this methodological, antitheoretical superficiality, while the apparently less manageable parts—in particular, the study of the mind—have suffered from that superficiality and also from the irrationalism inherited from the religious treatment of the soul. Accordingly, the addiction to surfaces, and the belief in the uniqueness and mysteriousness of man, have gone hand in hand and hindered all progress in our understanding of man. Such progress can only be expected when rational analysis is undertaken and opens the way for theory construction. This holds for the humanities in general, and for the study of mysticism in particular. What happens inside the sun is as unique, as different from ordinary experiences, and as susceptible of explanation in terms of a rational theory, as what happens in the depths of the human mind.

It is sometimes suggested that a further obstacle to the study of mystical experience is that it is not only irrational and unique but also rare, not easily repeatable, and perhaps not within reach of everybody; hence, so the suggestion goes, such experiences should be excluded from the realm of objective knowledge. We have already seen that experience in general, and mystical experience in particular, is neither rational nor irrational. But this last line of thought would also exclude astronomy, where experiences are often unique and experiments generally impossible; and the study of art, since good artists are rare. In physics, experiments like the Michelson-Morley experiment, designed to establish the existence of ether, but ultimately explicable only in terms of the special theory of relativity, generated the experience of an observation that is even rarer than mystical experiences. Moreover, Michelson and Morley were highly trained men and their experiment is not easily repeatable. True, in principle, many people could be trained as they were trained, and some might then succeed in doing the experiment again. But exactly the same may be said with regard to mystical experiences. Most people are able to learn certain techniques of concentration and in due course be in a position to submit at least some of the claims of mystics to a test. Not everyone's effort would have the guarantee of a beatific vision and not everyone would obtain *mokṣa* or *nirvāṇa*; but not everyone would be successful in the Michelson-Morley experiment, or be invited to join the Princeton Institute for Advanced Studies.

The point I am trying to make here is not new. In fact, after formulating it, I discovered that Bergson in a different context used almost identical phrases in the mid-1930's:

> It is alleged that the experiences of the great mystics are individual and exceptional, that they cannot be verified by the ordinary man, that they cannot therefore by compared to a scientific experiment and cannot possibly solve problems. There is a great deal to be said on this point. In

the first place, it is by no means certain that a scientific experiment, or more generally an observation recorded by science, can always be repeated or verified. In the days when Central Africa was a *terra incognita*, geography trusted to the account of one single explorer, if his honesty and competence seemed to be above suspicion. The route of Livingstone's journeys appeared for a long time on the maps and atlases. You may object that verification was potentially, if not actually, feasible, that other travellers could go and see if they liked, and that the map based on the indications of one traveller was a provisional one, waiting for subsequent exploration to make it definitive. I grant this: but the mystic too has gone on a journey that others can potentially, if not actually, undertake; and those who are actually capable of doing so are at least as many as those who possess the daring and energy of a Stanley setting out to find Livingstone. Indeed, that is an understatement. Along with the souls capable of following the mystic way to the end there are many who go at least part of the way: how numerous are those who take a few steps, either by an effort of will or from a natural disposition! (Bergson 1935, p. 210).

When I advocate a rational analysis of mystical experiences, it is not the fact of the experiences that is called into question, but their interpretation. Mystical experiences are just as common as certain diseases, or people with six or seven toes on one foot. But if we have no notion at all about what it could mean to have a mystical experience, it would not even be meaningful to ask whether what is allegedly a mystical experience is really a mystical experience—just as we can meaningfully ask whether a person diagnosed as having a rare disease may in the final analysis turn out to have merely a cold. But in order to settle such disputes, we need theories.

The prejudice that mysticism is irrational has become so widespread, that mysticism is now regarded as the antipode *par excellence* of logic, that embodiment of rationality itself. No less eminent and clear-headed a philosopher than Bertrand Russell has contrasted the two in his well-known essay, *Mysticism and Logic*. Further confusion has been the result. Russell believed that mysticism should be "commended as an attitude towards life, not as a creed about the world" (Russell 1953, p. 18). But mysticism is not an attitude towards life, and it deserves to be evaluated on what it claims to be, not on what it could conceivably lead into. Russell did not, in fact, pay much attention to what seems to be most central in many mystical doctrines. But he rightly began his analysis by denying that there is an opposition between the intuition that mysics advocate and the reason that scientists demand: "Instinct, intuition, or insight is what first leads to the beliefs which subsequent reason confirms or confutes" (Russell 1953, p. 19: quoted above, page 9). This applies to the heuristics of rational knowledge and to mysticism alike. Rational knowledge can be reached in a great many different ways. There is nothing inherently irrational, for example, in what Socrates said in Plato's *Phaedrus*: "Our greatest blessings come to us by way of madness" (*Phaedrus* 244A, quoted in Dodds 1957, p. 64).

If "mysticism" could be conceived of as consisting of ultimate elements, each a combination of a mystical experience and an interpretation of that experience, it is the experiences which are the primary objects of our analysis. This is another way of saying that it is the interpretations of these experiences which are under scrutiny, for our analysis would be one such interpretation. Of course, the experiences we choose to concentrate upon are selected in relation to a preliminary notion of what, when fully explicit, might be formulated as a theory. But when a theory is finally set up and ready to be tested, it should account for the experiences in the first place, though it would also throw light on the various existing interpretations of the experiences.

4

Appearance and Reality

So far I have been mainly concerned with the need for a rational exploration of mystical experiences. But the question also arises, whether the mystical doctrines invoked to account for such experiences can themselves be called rational in some sense or other. In order to answer this question one would need to know more about such mystical doctrines. In particular one would like to find characteristic features shared by all or most of these doctrines.

A clear candidate for such a characteristic of mystical doctrines is the distinction between appearance and reality. All mystics assert that there is something real which lies beyond the appearances and which is not experienced under normal circumstances. They may then go beyond this rather general statement and present certain claims about this underlying reality—for example, that it is one, undifferentiated, or timeless. Such claims may become unintelligible, as we have seen. But there is nothing either in this general method and approach, or in such particular assertions, whether true or false, that is irrational or that conflicts with the law of noncontradiction. Of course, reality presents itself to us as plural, differentiated, and, at least partly, embedded in the flow of time. But this does not logically conflict with the possibility that deeper analysis might show that reality is in all these respects different. What would be illogical and irrational would be to claim that reality is at the same time one and many, or temporary and eternal; in Averroism, dialectics, phenomenology, or existentialism such claims are possible.

Not only is the distinction between appearance and reality consistent with logic and the requirements of rationality; it is in fact exactly what is presupposed in most sciences and all rational inquiry. Scientists have shown that objects which present themselves to us as solid are permeated by space; that things which appear near in space or time, empty, or young, are far, full, or old, and conversely; that many events which appear in a certain way are quite different when subjected to deeper analysis. An illustration already referred to is provided by the distinction, in physics, between phenomenological and atomistic theories.

The distinction between reality and appearance, which science and mysticism share, is rejected by philosophies which confine themselves to "phenomena" as they present themselves, to ordinary experience, or to ordinary language. I have already drawn attention to the curious fact that almost all contemporary philosophies share precisely this one characteristic: they advocate that philosophers should limit themselves to ordinariness, surfaces, and appearances. Originally this narrowness was the outcome of a common reaction against the pompous claims and pseudoprofundities of traditional metaphysics, culminating in Hegel. As a result, phenomenologists now wish to confine themselves to the world of everyday experience, and ordinary language philosophers to ordinary language; both criticize science because it makes use of abstraction, formalization and theory construction.[1] Many positivist and behaviorist philosophers

1. These statements may sound incredible to non-philosophers, so let me give two representative examples. The French phenomenologist Merleau-Ponty advocates a return from the *constructa* of science to the *monde vécu* (Husserl's *Lebenswelt*) of everyday experience. This leads for example, to the following absurd characterization of some simple notions of geometry: "Let us, at the outset, reject any idea of a formal essence of the triangle. Although attempts at formalization may be conceived, it is in any case quite certain that they lay no claim to provide a logic of invention, and that no logical definition of a triangle could rival, for abundant variety, the actual sight of the figure, or enable us to reach, through a series of formal operations, conclusions not already established by the aid of intuition" (Merleau-Ponty 1962, p. 385). But most mathematics *is* the derivation, "through a series of formal operations," of conclusions *not* already established with the aid of intuition; one of the reasons, incidentally, that mathematics is not dull. It is true that we do in no science possess a "logic of invention." But if mathematics had confined itself to what is given in direct experience, it would not have arrived at theories and not have gone beyond the level it had already reached in ancient Egypt. Lastly, there is no such thing as *one* intuition (which, says Merleau-Ponty in the next sentence, has no place in logic): my intuition in mathematics is different from that of Euler. Does Merleau-Ponty claim that he knows by intuition all the

also urge that we confine ourselves to what is immediately presented to us in the form of data, facts, or behavior. Only they do not criticize the sciences, since they assume that science operates in exactly that way. But those sciences which have yielded the most spectacular insights, in particular the physical sciences, do not conform to this picture,[2] while the sciences that do (especially the behavioral sciences) have in general failed to produce interesting results.

Negligence of the distinction between appearance and reality prevents a rational interpretation of mysticism. In philosophy, a recent example is provided by Danto (1972). This author criticizes Oriental mysticism for reducing man to something inhuman or hardly human. But Danto's notion of "human" is a surface notion, derived from contemporary philosophy, while the Oriental notions of "human" refer in general to something that may come to the surface only under exceptional circumstances (cf. Staal 1974).

So, we arrive at the following division. On the one hand, rational analysis, most of the sciences (in particular the physical sciences), and also mysticism adhere to the distinction between reality and appearance; on the other hand, most contemporary philosophies and some of the sciences (in particular the behavioral sciences) re-

---

conclusions that can be derived from a definition (for that is what he says)? In that case, according to Leibniz and others, he would surely be divine. This quotation, lastly, is not an isolated passage; such passages are found throughout the work of Merleau-Ponty. Similarly antitheoretical statements are found in Wittgenstein, in his second period perhaps the most well-known ordinary language philosopher. Wittgenstein advocates that philosophy should leave everything as it is: "And we may not advance any kind of theory. There must not be anything hypothetical in our considerations. We must do away with all *explanation*, and description alone must take its place. And this description gets its light, that is to say its purpose, from the philosophical problems. These are, of course, not empirical problems; they are solved, rather, by looking into the workings of our language, and that in such a way as to make us recognize those workings: *in despite of* an urge to misunderstand them" (Wittgenstein 1958, p. 47).

2. This is clear from the facts from physics already referred to. Whitehead (1933, chap. 8), more specificially drew attention to the fact that the astronomers who discovered deviations in the orbits of the planets Uranus and Neptune did not rest content with the mere mathematical description of these observations but tried to explain them by postulating an imaginary point moving around the sun beyond the orbit of Neptune. When this unobservable phenomenon was correlated with certain dots on photographic plates, a new planet was discovered.

ject that distinction, eschew theory formation, and adhere to the study of surfaces only. The former, therefore, may be literally characterized as deep, the latter literally as superficial. This explains, incidentally, why the claims made by, say, physics, astronomy, Taoism, or Yoga are often challenging, while the descriptions produced by phenomenology, ordinary language philosophy, positivist sociology, or behaviorist psychology are generally boring. The former, right or wrong, say something that is new; the latter keep telling us what we know already.

While mystical doctrines purport to deal with objective reality, mystical experiences have a subjective quality, which, as we shall see, is an important feature that stands in need of further investigation. The distinction between appearance and reality, which primarily characterizes the objective claims made in mystical doctrines, is itself applicable to this subjective feature of mystical experiences, sometimes characterized by saying that these experiences are among the "altered states of consciousness."

That scholars and scientists are generally suspicious of the "subjective" is not only due to the difficulty of checking or testing in such cases. There is also some semantic confusion. "Subjective" means at least two things: (1) "subjective" as *opposed* to "objective," where "objective" means "objectively true" and "subjective" therefore means "false"; (2) "subjective" in the sense of "relating to the subject," which is *complemented* by "objective" in the sense of "relating to the object." In this essay, the term is used in this second sense in such expressions as "subjective experience," "subjective criterion," etc. Therefore, this use of the term does not imply that subjective experiences and criteria are false, and does not preempt the discussion about their validity.

The expression "altered states of consciousness" suggest that the waking state of consciousness, the state, for example, in which I am when writing and you when reading this, is normal and normative, while mystical and other states are alterations of it. But, of course, here too the appearances might deceive, and it is possible that the reverse is true—that the mystical state of consciousness is more basic, while the waking state is one of its offshoots or modifications. Such a possibility might be interpreted in psychological or historical terms. It could mean, among other things, that in the history of mankind, consciousness appeared first as what is now called the mystical state of consciousness. This hypothesis might explain some of the archaic features of mysticism and also, for example, why mystics often claim that there was a golden age when mystical insights were common.

I do not at all claim that this fairly mystical theory is correct. But since little is known about the phylogenetic origin of consciousness, the distinction between appearance and reality should alert us that the phrase "altered state of consciousness" might be misleading. We know for certain that mankind's priorities have changed frequently and profoundly. It would not be surprising if it were found that we ourselves are very different from what we appear to be. We should at least be prepared to learn from Chuang Tzu's story about the man who dreamed that he was a butterfly, and then wondered whether he was perhaps in fact a butterfly dreaming that it was a man (plate 13).

All these considerations show that many of the claims contained in mystical doctrines, whether true or false, are not only not irrational, but that their rationality is similar in structure to that of the sciences. I do not claim that this is something that makes mysticism more respectable or for which it is necessarily to be commended. Nor does it establish that mysticism *is* rational. But it shows that mysticism and rationality are compatible, and it indicates that it is entirely erroneous to suppose that mysticism cannot be studied at all. It should also be taken into account when we wish to find out how mysticism can be more adequately explored.

PART II

How Not to Study Mysticism

> A philosopher talked about celestial matters. Diogenes asked him: "When did you come back from heaven?"
>
> DIOGENES OF SINOPE

That mystical experiences and theories should be susceptible of rational analysis could have been expected on general grounds. For, as I mentioned earlier, most objects are neither rational nor irrational, and yet can be the object of rational inquiry: witness plants, which do not resist botanical analysis. The first part of this essay was designed to show that there is no special reason that would force us to move mysticism out of the domain of rational inquiry. The existence in this area of a special threshold, beyond which the unintelligible begins, has not been established. Yet it is precisely the contrary assumption—that mysticism cannot be rationally understood—which underlies and undermines all existing approaches to its study. I shall now review and illustrate four of these approaches and point out their inadequacies. This will at the same time enable me to introduce and illustrate a different approach.

5

Dogmatic Approaches

1. Mysticism in Christianity and Islam

Dogmatic approaches to the study of mysticism are those of theologians and orthodox believers in general, who wish either to reject or to incorporate mysticism, or those of some mystics, who wish to defend it. There are numerous forms of rejection, especially in the Judaic, Christian, and Muslim traditions. This is not surprising, for, although Islam is not as irrational as Christianity, as we have already noted (Muslims chide Christians for their belief in miracles, claiming miraculousness only for the revelation of the Koran), both religions are bound by a strict scriptural tradition which leaves little room for mysticism. The Muslim characterization of Muslims, Christians, and Jews (unlike its characterization of Hindus or Buddhists) as *ahl al-kitāb* "people of the book" underlines this in correct fashion. The more independent forms of mysticism, which interpret dogma in the light of experience, have therefore in both religions been charged with heresy.

The irrationality of the dogmatism of Islam and Christianity is not only often self-avowed; it is also apparent from the fact that what Muslims and Christians consider incompatible with their religious traditions, and therefore heretical, varies over the centuries and from person to person. In Islam, we see Najm ad-Dīn Rāzī in the thirteenth-century struggle with the fact that mysticism is by no means confined to Islam. He solves this problem in a purely arbitrary way by distinguishing between two kinds of mysticism, which are, for him, the good kind and the bad kind—the first being Muslim and the second non-Muslim. Zaehner comments on this as follows:

The essential difference between the two types of experience, Najm al-Dīn says, is that Brahmans, ascetics, Hindus, and philosophers always retain a sense of duality and "never experience visions of the lights of the attributes of oneness." Here, unfortunately, Najm al-Dīn is quite wrong, for whatever criticism one may make of Brahmanical mysticism, it is certainly not that it pays insufficient attention to oneness, for even those sects which have a pluralistic philosophy conceive of liberation as the attainment of an indifferentiable unity, even though that may not be absolute metaphysical unity. He is, however, nearer the mark when he says that they "do not come forth from their own being"; but can one be certain that the same is not true of his superior Muslim mystic whose "humanity is destroyed in the revelation of the light of the attributes of oneness and who enjoys the manifestation of the world of lordship" where "the tongue which speaks the absolute mystery, does right to say, 'I am the Truth' " (Zaehner 1960, p. 181).

Zaehner apparently wields a distinction of his own between good and bad mysticism in this attempt to interpret and elucidate Rāzī's own different, but equally arbitrary distinction. I have already mentioned Christian theologians, like Barth and Brunner, who rejected mysticism on grounds that are again different, though equally dogmatic. These evaluations in the light of what happens to be one's personal tradition, belief, or taste are incompatible with each other and are clear obstacles to the progress of understanding and to any rational inquiry.

Christian and Muslim mystics, because they were sincere believers or were afraid of excommunication if not martyrdom, had to find scriptural support for their mystical convictions and practices. Since few religious scriptures are entirely devoid of mystical utterances or utterances that can be interpreted within a mystical perspective, they were guaranteed some measure of success. The following cases illustrate the kind of difficulties encountered in the history of Christian mysticism. Many mystics have held the belief that there exists an impersonal divinity which is ineffable and which appears entirely different from the theistic and personal Christian Creator-God. This belief is partly based upon speculation, partly upon a mystical experience of emptiness, of "nonbeing," which is found all over the world and to which I shall return in chapter 12. In their incessant and paradoxical attempts to give expression to such an ineffable notion, the Christian mystics made use of Neoplatonic concepts. Plotinus, adopting an expression used in Plato's *Republic*, had said that the one, which is the Neoplatonic absolute, is beyond being (ἐπέκεινα ὄντος e.g., *Enneads* V.5.6.8–13; cf. Staal 1961b, pp. 185 ff.). One of the successors to Plato in the Academy, Speusippus, as well as some Neopythagoreans, called the supreme principle ἀνούσιον, "the supra-essential," or ὑπερούσιον, "the nonessential" (Dodds 1928, pp. 138–140; Merlan 1953, p. 117; cf. Gilson 1955, p. 598, n. 50). A Gnostic mystic of the second century, Basilides, went a step further and conceived of a divine "nonbeing" (Gilson 1952, p. 36). Scotus Erigena, in the ninth century, introduced these Neoplatonic ideas into the mainstream of medieval Christian mysticism. He said that God *est qui plus quam esse est* "is he who is more than being." Gilson, after describing Scotus Erigena's doctrine, states that it "was to remain a sort of permanent temptation against which, from century to century, doctrinal authorities were never to cease struggling, without ever succeeding in killing it" (Gilson 1955, p. 128; cf. Gilson 1952, p. 222).

One of the difficulties of this doctrine, apart from its paradoxical character, is that it seems to be in direct contradiction not only with the spirit but also with the letter of the Christian scriptures. There is a well-known Biblical passage where the God of the Old Testament reveals himself by saying: *ego sum qui sum*, "I am that I am" (Exodus 3:14). The Neoplatonic divinity, when forced to speak, could at most have said: *ego sum qui non sum*, "I am that I am not." Whether or not this contradicts itself, it certainly contradicts Exodus 3:14. Meister Eckhart, who some four centuries after Scotus Erigena also held that God *est aliquid alitus ente* "is something higher than being," engaged in breathtaking spiritual gymnastics to defend his doctrine by relating it to precisely this Biblical passage (Gilson 1952, p. 696; 1955, p. 439). Other mystics did not go as far and followed the lead of the *Corpus Areopagiticum* (which unbeknownst to them was also of Neoplatonic origin), in which the deity had been described as *esse omnium* "the being of everything" (Gilson 1952, p. 383), an expression not so clearly inconsistent with orthodoxy, though here the heretical interpretations leaned toward pantheism.

These doctrines do not seem to lend much support to my earlier contention that mysticism is rational. If anything seems to clearly contradict the law of noncontradiction, it is the statement that there is something that is not. But let us look more closely. Many of these examples, which could easily be multiplied, suggest that the mystics became entangled in self-contradictions which were due either to the fact that their experiences could not be expressed successfully in ordinary language, or to the fact that they had to twist their statements in order to make them acceptable to the orthodox.

As I have already pointed out, and despite what is generally believed, the former difficulty is not at all incompatible with rational inquiry: in all domains of knowledge where entities are dealt with which are not easily expressible in ordinary language (e.g., in mathematics), an artificial language is created to perform this function. To evolve such a language is an important part of theory formation and by no means irrational. Mystical experiences by themselves, just like ordinary perceptions, are neither rational nor irrational; but the mystics, especially in the West, often failed to find rational expressions to refer to their experiences. It is not obvious, anyway, that mystics should be in possession of the best theories about mysticism. Artists, scientists, lovers, patients, and animals do not have the best theories about art, science, love, illness, and the animal kingdom, respectively, nor are they generally interested. It is the students of mysticism whose task it is to evolve a theory.[1]

The second difficulty—that the mystics' statements needed to appear orthodox—does not arise in religious traditions where the scriptures are less binding or not taken literally, as in Taoism or Hinduism. Schomerus showed that the main differences between Eckhart and the Tamil mystic Manikka-Vasagar are not doctrinal

1. The point is familiar, but not to students of religion, who tend to insist that the student needs a "religious sense." Noam Chomsky related the following story to Ved Mehta: "Once, the Slavic Department at Harvard was thinking of offering Vladimir Nabokov an appointment. Roman Jakobson, the linguist, who was in the department then, said that he didn't have anything against elephants but he wouldn't appoint one a professor of zoology" (*New Yorker*, May 8, 1971, p. 50). But this is not all; for further discussion, see chap. 9.

but are merely due to their relationship to their respective religious traditions: Manikka–Vasagar was easily accepted as a Hindu in the tradition of the Upaniṣads; Meister Eckhart had to go out of his way to appear a Christian (Schomerus 1936). This partly accounts for the fact that Eckhart's expressions appear more paradoxical than Manikka–Vasagar's.

In Islam, some mystics traced Muslim mysticism, Sufism or *taṣawwuf*, back to Koranic utterances such as "We are nearer to him than his own jugular vein" (Koran 50:15; see also Massignon 1954, pp. 139–153). Others preferred to regard as a heresy, not the adoption of certain doctrines, but their expression in public. According to al-Ghazzalī (around A.D. 1100), who did much to make Sufism acceptable to orthodox Islam, "It is not permissible to commit one's secrets to writing. For the initiates say: 'To divulge the secret of the divinity is heresy' " (quoted in Wensinck 1940, p. 154). This led to such niceties as Majdhūb's saying: "Bury your secret, under seventy yards of earth, and let the creatures sigh until the Day of Judgment" (quoted in Massignon 1954, p. 17). Mysticism in Islam, by the twelfth century, had become an esoteric tradition.

One example will illustrate the unhampered development of mysticism in religions where scriptural orthodoxy is nonexistent, different in character, or less binding. In Hinduism, Śaivism and Vaiṣṇavism are distinct traditions, and sometimes develop as competing sects. But the adepts of Haṭhayoga could without fear of excommunication and with complete unconcern (also for the rules of grammar[2]) adhere to the maxim: "Śiva is the heart of Viṣṇu: Viṣṇu is the heart of Śiva": *viṣṇusya hṛdayaṃ śivaḥ śivasya hṛdayaṃ viṣṇuḥ* (quoted in Iyângâr 1893, p. ix).

2. *viṣṇusya* is not the genitive of *viṣṇuḥ* (as *śivasya* is of *śivaḥ*); the correct form is *viṣṇoḥ*. The logicians were similarly scornful of grammar: *asmākeṣāṃ naiyāyikeṣāṃ arthani tatpāryam/ śabdani kaś cintā?* which could be approximately rendered as: "us logickers is intend in meening—what kare is saund?" (The correct form would be: *asmākaṃ naiyāyikānām arthe tātparyam / śabde kā cintā?* "we logicians are intent on meaning—who cares for sound?"). The following lines are attributed to Śaṅkara: *prāpte saṃnihite 'tra maraṇe / na hi rakṣati ḍukṛñ karaṇe* "when death which is always near comes close (grammatical expressions like) *ḍukṛñ karaṇe* do not save." But since *ḍukṛñ karaṇe*, with locative ending, is not easily construed as the subject of the verb *rakṣati* "saves," Yutaka Ojihara (personal communication) proposes to read for *rakṣati*: *rajyati*, so that the second line means: "one is no longer attached to *ḍukṛñ karaṇe*." Since *karaṇam* means "activity" (in this particular grammati-

In Indian religions, freedom of religion and religious tolerance have been accepted values since the earliest times. Lack of dogmatism has been the result. A Hindu, in particular, can practically believe what he likes. But that does not imply that he can do what he likes. The main current of Hinduism does not stress *orthodoxy* or "right opinion"; but it emphasizes *orthopraxy* or "right activity." What a Hindu should do, his *dharma* "duty," is *varṇāśramadharma*: it is determined by his position in the caste system (*varṇa*) and in life (*āśrama*: see chap. 13, n. 2, below). What he thinks is left to him. He can be an atheist, a communist, or a witch-doctor. We therefore come across much intolerance in the realm of action—caste rigidity, preoccupation with ritual, obsession with pollution—and much tolerance in the realm of doctrine—theism, monism, mysticism, animism, communism, and any kind of syncretism.

In the sects of Hinduism, and also in the religions of Jainism and Buddhism—originally sectarian movements themselves—the situation is reversed (cf. page 101). Members of all castes are welcome, ritual is initially excluded, but sectarian doctrines are emphasized, and a measure of religious intolerance, sometimes reminiscent of the Western monotheistic religions, makes its appearance. But since there are hardly any religious authorities to whom all Hindus owe allegiance, the development of Hindu mysticism remains unrestricted and mystical experiences continue to be accepted and incorporated.

The attitude toward mysticism which is found in Indian religions, even those that do not regard themselves as primarily mystical, is therefore very different from the attitude of the monotheistic religions of the West. It is true that the mystical doctrines of the Upaniṣads are secret doctrines, to be taught outside the village community and in the forest only. The commentators explain the term *upaniṣad* itself as *rahasyam* "secret." But the reason is not the opprobrium of orthodoxy, but the belief that these doctrines are readily misunderstood and misapplied. In Vedic recitation, similarly, certain mantras

---

cal context), and also "body," it would also suggest that one is no longer attached to activity or to the body. Lastly, the second line expresses that the form "*ḍukṛñ*" is not attached to or influenced by the form "*karaṇe*," for in Sanskrit, final palatals are assimilated to following velars, so that *ḍukṛñ karaṇe* should have been *ḍukṛṅ karaṇe*, with velar *ṅ* instead of palatal *ñ* (cf. above, page 14).

are hidden in *aniruktagāna* "unexpressed chant" to prevent abuse by outsiders (as can be heard on Levy-Staal 1968). They are chanted in a special way, with the natural syllables changed into something unintelligible (e.g., "*bi bi bi bī*"). The exception here is Tantrism, where certain mystical doctrines are held secret because they teach the exact opposite of what the religious lawbooks lay down and puritans preach.[3]

In the Upaniṣads and in Tantrism the existence of secret doctrines may deteriorate into the kind of esotericism with which Indian religions are often associated, though it belongs more properly to such movements as theosophy. There is a clear parallel between the doctrine of irrationalism, which entitles its advocates to get away without providing arguments, and the doctrine of esotericism, which entitles its advocates to get away without providing evidence.[4]

Many of the different views of mystics on mysticism are inconsistent with each other; most of them result from prior convictions and are mere dogmatic assertions. One may turn out to be the correct one; or all may be wrong; but, since they differ, they cannot all be right. Śaṅkara said the same of the various Vedānta texts: if all teach different cognitions of the absolute, "only one of them is the right one, the others are erroneous": *teṣām ekam abhrāntaṃ bhrāntānītarāṇi* (*Brahmasūtrabhāṣya* 3.3.1, quoted in Staal 1960, p. 227). For adequate evaluations of the views on mysticism, further investigations and investigations of a different kind are therefore clearly necessary.

3. On esotericism and *sandhābhāṣa* "esoteric language" in Tantrism, see Eliade 1954, pp. 251–256 and 394–395, and Bharati 1965 and 1970, pp. 164–184, 290–291. One function of the "secret" language of mystics is the possibility of referring to particular visions, e.g., the blue light that is experienced but not seen by others (see chap. 1, n. 3).

4. Esotericism has been exploited primarily by the Theosophists, but also by a host of others, e.g., René Guénon, F. Schuon, T. Burckhardt, and, to some extent, A. K. Coomaraswamy, who have taught the traditional unity of all religions. There is undoubtedly a considerable similarity between mystical experiences all over the world, and it is the aim of the student of mysticism to explore this and account for it. But there is, at present, no good reason to believe in a traditional unity which is visible only to those who are initiated into esoteric doctrines and which contradict the explicit pronouncements of many representatives of the religions concerned. The theory is of course unfalsifiable: whoever denies esoteric meanings can be held to be concerned with their concealment.

2. *Zaehner on Mysticism*

The best contemporary example of the dogmatic approach to the study of mysticism is contained in the work of Zaehner. While this is especially clear in his *Mysticism Sacred and Profane* (1961) to which I shall revert, it is in the present context sufficient to turn to his *Hindu and Muslim Mysticism* (1960). The main historical thesis of this book (put forward in chapter V) is that the monistic phase of Sufism was introduced into Islam by Abū Yazīd al-Bisṭāmī in the ninth century, and was in its entirety derived from the Hindu Vēdanta. That this view is untenable has been shown by several authors (such as Arberry 1962, and Gelblum 1962). But apart from such historical errors, the main difficulty with this book as a whole is the author's own religious allegiance, which clearly prevents a fair and adequate description and evaluation of differing points of view and which leads the author to a classification which is nothing but a reflection of his own belief. For Zaehner, the phenomena of Hinduism and Islam must needs be reduced to two main types, the personal and the impersonal. These types are not interpreted in a constructive or revealing way, but merely provided with epithets and predicates (not rarely invectives) which convey that the author likes the former and despises the latter. We learn from this book that Zaehner is in fundamental sympathy with orthodox Islam, but is greatly irritated by the monistic trends in Sufism. On the other hand, he is in basic disagreement with much in Hinduism but appears greatly relieved when dealing with Indian theism and *bhakti* movements.

Such emotionalism may sound incredible, so let me give a few examples (for further details see Staal 1962b). An essential prerequisite for the study of Indian thought is an understanding of the ritualism of the later Vedic period, as expressed, for example, in the literature of the Brāhmaṇas. But for Zaehner, the Brāhmaṇa literature is "of historical interest only" (p. 6), and he speaks about its "dreadfully tedious series of cosmic and ritual identifications" (p. 24). At this point Zaehner could either have tried to take these ritual identifications more seriously, remembering for instance the Christian Eucharist; or else he could have tried to take their tedium more seriously, and thereby come to understand the later reactions *against* the ritual. But he does neither. Despite his dislike of the Vedic ritual, he is scandalized by the idea that the liberated man may pass "beyond all the rites of religion" (p. 107). When he discerns this objectionable trait in Abū Yazīd, he does not hesitate to attribute it to Vedānta influence, though Śaṅkara, he says "does strongly recommend an intense and loving devotion to God and was himself the author of many strikingly beautiful hymns to both Viṣṇu and Śiva"—hymns, in fact, which belong to a much later period and are merely attributed to Śaṅkara. Here again, he might have remembered from his own religious tradition Christ's transgression of the Sabbath.

Time and again, Zaehner's general religious prejudices lead to misinterpretation and facile generalizations. "Creation out of nothing is foreign to all Hinduism" (p. 87) is refuted by the passage in *Chāndogyopaniṣad* 6.2.1–2, which refers to philosophers who held precisely that view. The term *nirvāṇa* (p. 64) is not exclusively Buddhist. It is common in the Hindu epic and occurs several times in the *Bhagavad Gītā*, which uses the compound *brahmanirvāṇa* "extinction in *brahman*." Ghazzālī's "almost paranoiac hatred of the world" (p. 160) does not need to be connected with Manicheism and Buddhism: it constitutes a development which is not unlikely to take place in any religion and is, for example, not rare in early Christianity. In Islam it might have developed from the commendable practice of *iʿtikāf* "spiritual retreat," especially during Ramaḍān, the month of fasting.

Zaehner's book mixes dogmatism with emotionalism. Most Muslims and Hindus could from their own tradition provide refutations of such sweeping statements as: "of the monotheistic creeds it is only Christianity that builds a bridge between God, the Eternal, and man, the temporal . . ." (p. 86). Some doctrines are described by Zaehner in emotional terms which are reminiscent of the style some fathers of the church used when writing against heresies: "a rather silly quibble" (p. 90); "endless confusion" (p. 43); "maddeningly imprecise" (p. 54); "the usual maddening sentence" (p. 165); "slogans" (p. 195), for what in Islam is called *sh͟aṭaḥāt*; "flirtation" (p. 175)—expressions used only with regard to impersonalist trends. Especially the final sentences of chapters are suggestive: "So did Indian monism make its way into the Muslim creed which should have abhorred it" (p. 109). And *in fine*: "Both Najm al-Dīn Rāzī, defending Islamic orthodoxy, and Ibn Ṭufayl, defending sanity, expose the monist's pretension to be God as the 'misgrounded conceit' it so manifestly is" (p. 188). Zaehner might have followed instead the example of another father of the church, and made his own the dictum of Augustine: *non intratur in veritatem nisi per charitatem,* "truth is not reached unless through charity."

Zaehner's approach contributes little to the serious study of mysticism. It does not establish a position from which one can do more than scratch the surface of Hindu and Muslim forms of mysticism. The fact that such a testimony of faith is accepted without surprise or protest by a scholarly public as a possible contribution to our understanding seems only intelligible if it is assumed that, in the realm of religion and mysticism, argument and rational inquiry are inappropriate and faith is all that counts.

3. Panikkar on Hinduism

Zaehner is perhaps the best example of contemporary Roman Catholic dogmatism in the study of oriental mysticism. But even in those whose underlying attitude is more charitable and sympathetic, the limitations of such a dogmatic approach are obstacles to an adequate understanding and evaluation. This may be illustrated from the work of Raymond Panikkar (e.g., 1964a, 1964b). While Zaehner writes as if he had never met a Hindu in the flesh, Panikkar, not unlike Najm ad-Dīn Rāzī in Islam, obviously struggles with the fact that true religiosity, in his sense, does not seem to be confined to those of his own faith.

In Christian terms, says Panikkar, there are only two possible kinds of answer to this problem: "either we exclude from Hinduism any possible action of Christ altogether (i.e., Christ would save good Hindus in spite of and against their Hinduism); or we *somehow* incorporate Hinduism into the universal economy of salvation by God through Christ, of which Christianity is the summit" (Panikkar 1964a, p. 34).

While Zaehner's position seems aptly described by the former alternative, Panikkar opts for the latter. More explicitly, he regards Christianity as the end and fulfillment of Hinduism. This thesis is developed, for example, through an analysis of a text from the *Brahmasūtra.* Of course, Panikkar does not claim that the author of this text, or the commentators, "thought for a moment of Christ explicitly" (1964a, p. 132). But all the same, Panikkar tries to show that Christ was already at work there. He says about his work: "It would not be difficult to prove that we have been doing less violence to our text than Thomas Aquinas was in distorting Aristotelian thought . . ." (1964a, p. 135). In the last resort such distortions are perhaps not too important, for Panikkar believes, like all religious students of religion that "because we are dealing with the meeting of religions, the encounter is not merely rational . . . Hence it is in the depths of the dark and yet more sure knowledge where both spiritualities can meet" (1964a, p. 57).

In another book, which deals with this "meeting in depth of Hinduism and Christianity" (1964b, p. 9: *Begegnung in der Tiefe*), Panikkar states more explicitly what his work is about. If Hinduism selected a name for itself, it would prefer the name "catholic-universal-religion." If it lived up to this name, "Hinduism would meet the law of the cross as the road to resurrection, and it would not be able to avoid it . . . The present book aims to be a contribution to such a conversion" (Panikkar 1964b, p. 125).

While such an approach may have some validity for those who share Panikkar's Christian faith and his interest in Hinduism, it is obvious that it is of no interest to others, and has very little to contribute to the understanding of Hinduism.

Though the dogmatic approach to the study of mysticism seems misguided and barren, I shall in chapter 9 discuss a view that seems to be rational (though not necessarily correct; cf. chap. 5, n. 1) and that has been expressed by several mystics: the view that mysticism cannot be understood by those who lack mystical experience, and that no one can attain such an experience unless he is guided by some kind of faith.

6

Philological and Historical Approaches

Philological and historical studies provide the explorer of mysticism with some of his indispensable data. Yet these studies reflect a particular background and are of limited relevance, and that only for religions where texts and history play an important part. This is especially the case with the religions of the "people of the book," the Western monotheistic religions: Judaism, Christianity, and Islam, which are also those that pay most attention to history. But the present links between philology, history, and the study of religion are themselves susceptible to a historical explanation.

Religious studies as a branch of scholarship developed in the West in the wake of the study of the Bible, revived by Protestantism. This led to the study of Hebrew and Judaism, and of Arabic and Islam. Sanskrit, Vedic, Vedic religion, Hinduism, and Buddhism became objects of study during the Romantic movement (though British administrators in India had paved the way). Studies of the languages and religions of the Far East, especially Chinese, were undertaken during the Enlightenment. Though all these studies dealt with many aspects of civilization, they remained textually and historically oriented, an attitude inappropriate for many of the religious phenomena of South and Southeast Asia and the Far East, which are not concerned with texts or history.

However, even the published texts from these areas are often ill-suited to a strict philological treatment. The Indian epic as well as the *Purāṇas*, orally transmitted texts containing legends and myths, are not clearly defined or historically, geographically, or socially determined, nor are they uniquely named or attributed to one human author. They were often transmitted on festive and popular occasions by wandering bards, unlike the Vedas, for example, which were scrupulously transmitted inside orthodox homes and by trained reciters. Van Buitenen, the author of the new translation into English of the *Mahābhārata*, of which the first volume has now appeared, is eloquent on this point:

> One cannot expect that this transmission was a literal one, as it has been in the case of the Veda. A reciter's reputation was based on his skill in bringing the old stories to life again. Successive generations would add, embellish, digress; but also understate what might have been emphasized before.
>
> In a number of typical instances . . . the reciter would first give a resumé, a brief summary containing the salient features and little more. Then he would be prevailed upon to give the fuller story with all the detail he could think of. Even then his audience might interrupt him and ask for more information on certain points. All this creates the impression that what would come down from generation to generation were, first, the summaries, and, second, the technique of spinning out a tale to please the listeners. The reciter was thus also a creative poet, within the idiom of his craft (van Buitenen 1973, xxiii–xxiv).

Despite the floating character of such "texts," Paul Hacker applied the same philological criteria to the study of published (though uncritical) editions of the *Purāṇas* as he had earlier—and very successfully—applied to the study of philosophical texts. He set up an elaborate and intricate scheme establishing numerous historical relationships between various *Purāṇas* (Hacker 1960). The method is extremely precise, but the material is rather loose and so the conclusions, presented with great care, remain in fact indefinite (cf. Staal 1964b).

In the exploration of mysticism, historical and textual approaches are even less appropriate. Not only do the mystics claim that their experiences are timeless and inexpressible, but we know for certain that mystical experiences in very similar forms are found throughout history and all over the world, and that many mystics are careless about language and not interested in texts. Whatever it is, mysticism is mainly concerned with something quite different from whatever can be learned from the study of texts and history. Massignon quotes with approval what the Sufi Junaid said to Jurairī: "We have not learned Sufism by listening to 'they say this' or 'they say that,' but by fasting, by renouncing the world, and by being separated from those who are close to us and from pleasant things" (Massignon 1954, p. 17). A fact is that mystical experiences often follow dramatic, if not tragic, events (cf. plates 14a–b, 16).

Though most philologists and historians do not attempt to evaluate the validity of the experiences they describe, there are exceptions. Among these, some try to arrive at explanations by applying concepts borrowed from other branches of scholarship; others by adopting views from mystics they study. The former tend to take for granted the concepts they have adopted, assigning to them an explicatory function. This leads in general to new unresolved problems, sometimes conceptual in nature. The latter tend to become dogmatic, not in the realm of philology or history, but in that of interpretation and evaluation. In the following two sections I shall give examples of these two approaches. In the third section I shall discuss recent interpretations of the *Yogasūtra* which have been defended on philological and historical grounds alone.

1. Ruben and Lindquist on Yoga, Shamanism, and Hypnosis

In 1940 Ruben published an article in which he traced several mystic notions of Indian texts, and also the idea of transmigration, back to shamanistic beliefs that had originated in central Asia. His predecessor in these studies was Meuli (1935), who had carried out a similar investigation with respect to Greek religious ideas, especially in Orphism (these theories were given wider currency in Dodds 1957, chap. V; "The Greek Shamans and Puritanism"). Ruben, who also used ethnographic data (like later Indologists, such as Gonda and Kosambi), started with a consideration of the ascent to heaven (*Himmelsreise*) of the shamans, a journey supposedly similar to the psychic excursion they believed to take place in sleep. Ruben found this notion in the earliest Indian text, the *Ṛgveda* (10.136) (see pages 197–198). He suggested that the stages of yogic contemplation, which are parallel to the various planes distinguished in Indian cosmology, can also be traced back to the stages of the shamans' heavenly journey. Some of the alleged evidence is linguistic: in Buddhist Yoga treatises, the yogin is said to reach (*upasampad-*) one stage of concentration, stay (*vihar-*) there, and then ascend (*samatikram-*) to the next one.[1]

The ascent to heaven is an almost universal motif in the religions of the world. Even in Judaism and Islam, where mystical notions or notions susceptible of a mystical interpretation are relatively few, we find Jacob's ladder (Genesis 28) and Muhammad's nocturnal journey (*isrā'*), which is often interpreted as a mystic ascent (*mi'rāj*) (see plate 12; B. Schrieke and J. Horovitz in Wensinck and Kramers 1941, pp. 227–228, 509–511).

S. Lindquist, in his dissertation of 1932 and in a book of 1935, undertook a detailed study of many texts on Yoga, Hindu as well as Buddhist, and also sought to provide an explanation for the phenomena he met with (including some travel accounts of witnesses of yogic miracles). He arrived at the conclusion that these texts deal with techniques of autosuggestion, which often result in hallucinations and culminate in a state of autohypnosis which is repeatable at will. In going through these processes, the yogin also gains complete control over his subconscious. Lindquist interpreted many ill-understood technical terms of the Yoga within this perspective: *samāpatti*, according to him, refers to a hallucination; *prajñā* is the intellectual awareness of such a hallucination, and so on.

A brief comparison of Ruben's and Lindquist's results makes clear what problems we are faced with in this area. It is one thing to say that the Yoga can be traced back to shamanistic beliefs, another to say what these are. Ruben describes a variety of shamanistic phenomena, but says nothing about how they are to be

1. Similar ideas were propounded by W. Nölle in his Tübingen dissertation *Lehre und Kult der Kaulas* (referred to in Ruben 1954, p. 42, n. 39). Ruben himself developed his ideas later within a Marxist perspective. According to him, the original shamans recognized the soul as an active principle, but the mysticism of the Upaniṣads introduced the idea of quietism, which enabled Buddhists, Jains, and Brahmans to preach to the people that the perfect man does not allow his soul to be affected by any kind of suffering or exploitation (Ruben 1954, p. 144). Kosambi (1965, and in other works) has used Marxist ideas in a less orthodox and more fruitful manner. As we shall see in chapter 14, the Marxist dictum, that religion is the opium of the people, acquires special significance in the exploration of mysticism.

1. Viṣṇu asleep between creations.

See the complete descriptions of all the illustrations that follow the Contents page.

2. The force of *tapas:* descent of the Ganges.

3. Śiva, the divine yogin (*bhikṣāṭanamūrti*).

4. Śiva's dance of destruction (*gajasaṃhāramūrti*).

5. Śiva, the divine preceptor (*vyākhyāna-dakṣiṇāmūrti*).

6. Karman: ritual activity in a Vedic sacrifice.

7. Prapatti: surrender to God (the philosopher Rāmānuja).

8. Prajñā: spiritual wisdom (Buddha).

interpreted. Implicit in his investigation appears to be a vague conviction that shamanistic practices and beliefs are superstitions perhaps suggested by other primitive notions about dreams. But the significance of his investigations—granting for the moment that his correlations are valid—would lie precisely here. That significance would be quite different, for example, if shamanism were interpreted (with Eliade) as a reenactment of man's paradisal state, which is central to all religions, "primitive" as well as highly developed. In that case we would not have a simple though rather vague case of "reduction," as in positivism, but a complicated through perhaps empty substitution of one set of unanalyzed concepts for another. Shamanism might also be interpreted in the terms which Lindquist used to interpret Yoga, that is, suggestion and hypnosis. Empirical problems aside (see chap. 8, sec. 1, below), we are here faced with grave conceptual difficulties. Though a great deal is known about hypnotic phenomena, there is no generally accepted idea about what hypnosis is; "autohypnosis" is even more puzzling, not to mention that notoriously obscure, and perhaps empty, concept, the "subconscious." In all these attempts we arrive at unresolved problems, if not at cases of explaining *obscurum per obscurius*—"the obscure by the more obscure." We may learn just as much or as little about mysticism from studying hypnosis, as about hypnosis from studying mysticism. The data provided by the study of mysticism, hypnosis, and shamanism stand in equal need of further analysis and clarification; in all these cases we hardly know what we are talking about. We are certainly not in a position to evaluate the alleged correlations between them.

Though investigations like those of Ruben and Lindquist do not elucidate the nature of Yoga, they throw light on the close historical and geographical relations between the Indian Yoga and patterns of culture found all over central and northern Asia. These findings cast doubt, in turn, on a widespread speculation according to which Yoga represents the Dravidian element in Indian civilization. This theory, defended, for example, by Zimmer (1951: index, under "Dravidian factor"), is a recent variant on a traditional theme in the Western study of Indian civilization. This theme—no more than pure prejudice—is that everything Indian that is also found in the West was brought to India by the Aryan invaders, while everything else must be Dravidian.

It is worthwhile to pursue this historical topic a little further. We are seeking, among other things, greater conceptual clarity about Yoga. In such an abstract search one is wont to cling to whatever concrete evidence is at hand. The historical perspective in which we visualize the Yoga appears to afford such evidence, but by restricting our imagination, it also affects what we are prepared to find out about Yoga itself. It makes a lot of difference, for example, whether one tries to discover specific historical origins for the Indian Yoga or whether one explores Yoga as a general dimension of the human mind. Since we understand so little about Yoga, we are in need not only of more facts but also of an open mind and a flexibility of approach. One method that may assist us to attain these goals is through realizing that most theories about the historical background and origins of the Yoga rest on just as flimsy grounds as most of the theoretical and conceptual speculations about Yoga in particular and about mysticism in general.

The prejudice that Yoga is of Dravidian origin becomes more questionable still when linked with another unproven assumption: that the Harappā civilization was Dravidian (for a balanced evaluation of the evidence from the Harappā "script," see Zide and Zvelebil 1970). The fact always alluded to in this context is the existence of a Harappā seal with a representation of a horned figure, quite possibly a deity, sitting cross-legged (plate 10a). Though this figure also occurs on two other Harappā seals, the particular position represented here is often interpreted as a yogic position (e.g., Eliade 1954, pp. 349–354; 1969, pp. 355–356). This interpretation would in turn try to establish that Yoga was a feature of the Harappā civilization. "These facts can hardly be belittled, and their bearing is immense," says Eliade (1969, p. 356). Now it is true that squatting in such a position is in the West often associated with Yoga and meditation, but all over South and Southeast Asia people sit cross-legged when talking, eating, shaving, reading, teaching, and singing. Sitting cross-legged, in other words, proves nothing.

A distinctive feature of the representation of this seated figure is that it is ithyphallic, or represented as having an erection. This is hardly appropriate for a person engaged in Yoga. Moreover, several terracotta figurines of nude, very fat, ithyphallic males, often with animal heads and what appears to be a tail, have been found in Mohenjo-daro and Chanhu-daro (as well as in Nippur: Dales 1968).

The advocates of the theory of Harappā Yoga have nothing to say about such possible parallels. Or is there no difficulty?

One might make the attempt to save one fanciful theory by creating another. Some facts are suggestive. In a late Vedic text, the *Taittirīya Āraṇyaka* (10.12), we meet with the term *ūrdhva-retas*, literally "with erect semen." In later texts this becomes a relatively common epithet of sages and ascetics. The *Mahābhārata* epic, for example, refers to sages (*yati*) who are *ūrdhva-retas*. In similar contexts we also find the term *ūrdhva-liṅga*, which could literally mean "with erect penis." Both terms are also used of the Hindu God Śiva.

Despite what appears to be the literal meaning of these terms, they are not interpreted to mean that these sages are having an erection. Rather the opposite: they are said to keep their semen or penis "above" or "up"; that is, they live in chastity. The underlying idea, widespread in India, is that an ascetic gains power by controlling his semen and sending it upward, a practice which is often taken literally (Bharati 1965, pp. 91–96). Bharati refers in this connection to the practice of non-ejaculatory intercourse as part of a religious discipline, not only in India but also among Christian sects. In the Christian middle ages, virtuous men slept next to, but not with a woman, to test their resolve (Huizinga 1947, p. 313). In Tantrism, the ascetic may proceed to ejaculation, but the information on this alternative is recent. (A follower of the Tantra told Bharati in 1954: *ūrdhvaṃ gacched vā adhaḥ pated retaḥ/brahmānando bhavaty ubhayoḥ* "whether the semen goes up or falls down, *brahma*-bliss results from either"; Bharati 1965, p. 91).

The *Kāmasūtra*, the classical text on Indian erotics, as well as the epic on the subject, refers to erections by means of another term, *sthira-liṅga*, literally, "with firm, hard penis." In Indian semantics this notion is associated not with the idea expressed by the conventional term "erection," but is closer to the idea of the American colloquial "hard on." So we can only save the fanciful theory that the Harappā figure represents a yogin by other flights of fancy: that Indian semantics is in this area different from what it is, or that this ithyphallic representation expresses continence.

It would be safe to conclude that solid evidence for Yoga in the Harappā civilization is lacking. Connections with Dravidian civilization are not to be excluded, but hard evidence is not available. The connection of Yoga with the shamanistic cultures of central and northern Asia, stressed by Ruben and later, though with reservations, by Eliade, seems less speculative. But in the face of all these speculations it should be borne in mind that Yogalike phenomena are not absent from the core of the so-called "Aryan" civilization, from the Vedas themselves. These connections were perhaps first pointed out by Hauer (1932, 1958) who went, however, further than most scholars would nowadays be willing to go. I shall later refer to long-haired sages, akin to yogins, mentioned in a hymn of the *Ṛgveda.* I shall now briefly mention a few other facts that are not open to doubt.

The term *brahmacārin*, literally, "who is walking with *brahman*," is used in later Hinduism to denote the first of the four stages of life of an orthodox Hindu: the student stage. The term *brahmacarya* is also in later times associated with continence or sexual abstinence. In the *Atharvaveda, brahmacarya* still has its literal meaning, but it is there connected with *tapas* "austerity" (for the following, see Gonda 1965, pp. 286 ff.). This relationship is often mentioned in later texts. In the Upaniṣads it is said that *brahman* is reached by *satyam* ("truth"), *brahmacarya*, and *tapas* (Gonda 1965, pp. 294–296). Lüders (1959, pp. 644–652) has shown that *tapas* resembles the Vedic idea of the *brahman*-force which inheres in the mantras recited by Brahman priests during the ritual.

In the epic, *tapas* refers to the practice of asceticism and also to its result, that is, merit. In the latter sense it is a potent entity which can be transferred from person to person (Hara 1968–1969). In several articles and in unpublished work, Hara has studied the occurrences of *tapas* in the epics. It is the property especially of Brahman ascetics; it yields particular, often supernatural powers (*prabhāva*); and it is *duścara* "difficult to perform" and *sudāruṇa* "severe" (Hara 1968–1969, pp. 390–392; 1970, p. 64).

The force of *tapas* is a distinctive theme in many Indian legends, myths, and stories. A typical example is the legend of the royal sage Bhagīratha who, at a time of great drought and famine, through performing *tapas* urged the Gods to release the river Ganges which originally flowed in heaven (plate 2). Bhagīratha kept his arms raised for a thousand years, and in addition stood on one foot for another thousand. When the Gods at last granted his request, the force of the water which came pouring down was so strong that Śiva had to catch it on his head and reduce its power by diverting its descent through the labyrinth of his long, matted hair (see Zimmer 1946, pp. 109–121).

Since we do not know much about what *brahman*-force, *tapas*, and Yoga are, it is fruitless to speculate exactly how they were related. There is no insight gained by, and it is easy to find counterexamples to, general and emotional impressions (for example, "the ascetic collects in himself by means of fasting and austerities magical heat" versus "the yogī attempts by means of serene recollection to contemplate the highest," as is Frauwallner 1953, p. 134). But the mere similarity of the contexts in which these concepts occur suggests that *tapas*, though not the same as Yoga, represents a close Brahman relative. Though many of the terms of the later developments and of the *Yogasūtra* do not occur in their technical meanings in the Veda or in the epic, the function of *brahmacarya* and especially of *tapas* are clearly reminiscent of the Yoga. The supernatural powers *(prabhāva)* which result from *tapas* correspond to the supernatural powers (*siddhi*; *vibhūti*) which accompany Yoga.

Another term which is basic to the Yoga, Hindu as well as Buddhist, is *dhyāna* "meditation," derived from a root *dhyai*. It is related to several Vedic terms derived from the root *dhī* which express similar notions. According to Gonda, who devoted a monograph to this topic (Gonda 1963), the noun *dhī* denotes a vision, while the corresponding verb means "to have a vision," "to have an inspiration." The *dhītayaḥ* (plural of *dhītiḥ*) refer to materialized visions, often inspired hymns. The term *dhīta* denotes "an object of visionary sight"; the adjective *dhīra* means "gifted with vision" and hence "able on account of the possession of a vision." The quality expressed by *dhīra* may enable a sage to overcome practical difficulties of various kinds. And so we have a whole family of concepts which originate in the *Ṛgveda* and which pave the way for the related term *dhyāna* of classical times.

Since Lindquist's speculations on Yoga and hypnotism might be relevant for a future theory of mysticism in which such terms would be provided with clear interpretations, it befits us to study what the Indian texts have to say on hypnotism and related phenomena. The older Buddhist texts describe a type of clairvoyance, or the ability to look into other minds. These powers are attributed to persons who have attained a special state of consciousness, but they are not confounded with that state itself. Similar powers are attributed to the Christian saints (the term used is *καρδιογνωσία* "insight in the heart"). When the Buddhist monks mind is "concentrated, purified, clear, spotless, receptive, steady, . . ." he obtains many special faculties which are enumerated in *Dīgha-nikāya* II.83 and following. Of each of these it is said: "This also is a mundane fruit of the monk's life, which is better and more beautiful than the previous one." Among these is the faculty by which the mind knows the qualities of other minds, and sees into them.

Various texts refer to the ability to enter another body (*paraśarīrāveśa*), even a dead body. The ability to enter another body is often regarded as a special power obtained by those who are engaged in Yoga. *Yogasūtra* 3.38 says: "When the causes of bondage are loosened and when this procedure is perceived, the mind enters another body." According to most of Indian thought, bondage in the body is due to the effects of past activity. Through Yoga these effects can be undone and the mind thereby gains independence from the body. If the yogin adopts this procedure and is fully aware of the way it works, a side effect is that his mind can enter another body (*paraśarīrāveśa*) and control it.

A detailed description of a yogin entering a body occurs in the *Mahābhārata* epic (*Anuśāsanaparvan* XIII, 40 and 41; see Hopkins 1901, upon which Eliade 1954, p. 91 [= 1969, pp. 78–79] is based). Bhārgava Vipula was left to look after the wife of his guru, who had to attend a sacrifice. The God Indra, always interested in amorous adventures, appeared at the gate in beautiful shape, and Ruci, the guru's wife, was immediately taken by his charms. But the virtuous pupil "restrained her senses by the bonds of yoga." More than that, through Yoga-power his mind left his own body and entered hers:

> He abides in her limb by limb, like a shadow, like a person stopping in an empty house which he finds on his way, soiling her as little as a drop of water soils a lotus-leaf, standing in her like a reflection in a mirror.

In that state he changed the words she wished to utter, with the result that she, against her own inclinations and "under another's will" (*paravaśā*), addressed Indra with "Sir, what business have you to come here?" And since these words were prompted by the learned yogin, they were spoken in excellent Sanskrit.

2. *Massignon on Sufism and Conze on Buddhism*

I shall now briefly discuss two examples of scholars who have adopted views from the mystics they study and who are personally involved in the mystical experience, unlike, for example, Ruben or Lindquist. Despite their personal orientations, these scholars, though they are ultimately interested in other things, use primarily historical and philological methods. The subtitle of Massignon's main work is "A Study in Religious History," and that of Conze's principal book, "Three Phases of Buddhist Philosophy."

Louis Massignon devoted a series of publications to the Muslim martyr Mansūr al-Ḥallāj (executed in A.D. 922). The most important of these works are Massignon 1922 and 1954 (the latter originally published in 1922 also). Massignon's work manifests an extraordinary combination of devotion and scholarship. For him, the divine love of the mystic is the highest religious value. Like all religious values, he believes, mystical love is unique and *sui generis*, and it cannot be reduced to historical, literary, sociological, or psychological causes. It can be studied and followed, but it cannot be questioned. At the same time, Massignon has abiding faith in the religious mission of the Semitic tradition, and he approaches Islam as that branch of the tradition which inherited from Israel an exclusive faith in divine transcendence (e.g., Massignon 1963, p. 429).

These presuppositions deny to Massignon the unprejudiced study of any other religious tradition, but they enable him to penetrate into Islam like a believer. Disregarding the purely individualistic theories of philologists, Massignon stresses the need to reconstruct through introspection what he regards as a fact of sociology: the dogma that has resulted from centuries of "collective meditation" by Muslim society with the help of the Koran. Thus, when discussing Muhammad's night journey (*isrāʾ*) or ascension (*miʿrāj*), which the mystics of Islam have always regarded as the Prophet's supreme mystical experience (plate 12), Massignon brushes aside philological interpretations:

We shall not adopt the ingenuous philological conjectures of Bevan and Schrieke regarding a 'new' [*sic*] theory of the Nocturnal Ascent. We cannot simply substitute an individual interpretation, however ingenious, constructed by these Orientalists, for the sociological fact of a *dogma* that has been gradually arrived at through the collective meditation of a society of believers with the help of the text of the Koran. That would be to situate ourselves outside the only perspective which counts here: *the introspective reconstruction of the Muslim meditation ["l'introspection de la méditation islamique"] of the Koran (*Massignon 1922, p. 848).

This attitude leads to many valuable assertions and remarks, but they appear idiosyncratic to anyone but a believer. Such an approach also places philology in a special perspective. Massignon emphasizes, for example, that the Koran was not fabricated by Muhammad. The reconstruction of Muhammad's mental evolution, even if it could be carried out successfully, can therefore not throw any light on the internal chronology of the Koran. And so we meet with the kind of remark which is typical of the dogmatic obscurity that pervades much of Massignon's work and surrounds it with an aura of profundity. He protests against Goldziher, who advocated the study of Muhammad's internal development for establishing the chronology of the *sūra*'s: ". . . if one bases oneself upon this axiom that there is a contradiction between predestination and freedom; an axiom against which the entire religious experience of the believers protests . . ." (Massignon 1954, p. 143, n. 2).

In another footnote, Massignon expounds remarkable views on the psychological interpretations of Muhammad's mission and religiosity: "The hypotheses of epilepsy, autosuggestion, excessive imagination, have been propounded by sedentary psychiatrists, who do not know the life of the desert or the positive ingenuity required in order to simply remain the chieftain of a tribe of Bedouins" (Massignon 1954, p. 144, n. 5). I find such thoughts very attractive and suggestive, and yet it would be difficult to evaluate them without extensive and thorough investigations by sedentary and nomadic investigators alike. I shall return to a similar idea in a different context: we shall see that there is a relation between the motif of the wandering ascetic and the nomadic reminiscences of a sedentary society.

Though Massignon provided as many data on al-Hallāj as his

philological and historical methods could make available, to him the study of al-Ḥallāj is ultimately a discovery of the action of divine grace; its understanding and success depend on the scholar's own participation in that state of grace. This is possible only because it is in accordance with the doctrine of the Catholic church (cf. Waardenburg 1961, p. 307). These presuppositions enabled Massignon to approximate al-Ḥallāj's own interpretations of his experiences. But within this perspective, such presuppositions can hardly be questioned; any explanation along different lines is ruled out in advance. The difference between the dogmatic approaches of Massignon and Zaehner is that, apart from the mass of documents Massignon made available for the first time, his evaluations are approximations of those of al-Ḥallāj himself; while Zaehner's evaluations approximate in only a few cases, and are elsewhere incompatible with what the mystics have themselves declared. Neither approach is on these counts necessarily correct or incorrect.

The approach of Edward Conze is equally difficult to evaluate. Conze devoted a series of publications to Buddhism, especially to Mahāyāna Buddhism and the Mādhyamika. The most important of these is Conze 1962, but Conze 1951 and 1956 are relevant in the present context. All these are based at least in part upon philological and historical scholarship, but they also go beyond this. For Conze, the core of Buddhist mysticism is meditation, which can thrive only in the climate of a living spiritual tradition. Almost equally basic, at least for the modern Western readers these books address, is the realization that modern Western civilization not only fails to provide such a milieu, but is bankrupt. This is of course consistent with the Buddhist view that the world is wholly ill.[2] Conze also sees in Buddhism the answer to the basic anxiety existentialist philosophers have drawn attention to. "In its pure form, this anxiety is experienced only by people with an introspective and philosophical turn of mind, and even then only rarely" (Conze 1951, p. 23).

2. Unlike some contemporary prophets of doom, the Buddha did not regard this view as obvious: "It is difficult to shoot from a distance arrow after arrow through a narrow key hole, and miss not once. It is more difficult to shoot and penetrate with the tip of hair split a hundred times a piece of hair similarly split. It is still more difficult to penetrate to the fact that 'all this is ill' " (quoted Conze 1951, p. 45). Contrast the facile misrepresentation of Danto (1972, p. 67): "The First Noble Truth is that suffering exists. This may be thought obvious enough. . . ."

That existentialism is linked with the German medieval mystics, even historically, is quite likely. Heidegger once planned a study of Meister Eckhart, and the Christian mystics' "dark night of the soul" can be found back in Heidegger's grand design of the *Weltnacht der Seinsvergessenheit* ("world night of the oblivion of being"). It is of course very difficult to determine whether an experience of anxiety, even when felt, is "basic." But if mysticism in general, and Buddhist mysticism in particular, has something to do with a transformation of the human mind or spirit—the minimum the explorer of mysticism should be willing to grant—it would be premature to confine its understanding to those who indulge in such far-reaching evaluations as the primacy of such an existentialist experience, or the bankruptcy of Western civilization (though it is no doubt easy to adduce evidence that would seem to support the latter view). Also, such stern moralizing seems difficult to reconcile with a religion which, like most forms of mysticism, moves mostly beyond the level of ethics and society, and which stresses tolerance and compassion once it descends to that level. It is likely that a mind affected by anxiety and the gloom of bankruptcy is conducive to otherworldliness, increases the desire for seclusion and isolation, and facilitates the first steps on the mystic's path, if indeed it is a path. But the study and eventual explanation of mysticism on the one hand, and its advocacy as a cure for whatever ills it is supposed to cure on the other, are independent from each other. Even if we were to find that mysticism can cure certain ills, that would not necessarily throw much light on it. Medical science, as distinct from medical practice, is not satisfied with the knowledge that there is a high correlation between the administration of certain drugs and the cure of certain diseases. We want to know why.

It may be noted in passing that Buddhism itself seems to favor a more rational and less pragmatic approach. It is true that the Buddha ridiculed the man who, when wounded by a poisonous arrow, insisted on knowing whether it was an ordinary, an iron, a claw-headed, or a calf-tooth arrow which struck him, whence it came, who aimed it, and so on: "That man would die without ever having learnt this" (*Majjhima-nikāya* 63). But it has been convincingly shown, by T. R. V. Murti and others, that the Buddha's teaching cannot be adequately interpreted as pragmatism, agnosticism, or nihilism, but implies an analysis of the very cure it prescribes (Murti 1955, pp. 36–54). The Mādhyamika philosophers addressed themselves to precisely such questions.

Despite Conze's dogmatic acceptance of the Mādhyamika school of Mahāyāna Buddhism (which claims to be not a philosophy, but a criticism of all philosophy) as a superior form of religion and philosophy, his attitude is less dogmatic than that of Massignon. The reason is that Buddhism even in its most dogmatic form (Mahāyāna) is less dogmatic than Islam even in its least dogmatic form (Sufism). Though Buddhism, at various periods, recognized three treasurers, four holy truths (each with four aspects), five *skandhas* and five hindrances, eight stages of apperception and eight stages of trance, twelve links of the chain of causation, fourteen "inexpressibles," eighteen special *dharmas*, thirty-two parts of the body, and other enumerations, all such assertions may be taken with a pinch of salt. Moreover, the Buddha does not seem to have encouraged people to follow him blindly (see below, page 146). It is characteristic especially of Theravāda Buddhism to stress the value of experimentation. In the Pāli Canon, the prevalent opinion seems to have been that statements of which the truth is claimed on authority should be accepted or rejected only after they have been personally tested (cf. Jayatilleke 1963, pp. 369–401).

Conze's remarks, addressed to modern "empiricists," "humanists," and "scientists," are consistent with this Theravāda trend and can pave the way for the rational approach to the exploration of mysticism which I am here advocating:

> But though I were to speak with the tongues of angels, my "empiricist" friends will continue to shrug their shoulders at the suggestion that Yoga and other nonscientific techniques should be taken seriously. As professed "humanists" they might be expected to have a greater faith in the depth and breadth of the human spirit and its modalities. As "empiricists" they might have a more catholic notion of "experience," and as "positivists" a clearer conception of what is, and what is not, a "verifiable" fact. And even as "scientists" they ought to have some doubts as to whether the world of sense-bound consciousness is really the whole of reality. But alas, a staggering hypertrophy of the critical faculties has choked all the other virtues. Contemporary empiricist and positivist philosophers, in their exclusive reliance on scientific knowledge, are guilty of what Whitehead has charitably called a "narrow provincialism." Usually unfamiliar with the traditional nonscientific techniques of mankind, they are also, what is worse, quite incurious about them. At

best these techniques, if noticed at all, are hastily interpreted as approximations to scientific ones, worked out by ignorant and bungling natives groping in the dark (Conze 1962, pp. 20–21).

3. *The Structure of the* Yogasūtra

The normal occupation of philologists is the analysis of texts, and the most spectacular job a philologist can perform is to take a text to pieces and show that these pieces came from other texts which, when not found, have to be postulated as lost. In the field of Sanskrit philology, the easiest prey for such hunts is the *Bhagavad Gītā*, and the crown on the philologists' dissection game was placed by a well-known phenomenologist of religion to whom I shall return in the next section. The original problem which the *Gītā* presents to a Western monotheistic mind is that it juxtaposed so-called theistic and so-called pantheistic elements. The first hypothesis offered by philologists was that it had originally been a pantheistic text, to which theistic passages were added. The German scholar Richard Garbe reversed this hypothesis: according to him the original *Gītā* was theistic, and the "pantheistic" passages were added under the influence of the Vedānta. Garbe was followed by many German scholars, including the author of the most authoritative history of Sanskrit literature, Moritz Winternitz. But once such kinds of analysis begin, it is hard to stop them. Scholars with neater minds suggested that the original *Gītā* had ended with verse 38 of the second chapter, to which first the chapters III–XII, and later the chapters XIII–XVIII were added. The *Gītā* is indeed plain sailing up to II.39, when the word *sāṃkhya* occurs, for this term means "number, enumeration," but may also refer to the name of a system of philosophy. The famous German phenomenologist of religion, Rudolf Otto, put all these earlier efforts to shame by offering a demonstration that the *Bhagavad Gītā* was derived from an original *Ur-Gītā*, to which materials from eight different lost treatises were subsequently added.

Even philologists cannot be all deceived. The French Sanskritist, Émile Senart, noted simply in the Introduction to his translation of the *Gītā*: "Efforts have been made to distinguish pieces of different origin; attempts that are ephemeral as well as arbitrary."

The *Yogasūtra* deals with topics considerably less known and understood than the *Bhagavad Gītā*; it is, as a *sūtra* text, much more concise and abbreviated; and it abounds in technical terms. The techniques of philologists are therefore bound to be even more unsuccessful here. But the attempts have not been lacking. The challenge was provided by a remark of a great nineteenth-century German scholar, Hermann Oldenberg, according to whom the Yoga is *eine unentwirrbare Mischung von Philosophie und Zauber* ("an inextricable mixture of philosophy and magic," a view quoted with approval in Heiler 1918, p. 87, n. 236).

The German scholar who devoted most attention to the *Yogasūtra* is J. W. Hauer (1932, 1958), who divided the text in five portions. The first of these is the "*nirodha*-text," that is, the first twenty-two *sūtras* of the first book, which introduce the notion of *nirodha* "cessation" and elaborate on the definition of Yoga as *citta-vṛtti-nirodhaḥ* "cessation of the fluctuations of the mind."

Hauer's historical perspective is implicit in the first move he makes in attempting to set this portion apart from the rest and assign it a definite time: "This text must therefore belong to a period, when yoga resisted the excessive cultivation of consciousness; a period, therefore, judged by Indian standards, given to greatly increased dialectical and speculative activity which, after all, at several times during the course of Indian history, had been regarded as conducive to salvation" (Hauer 1958, p. 227).

It would take much time to follow Hauer step-by-step in his dissecting activity, which provides us with detailed information about his prejudices. The most disconcerting feature of this dismemberment is that the next scholars who continued that trend, though they also dissected, dissected differently. Frauwallner in his history of Indian philosophy (1953, pp. 427–443), followed by Oberhammer (1965), also sets apart the section which deals with *nirodha*, though Hauer and he regard different *sūtras* as its end (of course, everybody tends to begin where the text begins). The only other respect in which Frauwallner is relatively close to Hauer is in his separation of a theistic portion, Hauer's *Īśvarapraṇidhāna* ("devotion to God") text, that is, *Yogasūtra* I.23–51. Here, one suspects, they might well be right, at least in one sense (see below, page 195). Though Frauwallner and Oberhammer did not specify as much detail as Hauer did, it is clear from the following table that the rest of their dissections diverge considerably:

Hauer	*Frauwallner and Oberhammer*
I.2–22	I.2–18
I.23–51	I.41–50
II.1–27	II.54–III.7
II.28–III.55	
IV	

One need not know anything about the text and yet be in a position to suspect arbitrariness here.

It would be fruitless, and uncalled for in the present context, to follow these various cuts and excisions in greater detail. But there is a basic distinction between two kinds of Yoga which all these scholars have found difficult to accept and which is of philosophic significance. This is the distinction between, on the one hand, the *nirodha,* interpreted as "suppression" (*Unterdrückung*) by Frauwallner and Oberhammer, elucidated in the beginning of the *Yogasūtra,* and, on the other hand, the eight-limbed (*aṣṭāṅga*) Yoga expounded later. The latter kind, which all these scholars declare similar to the Buddhist Yoga, is characterized by the terms *saṃyama* (which refers to the last three stages of the eight-limbed Yoga) and *samāpatti* "contemplation," and is described by Frauwallner in terms of "knowledge" (*Erkenntnis*). Oberhammer described the differences between the two kinds of Yoga as follows in the English summary of his article:

> The *samādhiḥ* of the Nirodhayoga may possibly be called a "natural mysticism," while the *samāpattiḥ* represents only a method to "appropriate" existentially a certain belief or truth being a part of a philosophical or theological system. Thus the *samāpattiḥ* having no real object, but only representations and ideas, i.e. finite contents of cognition, cannot be called a mystical experience. The *samādhiḥ* of the Nirodhayoga on the contrary—not the *samādhiḥ* of the *saṃyamaḥ*—is a meditation of a completely different structure. In it the cognition transcending all finite objects in direction of the "Being," which as "sky-line" of cognition is a necessary apriori of each act of cognition, reaches this very "Being" in a sort of direct experience, since every content of the act of cognition is eliminated, in spite of the fact that this "Being" on principle can never become the explicit object of human cognition (Oberhammer 1965, p. 118).

In order to evaluate this description, it is obvious that we have first of all to delete terms which have nothing whatsoever to do with

Yoga, like the expression "natural mysticism" (intelligible only within the context of what is called "natural" in Christian theology, namely, "non-Christian"), or terms which appeal to an existentialist or Heideggerian audience: "sky-line" = *Horizont*, "Being" = *Sein*, etc. Once we have done this, we have to face the question whether it is true that we are left with two irreconcilable trends, symbolized by the terms *nirodha* and *samāpatti*.

It should be clear, first of all, that the author or compiler of the *Yogasūtra*, in the form in which we know it, does not think so. On the contrary, there are *sūtras* which state that there is a close connection between the two. *Sūtra* I.41, for example, which according to Oberhammer is the beginning of the *samāpatti* exposition, states unambiguously that the mind is in the *samāpatti* state "since its fluctuations have been destroyed" (*kṣīṇavṛtteḥ*), a clear reference to the so-called *nirodha* Yoga. Another *sūtra*, II.11, which according to Hauer, Frauwallner, and Oberhammer does not belong to the *samāpatti*-text, says that "the fluctuations of these" (i.e., fluctuations of the mind due to certain obstacles) "are abandoned by means of meditation" (*dhyāna-heyās tadvṛttayaḥ*). The term "meditation" (*dhyāna*) which is used here is the same as the seventh step of the eight-limbed Yoga, and this *sūtra* therefore refers to the so-called *samāpatti* Yoga. Even more strikingly, *sūtra* III.9, in the middle of an exposition of the *saṃyama* stages, refers back to *nirodha*. In other words, there are *sūtras* in both parts of the text which refer to the other, allegedly irreconcilable part .

Now it is of course possible to say that such references were inserted by a compiler who wished to obscure the fact that there are two irreconcilable kinds of Yoga. But to make such claims is a very dangerous game, unless one knows exactly what the text means. As a matter of fact, we can easily talk about "cessation of fluctuations" and "meditation," but that does not disguise the fact that we do not really know what such expressions refer to. The interpretation of the *Yogasūtra* by philologists amounts to little more than consistently translating certain technical terms in the Sanskrit original by certain German or English terms (as in Woods' 1927 translation). But what these terms in turn denote can only be determined when we explore not texts about Yoga, but Yoga itself. Until we do that, it is pointless to divide a text into portions.

Another fact makes this particular interpretation of the distinction between *nirodha* and *samāpatti* Yoga as two irreconcilable kinds of Yoga even more hazardous. The Buddhists also distinguish between these two, and also regard them as quite compatible. That the term *samāpatti* is common in the Buddhist texts is admitted by all students of the *Yogasūtra*. Whether it expresses the same in both traditions is of course not obvious; but we can only determine this when we know what it might refer to at all. Parallels to *nirodha* Yoga are also common in Buddhism. In Mahāyāna, for example, *nirvāṇa* is considered as *prahāṇa* (vanishing), *virāga* (detachment), and *nirodha* (cessation) (Lamotte 1970, pp. 1461–1463). Now, *nirvāṇa* is the goal of the Buddhist Yoga, which passes through stages that closely resemble the stages of the eight-limbed Yoga (see, e.g., Heiler 1918, pp. 44–46). There is much scope for detailed comparison between Yoga and Buddhism, and interesting beginnings have already been made (see, e.g., the bibliographical survey in Eliade 1954, pp. 382–383). But the significance of such comparisons depends on our understanding not of the texts, but of what the texts deal with.

A Sanskrit scholar who knows nothing about the structure of the human body may take it upon himself to analyze a Sanskrit text on anatomy. He will be surprised to find a certain amount of repetitiveness. The arms of the body, as seen through the text, look like the legs. But such repetitions are never exact: there are small differences, subtle variants, apparent inconsistencies. Then he meets with a description of the nervous system. Its function is unclear, its relationship to other parts of the body obscured by technical terms which are unintelligible. And now comes the description of the head. Though it still has muscles on the face, its inside is described in very different terms from the heart, lungs, and intestines which were described before. The text claims the head to be hard outside, to have gray matter as well as teeth inside; a portion of the brain protrudes and perceives form and color, a tongue produces sounds, ears register them—in brief, "an inextricable mixture of philosophy and magic."

What can a philologist do but assign the different passages to different lost works, each of which is postulated to have dealt in a neat and intelligible manner with a single limb? Our *Yogasūtra* scholars are in much the same position. We shall never understand texts like the *Yogasūtra* by studying the Sanskrit expressions until we know a great deal more about the subject they deal with.[3]

3. It is not only in the study of Yoga that we find a difference of perspective between philologists, who wish to confine themselves to texts in order to be able to discuss what the texts deal with, and scholars, who try to treat a subject matter systematically and from other points of view in order to understand texts as well as their contents. In the study of Indian logic there are similar differences of approach. We know from the study of the history of Western logic that logical theorems can only be recognized and evaluated by logicians, and only to the extent that the level of logic reflected in the texts they study is not higher than that of the logic they are familiar with. Prantl, for example, regarded all medieval logic as worthless, since he was no logician but a follower of Kant, who had stated that logic had made no progress since Aristotle. In the study of Indian logic, similar mistakes were made by S. C. Vidyabhusana, followed by a host of others (see Staal 1973). A similar situation prevails in the study of the Sanskrit grammarians. Philologists like Whitney, held back by inadequate notions of the goals of linguistics, failed to recognize and appreciate the linguistic insights of the Sanskrit grammarians (see Staal 1970b; 1972, Preface and pp. 138–141).

7

Phenomenological and Sociological Approaches

1. Phenomenology of Mysticism

Like phenomenology as a trend within philosophy, the phenomenology of religion often associates itself with the kind of irrationalism exemplified by the views of van der Leeuw referred to at the beginning of this essay. However, such an alliance is not necessary. The phenomenology of religion, which has closely allied itself with the study of the history of religions, is historically a reaction against the missionary attitude of earlier Christian apologists toward "pagan" religions. It expresses a helpful methodological insight, provided it is treated in the right perspective, namely, as a mere beginning. Disposing of prejudices by an "epoche" of evaluation is useful only if, after the phenomena have been collected and classified, the real task of their evaluation is undertaken. Without that we are generally left with implicit evaluations, which can often be shown to be prejudices once again. So the phenomenology and history of religion is (1) always unsatisfactory and insufficient because it does not investigate the validity of the phenomena it studies, and (2) often wrong because of incorrect implicit evaluations. Since the premise of the first point is accepted by proponents and critics alike, I shall briefly discuss two representative examples of the second only.

Rudolf Otto, whose most well-known work, *Das Heilige* (1917), "The Holy," dealt with the "irrational in the idea of the divine and its relation to the rational," devoted a special monograph to mysticism, entitled *Mysticism East and West: A Comparative Analysis of the Nature of Mysticism* (I quote from the English paperback edition of 1959). This is a perceptive book, and yet it tries at great length to establish a thesis which is either patently false or, interpreted charitably, highly misleading: that there is a "common theistic foundation" of, in the first place, the mysticism of Eckhart and Śaṅkara, and, by generalization, of all "higher" forms of mysticism.

Though Otto's 1959 publication originally appeared in 1926, this particular interpretation cannot be brushed aside as ancient history. Not only has it been given wide currency through its paperback edition, but it also continues to be taken seriously by scholars. In 1965, for example, Paul Hacker, a scholar of Śaṅkara's Advaita Vedānta, regarded this work of Otto as "a penetrating and elaborate study of the theistic basis or background perceptible in Śaṅkara's monistic thought" (Hacker 1965, p. 147). Five years later, Hacker (1970, p. 121) again referred approvingly to Otto, this time in an article in which he defended Śaṅkara's authorship of the *Yogabhāṣyavivaraṇa*, a subcommentary on Vyāsa's commentary on the *Yogasūtra*; traced similarities between the *Yogasūtra* and other works of Śaṅkara (distinct in this respect from other Advaitins); and arrived at the conclusion that Śaṅkara had been an adherent of the Yoga system before he became an Advaitin.

Otto was well aware that his interpretation, especially with regard to Śaṅkara, was far fetched and difficult to maintain. One interpretation of his thesis would be to stress (as he sometimes does himself) that "theism" in this context does not mean "personal theism," and that "theistic foundation" merely means that these forms of mysticism "tower above a theistic basis." But the former negation raises the question (which Otto never answers) of what this "theism" is; and "towering" is merely a metaphor, which he exchanges for other similar metaphors but never explains. That Otto has a more specific interpretation in mind—that, for Śaṅkara, God (*īśvara*) is as real, important, and central is *brahman*—may be inferred from the fact that he leans heavily on suggestions purporting to show that the main notions that could establish such primacy for *īśvara*, namely *aparavidyā* (which actually means "lower, erroneous knowledge") and *māyā* (which means "appearance, magic, unreality"), denote in fact "(valid) knowledge" and "reality," respectively (Otto 1959, pp. 110–111, 117–118, 153, etc.). But these interpretations cannot be justified unless one ignores most of the evidence.

Otto tries to clarify his thesis by contrasting the basic ideas of Śaṅkara with those of other mystical systems, such as Yoga, Mahāyāna, Buddhism, and Taoism. Unfortunately, his clarifications are irrational and tend to be sentimental: "Brahman mysticism is qualitatively different from Ātman mysticism . . . the difference between them, however, is itself as non-rational as the difference in character of the two mysticisms; it is not to be reproduced in intellectual conceptions and is only comprehensible in mystical experience itself" (p. 146; a rather implausible suggestion that a person possessing or undergoing a mystical experience would be at the same time interested in, or even capable of, comparing it with other mystical experiences); "within Vedānta and Mahāyāna, in spite of mutual convergence, there lives an entirely different spirit, which needs to be perceived in its essence and cannot be exhausted by generalities" (p. 149); "yet Tao is fundamentally different from Brahman. Since it concerns the absolutely non-rational it is again only possible tentatively to indicate these differences and to understand them by feeling rather than through the intellect" (p. 148).

Results so thin are better left unpublished. But that fuzziness and obscurity are not at all necessary follows from the work of others who have interpreted the same material with much precision, and have accordingly gone much deeper (e.g., Murti 1955). Moreover, even if Śaṅkara himself is sometimes not very clear in his writings, students of Indian philosophy know that they should look at the commentaries and see whether these throw light on inexplicit passages. Of course, commentators may be wrong; but this can only be established when their elucidations are clearly understood and compared with the texts they comment upon. As matters stand, the later commentators and philosophers of Advaita often make sense of what is otherwise difficult to understand. Now, Vidyāraṇya states in his *Pañcadaśī*: "*māyā* is understood in three ways: by the man in the street as real, by the logician as undeterminable, by the follower of the scripture as non-existent" (quoted above, page 35).

So Otto forces upon a key concept of Śaṅkara (that of *māyā*) the one interpretation Śaṅkara's followers quote as a popular misconception that it is real). A dubious foundation for such far-reaching evaluations.

This brief analysis leads to a simple conclusion: Otto's emphasis on theism is not based upon an open-minded study of Śaṅkara, but reflects the emphasis in his other studies which deal primarily with Indian theism and, ultimately, his own Christian theism. Otto's publications on Indian theism (Otto 1916, 1923a, 1923b, 1930) are accordingly much better suited to their subject. It is, moreover, not surprising that Otto, in his book on the mystical systems of Eckhart and Śaṅkara (1959), interprets Śaṅkara mainly in the light of his commentary on the *Bhagavad Gītā*. The *Bhagavad Gītā*, and Śaṅkara's commentary upon it, emphasized theism and dealt primarily with ethics as distinct from Śaṅkara's *Brahmasūtrabhāṣya*, which mainly treated theoretical issues (see Faddegon 1906).

Later in his book, Otto's Christian bias becomes the more unmistakable, the more he emphasizes the differences between Eckhart and Śaṅkara. In these later chapters we are told (as the headings suggest) not merely about the differences between Eckhart and Śaṅkara but about the superiority of the former over the latter. This comparison is first expressed haltingly, but becomes increasingly explicit: "The whole construction of his (i.e., Śaṅkara's) doctrine of salvation, and of the Indian teaching of salvation, is based upon the subjective element" (p. 189). This is quite untrue, as we shall see (below, pages 176–177); Śaṅkara, unlike Otto, distinguishes very clearly between subjective and objective. Otto then refers to the Christian concept of soul, to Eckhart's notion of *Gemüt*, and to conscience, justification, and sanctification, after which he says: "Śaṅkara's mysticism is none of these things because it springs not from the soil of Palestine, but from the soil of India" (p. 206). And about *agápē*: "a love of a kind which neither Plotinus nor Śaṅkara mentions or knows" (p. 214). All of this may be true or may be false. But why are we nowhere told that Eckhart "neither mentions nor knows" *adhyāropa, vivarta, vyavahāra, pratibhāsa, paramārtha*, and a host of other concepts "which spring from the soil of India"? By now the spirit of phenomenology has entirely evaporated.

The pattern exhibited in these investigations is distressingly similar to the general development of the Christian preoccupation with non-Christian religions. First Christians thought that only Christianity recognizes a God; but when it was discovered that also other people have Gods, it was maintained that only Christianity has monotheism. And when it was discovered that others also have that, it was maintained that only Christianity possesses an incarnated God. When it was discovered that others have that too, it was said that only Christianity has an incarnated God who suffers; when that was discovered elsewhere, its essence became a God who saves mankind; etc. The general pattern is: first the apologist tries to state what is most central in Christianity, and then to discover whether that may also be found in other religions. But when, with increasing knowledge, this test establishes again and again that allegedly fundamental characteristics are found elsewhere, the position is reversed: now the apologist tries to discover what feature occurs in Christianity and is not found elsewhere, and then he argues that it is that feature which is the basic and superior characteristic of Christianity.

Naturally, not only a Christian bias prevents the rational study of religious phenomena; other religious prejudices are obstacles as well. Most religions seem to have similar feelings of superiority, though in varying degrees, and sometimes in disguise. In Hinduism, for example, where tolerance is greatly stressed (cf. Staal 1959), feelings of superiority are not stated so bluntly: Hindus do not say that Hinduism possesses the only truth, and other religions nothing; rather, they tend to say that all religions have the truth, but Hinduism has the highest truth. To make sense of this, it will have to be interpreted in terms of the traditional distinction between lower knowledge *(aparavidyā)* and higher knowledge *(paravidyā)*, which Śaṅkara inherited from Nāgārjuna. As we have just seen, the lower knowledge is ultimately false. It follows that Hindu orthodoxy, in the final analysis, is no better than Christian orthodoxy.

In all these religious utterances we do not find a single indication to show that mysticism itself is irrational. We only find that mysticism tends to be studied in an irrational fashion.

My second example of an implicit evaluation which is untenable is taken from the work of Mircea Eliade and brought to light by Wasson. According to Eliade, the use of the fly-agaric among Siberian shamans as a method to induce a state of ecstasy is of recent origin, derivative, decadent, and vulgar (Eliade 1951, pp. 202, 360, 415 = 1964, pp. 223, 401; 1954, p. 335 = 1969, p. 338). Eliade adduces no evidence in support of this view. Wasson, on the other hand, has shown that at least the historical thesis is untenable; such a use of mushrooms in Siberia appears in fact to be very ancient. After discussing Eliade's statements in detail, Wasson (1968), rightly concludes that Eliade's "preference on moral grounds for other techniques to attain ecstasy has affected his critical faculty" (p. 331).

Eliade in fact goes so far as to say: "In ancient and modern India, and indeed all through the East, we constantly find this strange mixture of 'difficult ways' and 'easy ways' of realizing mystical ecstasy or some other decisive experience" (Eliade 1951, p. 360 = 1964, p. 401). This is in fact a significant distinction, to which I shall return in chapter 13. For Eliade, the "easy ways" are necessarily "decadence" and "vulgarization" of the "difficult ways." Such as evaluation, however, is not generally made in Asia, unless it has been recently introduced as part of the Protestant ethic.

This low evaluation of "easy" ways and of hallucinogenic plants is similar to the low evaluation of drugs among contemporary mystical cults and movements, which preach whatever they preach as the ultimate cure for drug addiction. The reasons here are rarely puritanical. Many young people, after experimenting with drugs, experiment with meditation, and those who find meditation more "satisfying" adopt a guru or join a movement. Of those others who prefer drugs we do not hear in the same context. But the fact that there are converts from drugs who are rehabilitated by meditational practices is in due course exploited by the proponents and missionaries of the various cults in their efforts to appear useful and respectable in the eyes of the establishment. These moves are of sociological interest but have nothing to do with a critical evaluation of and comparison between the effects of drugs and of meditation (a topic to which I shall return in chapter 12). The low evaluation of drugs also resembles, and is related to, the low evaluation of the yogic powers (*prabhāva, vibhūti,* and *siddhi* in Hinduism, *ṛddhi* and *abhijñā* in Buddhism). Here religious and moral prejudices, Indian as well as Western, have obscured the fact that these powers are an integral part of Yoga (see Pensa 1969, especially pp. 197–204).

2. Sociology of Mysticism

A less biased and more purely "phenomenological" approach to the study of mysticism than that of the professional scholars or religion is found among some anthropologists. One of the reasons for this is, probably, that anthropologists are aware of and concerned with the fact that people tend to have prejudices. In no book on the history or phenomenology of religion have I found remarks like: "The contributions . . . in this book add little to the sum of human knowledge but if they provoke some readers to doubt their sense of certainty then they will have served their purpose" (from the Preface of Leach 1961).

It is therefore not surprising to find the best phenomenology of popular Javanese mysticism based not so much upon textual studies (like Rinkes 1909 or, for Sumatra, van Nieuwenhuijze 1945) as upon direct observation of people's behavior and accounts of their beliefs, in the relevant chapters of Geertz' *The Religion of Java* (1960, pp. 309–352). Aside from describing mystical phenomena in their social setting, this study gives a good idea of the interaction between common forms of mysticism and daily life as it can also be found elsewhere in Asia. It is not impaired by religious prejudice. Another example of an open-minded exploration which is often concerned with mysticism is *Precept and Practice: Traditional Buddhism in the Rural Highlands of Ceylon* by R. F. Gombrich (1971), who was trained as an anthropologist and a classical Indologist.

Many sociological and anthropological studies of religion (sometimes grouped together under the label "sociology of religion") are not oriented toward phenomenology. I shall briefly comment on their possible significance for the study of mysticism. Since the sociology of religion deals primarily with the social aspects of religion, mysticism constitutes within this perspective a limiting case; for mysticism, looked at from the point of view of society, is mainly characterized by its asocial or antisocial outlook. Most mystics are drop-outs. Social reformers therefore tend to look upon mysticism as a form of egoism and escapism. The mystics themselves often express their dislike or contempt of the world, that is, the world of society. It is society (not nature or the cosmos) which is primarily had in view when the Buddha, for example, emphasizes that this world is suffering (see chap. 6, n. 2, above).

In Yoga, the first step on the mystic path is *vairāgya* "detachment, renunciation" (see pages 138–139, below), primarily directed away from our social attachments. Such an attitude is not confined to Indian forms of religion. Though modern Christianity stresses social responsibility, Jesus had also said: "If any man come to me and hate not his father, and mother, and wife, and children, and bretheren, and sisters, yea, and his own life also, he cannot be my disciple" (Luke 14:26), and to a man who wanted first to bury his father before following Jesus: "Let the dead bury their dead" (Matthew 8:22; Luke 9:60).

In Islam, Zaehner speaks about Ghazzālī's "almost paranoic hatred of the world" (Zaehner 1960, p. 160), connecting this attitude with Manicheism. I have already noted that such hatred of the world might in Islam have developed from the practice of *iʿtikāf* "spiritual retreat." But its occurrence is wide-spread and is very common, for example, in early Christianity. Taoism is noted for its anti-establishment, anarchist, and *laissez-faire* attitude. Levenson and Schurmann characterize Confucianism as a golden mean between the emphasis on law and order and the establishment values of the legalists on the one hand, and the individualism and anarchist egoism of the Taoists on the other hand (Levenson and Schurmann 1969, pp. 62–65). Watson describes how Taoist writings, though not actually suppressed, were not accorded any official recognition during the Han dynasty (Watson 1964, p. 9).

Waley, who regards Taoism primarily as quietism, relates how Han Fei Tzu addressed the king of Ch'in on this matter:

> I submit to your Majesty that this Quietness is of no practical value to any one . . . Man's duty in life is to serve his prince and nourish his parents, neither of which things can be done by Quietness. I further submit that it is man's duty, in all that he teaches, to promote loyalty and good faith and the Legal Constitution. This cannot be done in terms that are vague and mysterious. The doctrine of the Quietists is a false one, likely to lead the people astray (Waley n.d., p. 43).

The evaluation of mysticism as escapism may be justified when intended as a psychological evaluation of the attitude of individual mystics. As a general characteristic of mysticism it fails not only because it is not applicable in many individual cases, but also because it approaches mysticism from a perspective which is alien to it. It is true that some people have taken to mysticism out of despair, fear, or because of social failure; but others, like the Buddha, took to it despite their comfortable position in society, and in Indian civilization it is not uncommon for kings to meditate (see, e.g., the illustration of the Khmer monarch Jayavarman VII). Śiva, the divine renouncer, is also a beggar (plate 3). In Hinduism, where the prevailing ideal results from a synthesis or compromise between the requirements of asceticism and of society (cf. pages 181 ff., below), the mystical path of *saṃnyāsa* is generally advocated only for those who have gone through the entire gamut of social responsibilities (cf. chap. 13, n. 2). Those who take to *saṃnyāsa* without having discharged their social duty (*dharma*) are generally frowned upon. Such an attitude is strengthened by the fact that there is a marked difference in visibility between the two transitions: a prince's or retired banker's taking to *saṃnyāsa* is a spectacular event; a beggar turning into a *saṃnyāsin* goes unnoticed.

A person who in his search for mystical experience turns away from society cannot be expected to contribute directly to the solution of social problems. But it does not follow that mysticism does not have social implications, even constructive ones. Later Taoism, for instance, could become an expression of protest, not only for "escapist intelligentsia" but also for "rebellious peasantry" (Levenson and Schurmann 1969, pp. 117–118). Social reformers, anarchists, and mystics can meet in anti-establishment enterprises which, in contemporary society, resemble the uneasy alliances between political activists and hippies on university campuses (see Staal 1970a, pp. 144–145).

That mysticism constitutes within the perspective of the sociology of religion a limiting case does not imply that no light can be thrown upon it from that perspective. In the case of Indian religions, the position of the mystic in society and the implications of his ideas for the development of religion have been studied in an illuminating way by the French sociologist Louis Dumont (1959; 1960; 1966, pp. 324–350; cf. Staal 1961c). Dumont has drawn attention to certain structures which underlie the bewildering variety of religious phenomena in India. His point of departure is the observation that *saṃnyāsins* wish to renounce the world (the world of caste society), while Brahmans "are in general rather comfortably placed in the world" (Dumont 1966, p. 334). In leaving the world, the *saṃynāsin* "finds himself invested with an individuality which he apparently finds uncomfortable since all his efforts tend to its extinction or its transcendence" (Dumont 1960, p. 46). While the Western observer is used to the Western stress laid upon the individual-in-the-world, individuality in Hinduism exists only outside the world. Inside the world, the only reality of Gods or human beings lies in their relationships to others, not in their apparent individuality in isolation. To the renouncer, the world he has left behind appears as a world of transmigration; he thus establishes a relation between himself and the man-in-the-world, and therefore he does not feel inclined to deny the religion of the latter. Furthermore, the renouncer may himself found a "religion of salvation," which may be incorporated in the religion of the world as a sect, and offer the man-in-the-world a choice of religions for the individual. Thus individualism penetrates into the group religion. While orthodox Brahmanism is exclusive as regards the people who can be admitted among the faithful (the subjects of religion) but inclusive in the domain of belief (the object of religion), the sect is generally open to all castes but intolerant of other doctrines and of syncretism (cf. Staal 1959). We find accordingly that the founders of sects, and many *saṃnyāsins* in general, come from a low caste background (cf. plates 14a–b). Even the founders of Jainism and Buddhism belonged to the *kṣatriya* caste—a high caste no doubt, but not as high as that of the Brahmans.

Dumont thus views Hinduism as the dialogue between the renouncer and the man-in-the-world, and ultimately characterizes Indian religions through the interaction between the group religion of the caste society, supervised by the Brahman ritualists, and the "disciplines of salvation," founded by *saṃnyāsins* such as the Buddha, Mahāvīra, and the founders of the Hindu sects. This analysis clearly points to some of the ways in which mysticism has influenced the development of Indian religion. More important, it reveals mysticism as perhaps the major source of individualism in Indian civilization. It also assigns mysticism its proper place in Indian society, and, incidentally, enables us to imagine psychological motives which may have prompted Indians to leave the caste society and turn to mysticism. However, such an analysis throws no light on the nature of mysticism or on the validity of the mystical experience itself.

8

Physiological and Psychological Approaches

1. Brosse on Yoga and Wallace on Transcendental Meditation

Psychological approaches to the study of mysticism should be rewarding in principle if psychology is regarded as the science of the human mind, for mystical experiences are at least (whatever else they may be in addition) experiences which affect the mind. Moreover, the mystical experience may be said to bring about a mystical state, which as a state of mind or consciousness should be compared to the other states, such as the waking state, the states of sleep and dreaming, or the hypnotic state.[1] The oldest comparisons between mystical, dreaming, and sleep states occur in the Upaniṣads. They are also found in Chuang Tzu (plate 13). But so far, contemporary psychological approaches do not seem to have yielded many significant results in these areas. This lack seems to be due to the particular limitations which psychologists have imposed upon themselves. What the enforcement of these limitations

1. There are psychologists who object to the term "hypnotic state," and Hilgard (1971) has hence suggested using "hypnotic domain." Nothing hinges on such terms, unless it is assumed that a "state" must last for a specific period, be uninterrupted, be different from other states, etc.

generally amounts to is, that the subjective and experiential realm is excluded, since it is assumed that, in some sense or other, it resists rational analysis.

The most obvious among these limitations—now becoming outdated—is the behaviorist limitation. It is of *some* significance to find out how much mental states are manifest in overt behavior. But the identity or difference between two mental states is not established by the identity or difference between two sets of "corresponding" behavioral "criteria."[2] A simple analogy from linguistics may illustrate this. Synonyms are different sounds representing the same meaning; homonyms are identical sounds representing different meanings. The identity or difference between sounds cannot therefore serve as a criterion for the identity or difference between meanings.

The same holds for physiological criteria. Hence the study of the electroencephalograms and electrocardiograms of mystics or persons engaging in meditation is not going to establish whether the mystical state is the same or is different from other states. The reason for this limitation is simply that such methods tell us, for example, how meditation affects the body, not how it affects the mind. The influence exerted on the body by mystical experience, like the effect on the body of listening to music, can at best be described as a side effect. A balanced study of mental states can only result from fully taking into account not only behavioral and physiological, but also experiential or subjective, data.

Kamiya (1961), studying drowsiness and sleep, has clearly indicated the limitations of physiological criteria:

2. Wittgenstein and especially "linguistic behaviorists" such as Malcolm have introduced much confusion by claiming that descriptions of mental states (e.g., dreaming) are the sole criteria for these states: we learn the meaning of terms referring to these solely by learning what these criteria are. For nonbehavioristic criticism see Putnam 1962 and Chihara and Fodor 1965. Assuming that Wittgenstein (who is very unclear) expressed a single view of linguistic behaviorism, his is still no ordinary behaviorism. Wittgenstein is willing to say of a friend: "My attitude towards him is an attitude towards a soul" (Wittgenstein 1958, p. 178). In such passages (to which Hans Sluga drew my attention) Wittgenstein seems to suggest that we talk, behave, and function in a way which indicates that we take certain things for granted, for example, that a man has a soul. But he is not willing to say anything about *whether* a man has a soul. He therefore stays close to the surface and steers clear of such deeper problems as would involve theory construction (cf. chap. 4, n. 1).

> . . . the EEG . . . has increasingly come to be regarded as the criterion of sleep. But under conditions of extreme sleep deprivation, the EEG can indicate "deep sleep" when the subject is awake, at least by all the usual standards—talking, responding to instructions, etc. . . . Such dissolution between behavior and the EEG can also be produced pharmacologically or surgically . . . It would be confusing to reconcile these differences by distinguishing between "behavioral sleep" and "physiological sleep." They merely indicate imperfect validity of the physiological indicator (Kamiya 1961, pp. 155–156).

Within these limitations, physiological investigations may be taken to be suggestive, provided it is made clear of what. Take the very detailed and very careful researches of Brosse (1963), which he appropriately calls psychosomatic, with practitioners of *haṭhayoga* and *rājayoga*. These establish and confirm beyond reasonable doubt that a yogin can influence not only his breathing but his pulse and heartbeat as well as his brain waves, and in very specific ways, and can also bring about changes in his blood (e.g., increase of urea, sugar, potassium, and carbon dioxide, and decrease of nitrogen) (Brosse 1963, p. 73). Moreover, Brosse has been able to distinguish physiologically between different yogic states, such as the stages of *prāṇayāma*, the stages of the raising of the *kuṇḍalinī*, the effect of exercises such as *uḍḍiyāna-bandha*, or the *dhāraṇā* type of meditation. The term *dhāraṇā*, "concentration," denotes the first of the higher stages of yogic meditation (*saṃyama*): *dhāraṇā*, *dhyāna*, and *samādhi*. The reader need not ask what these terms mean; we don't know at present what they mean, and to replace them with English terms merely introduces misleading associations. Brosse recognizes this. As far as *dhyāna* and *samādhi* are concerned, he writes that, even if these could somehow be measured by physiological methods, we would measure "merely the effect on the organism of experiences of which we know nothing but their name" (Brosse 1963, p. 108). Despite the impressive amount of careful research that has gone into the study of Yoga, and of mysticism generally, through EEG, ECG, and similar methods, one cannot help feeling that it is like studying art through films of the eye movements of art viewers. Even if the results are valid, their significance is minute.

Brosse studied a few yogins in great depth over a period of twenty-five years, but others have studied larger numbers of subjects engaged in less strenuous forms of meditation. Wallace (1970a) has studied the physiological effects of the transcendental meditation introduced to the West by Maharishi Mahesh Yogi. Wallace claims to have established that the state of consciousness reached through transcendental meditation is different from the states of waking, sleeping, and dreaming, and from the states induced by hypnosis and autosuggestion. That the identity or difference among these states can never be established solely by studying their physiological manifestations does not seem to have occurred to him. Wallace, moreover, suggests that transcendental meditation is different (mainly because it is easier) from other forms of meditation, such as Yoga and Zen meditation, with which it shares certain physiological features. At the same time his work abounds in the kind of advertisement for transcendental meditation that might seem to make it palatable to television audiences: it is conducive to "rest and relaxation," and it "is practised as a preparation for successful activity and not as an escape from the problems of life" (Wallace 1970a, p. 43, quoting Maharishi). Such evaluations smack again of dogmatism, albeit less of the Christian than of the American variety (in the United States, music is also for relaxation, and so listening to music is not considered irresponsible). What seems particularly suspect is the air of certainty that pervades such investigations —a feature conspicuous in all dogmatic writings and significantly absent from Brosse's researches.

More careful study of Wallace's work confirms this impression. It emerges when we try to find out what is the precise evidence offered in support of the alleged differences between the transcendental and hypnotic states. In a general report on these findings (*Hospital Times*, London, May 1, 1970: "Towards Pinning Down Meditation"), we read that the EEG of transcendental meditation shows particular features, but "reports of physiological studies on hypnotic trance indicate that the hypnotic state *per se* is accompanied by no particular metabolic or electroencephalographic changes." In Wallace 1970b the formulations are a little more careful:

> the physiological changes induced during hypnosis vary in the same way as in different emotional states observed during wakefulness . . . Many

different EEG patterns have been reported during hypnosis, but most are identical with wakefulness patterns and all appear to be different from the patterns observed during meditation.

In his book (Wallace 1970a) the same statements occur, but the section which deals with the comparison between transcendental meditation and hypnosis ends with the following passage:

> Hypnosis and conditioning procedures seem to either produce altered substates of wakefulness or to involve selectively controlling and manipulating a particular aspect of the organism. The waking, dreaming, sleeping and transcendental states may be distinguished from these other states because of the unique and well-integrated combination of physiological changes which occur during these four major states of consciousness. Meditation techniques have sometimes been classified as altered states (Tart 1969). This classification is correct in the case of techniques which utilize control or manipulation of a particular aspect of body, such as breath control, concentrating the attention, or controlling thoughts. By attempting to reach this state by forcing, rather than allowing the individual to easily maintain the transcendental state, these techniques can strain the mind and create stresses. However, in the case of transcendental meditation, all subjects reported that the technique involves neither contemplation, concentration, nor any type of control or manipulation, but allows the mind to naturally experience "subtler" or more abstract levels of thinking. Since this experience is reported to be increasingly more enjoyable, the technique, by utilizing a strong tendency of the mind to seek fields of greater enjoyment or happiness, is an effortless process which employs a natural and spontaneous type of continual positive reinforcement. A few minutes after allowing this mental process to take place, a complex physiological condition is produced in which the metabolism has dramatically decreased and yet the mind is relaxed and awake. Without any attempt to manipulate the functioning of the body, transcendental meditation produces a unique physiological state (Wallace 1970a, 30).

I have quoted this passage in full in order to invite the reader to carry out a small experiment: see what remains when we delete all terms that do not convey information or contribute insight, terms which could also be used in an advertisement for Excedrin, on the positive side: *integrated, easily, enjoyment, happiness, effortless, natural, spontaneous, relaxed*, and on the negative side: *forcing, strain, stresses, control, manipulation*. The kind of advertisement for transcendental meditation that Wallace indulges in, and that acts instead on many as a deterrent, throws little light on transcendental meditation, or on meditation in general.

It is sobering to read in contrast the less conclusive but more reliable statements of careful researchers into the problem of the "supposed identity of hypnosis and the waking state on the one hand, and the non-identity of hypnosis and sleep on the other (e.g., Gorton 1962, pp. 40–43). It will be obvious from these that, though something is known, almost nothing is understood even of the waking state and of sleep. It will also be clear that, in the field of hypnosis (which covers a broad spectrum of altered states) the so-called autogenic training studied and practiced by Schultz and Luthe (1959) is closer to meditation practices than are some other kinds of hypnosis. But at the present state of our knowledge and understanding, it seems doubtful that one could go much beyond the not very spectacular, but at least well-considered, formulations of Filliozat (from the Preface to Brosse: 1963, p. xxiii; cf. also Filliozat 1946, p. 220):

> In the kind of hypnosis which has been regarded as the opposite of yoga, the subject abandons his will in a state of quasi-sleep in order to be receptive to external suggestions; or he confines his volitions to the putting into effect of the received suggestions. But if hypnosis is regarded merely as a state of volition in which the subject is willing to conform to a method of physical and physiological discipline, the yoga may well be regarded as such a kind of self-hypnosis. The difference between a person who undergoes autogenic training and a yogin who follows a prescribed discipline does not lie in the basic mechanism that is at work, but only in the goals that he has set himself at the beginning: relaxation or control.

In terms of this distinction, hypnosis is clearly different from Yoga. Hypnosis is more akin to devotional types of religiosity, where the devotee abandons his will entirely. Taken out of its context, "Thy will be done" is the kind of statement that is appropriate to a subject addressing his hypnotist or his *guru*.

It would be tempting, at this stage, to contrast many Oriental forms of mysticism with the American fads fashioned after them by characterizing the former by the desire for control and the latter by the desire for relaxation. But things are not that simple. First we must distinguish between relaxation as a means and relaxation as an end. Second, the starting point for mystical practices in the traditional East need not be the same as in the modern West.

Though Indian forms of mysticism, such as Yoga, aim at a certain kind of control, it does not follow that this aim can be reached only by methods which stress control. After all, a prerequisite for Yoga is that the "knots" of the mind be "released" (see next section). The transcendental meditation advocated by Maharishi follows this lead. It points at relaxation as a means to proper meditation and emphasizes that meditation itself is relaxing. Such relaxation may seem to be a desirable end itself to many modern Americans, Europeans, or Asians, who find themselves entrapped in stresses and neuroses. But that does not conflict with the fact that such relaxation is, for Yoga, in the first place, a prerequisite. Once a state of relaxation is reached, the modern adept may feel strong and fulfilled. But the yogin feels that only then has he reached the level from which he can go on to higher states of control, insight, and bliss. Otherwise, we would not come across such statements as "this self is not within the reach of the weak" (*nāyam ātmā balahīnena labhyaḥ*) (quoted in Daniélou 1955, p. 17).

It would be premature to try to decide at this stage whether the higher states of control, insight, and bliss would coincide with each other and with what could from another point of view be described as a state of complete relaxation. The ultimate in relaxation might be reinterpreted to mean the same as *nirodha* "cessation" or *nirvāṇa* "extinction." The aims of some modern psychotherapists and of some traditional forms of mysticism might then turn out to be similar. Such claims have of course been made by a variety of people, ranging from C. G. Jung to Alan Watts. At the present state of our understanding, however, all the key terms remain mere words. Such problems can be considered seriously only after the proper investigation of mysticism has effectively begun.

While the missionary zeal and Madison Avenue overtones of Wallace and similar researches become apparent in this context, the real significance of such physiological discoveries remains as unclear as that of Brosse's much more careful studies. The same verdict applies to other similar investigations. The study of the EEG pattern of Zen masters was undertaken by Kasamatsu and Hirai (1966), who found that, as practice in Zen meditation increased, there was an appearance of alpha waves (slow electric waves emitted by the brain) which slowly increased their amplitude and then decreased their frequency. In Zen masters with twenty years or more of practice, there also appeared theta waves, which are even slower than alpha waves.

Kamiya (1969) found that subjects can be trained by various feedback methods to regulate their alpha rhythm. His study concludes with the observation that nobody knows for sure what the significance of a changed alpha frequency is. The subjects themselves stress the ineffability of their experience in statements like: "In this experiment, you keep asking me to describe this darned alpha state. I can't do it; it has a certain feel about it, sure, but really, it's best left undescribed; when I try to analyse what it is I don't do well" (Kamiya 1969, p. 515). Kamiya hypothesizes that the experience is pleasant, since he is flooded with requests of people from all over the U.S. who volunteer to be guinea pigs.

The literature on such subjects is increasing rapidly, but it is doubtful whether there is, along with this increase in information, an increase in understanding.[3] Zen meditation has been especially studied by Japanese physiologists, psychologists, and psychotherapists. A bibliographical survey by Timmons and Kamiya (1970) lists a variety of studies without excluding many that are trivial or superficial. The best one can say for most of these studies is that they might broaden the minds of people who are disinclined to accept that meditation has any effects, like perhaps most regular readers of such magazines as *Science, American Scientist*, and *Scientific American*. Many people become interested in meditation only

3. Business, which does not need understanding, has not lagged behind. A Berkeley, California, firm offered for $70.00 (plus $2.00 postage and handling) a "Brainwave Monitor and Feedback Trainer: For Meditation and Relaxation—Alpha and Theta Rhythm Reinforcement." (The Theta Rhythm Reinforcement seems to be added especially for Zen monks with more than twenty years of experience.) This model "7000 incorporates all the features necessary for quick, efficient brainwave training. The amplifier hangs around the user's neck, eliminating any uncomfortable pressures on the head. Only two electrodes are used on a special Velcro headband, allowing quick and versatile positioning." The gadget appears to deteriorate rapidly, but this was advertised as a special advantage: "At later stages of training, the sensitivity is decreased to allow only the highest-amplitude bursts of alpha to be heard, thus training for a deeper state." One would have to search deep for a better example of California mysticism.

after it has been demonstrated to them that meditation has effects on the body. But to those not thus prejudiced and not primarily concerned with mere acquisition of knowledge already possessed by others, a much more basic feature of meditation is that it has definite effects on the mind. Larger issues are also involved. The Buddha sought the causes of suffering, and its elimination, not a feeling of relaxation. The physiological studies do not throw any light on such larger issues and are not in a position to provide even a first understanding of the phenomena they describe—let alone offer explanations in terms of theories. They have established that meditation has definite effects on the body, which remain unexplained and are probably side effects of little consequence. They do not say anything about its effects on the mind, which constitutes one reason, in general not the only one, for engaging in meditation in the first place.

2. *Psychology in the Upaniṣads*

The application of pschological methods to the study of mysticism should be more rewarding. After all, the links between mysticism, traditional psychology, psychotherapy, and psychoanalysis are close, suggestive, and ancient. Before considering contemporary psychological studies relating to mysticism, I shall therefore illustrate the kind of psychology one meets with in Indian mystical texts.

The seventh discourse of the *Chāndogyopaniṣad* consists of the teachings of Sanatkumāra, the eternal youth, son of the God Brahmā, to the sage Nārada. The last section of this discourse (*Chāndogyopaniṣad* 7.26.2) summarizes these teachings. It describes how Sanatkumāra finally showed Nārada "the other shore" (i.e., the goal of the mystic path) after Nārada's mind had been completely purified. About this purification the Upaniṣad says: *smṛti-lambhe sarvagranthīnāṃ vipramokṣaḥ* "by attaining memory all the knots are released."

Though some scholars (e.g., Senart, 1930, p. 106) take *smṛti* here in the sense of tradition, the term clearly refers here to the mental faculty of remembering. What are these knots (*granthinaḥ*)? The Upaniṣadic thinkers speculated on the theory of causality which underlies all activity. In doing so, they distinguished the effects which an act has on the outside world from its effects on the mind of the doer. In terms of the psychology of human activity, the knots are *karman*-knots (*karma-granthinaḥ*), i.e., knots in the mind which are the result of previous activity (*karman*). Many centuries later, the commentator Śaṅkara specifies that such knots are due to previous experiences and ultimately to ignorance, the metaphysical root of all evil in the Advaita Vedānta. Śaṅkara paraphrases *sarvagranthīnāṃ vipramokṣaḥ* "a release of all the knots" as follows: "a kind of releasing, a destruction, of all the knots which reside in the heart and which are hardened by impressions (*bhāvanā*) of experiences obtained during several previous births, in the form of fetters of evil due to ignorance" (*sarveṣām avidyākṛtānarthapāśarūpāṇām anekajanmāntarānubhavabhāvanākaṭhinīkṛtānāṃ hṛdayāśrayāṇāṃ granthīnāṃ vipramokṣo viśeṣeṇa pramokṣaṇaṃ vināśo*).

The word for "mental impression" used here, *bhāvanā*, is closely related in meaning to what other texts call *vāsanā* or *saṃskāra*. These terms refer to "subliminal" impressions, impressions of which one is unaware, but which exert specific influences and which may be recalled through an effort of remembering. The connection with *smṛti* "memory" is obvious, and is clearly formulated, for instance, in the later handbooks of Indian logic: "*bhāvanā*, which comes from experience and causes memory, operates only in the self" (*anubhavajanyā smṛtihetur bhāvanātmamātravṛttiḥ*) (*Tarka-saṃgraha*, sec. 75, "*saṃskāra*"). The term "hardening" underlines the traumatic nature of the original impressions.

Apart from such psychological ideas, there are many correlations between mystical and physiological notions referred to in later Indian traditions. Some of these should at least be mentioned. Even in earlier texts such references are not rare, though few would willingly follow Rele (1932), who provided detailed interpretations in neurological terms of the Vedic Gods: according to him, Pūṣan is the cerebellum, Viṣṇu the spinal cord, Agni the thalamus, Indra the cortex, etc. In Yoga and tantra, the most well-known development which stresses such connections is that of the *kuṇḍalinī*, the symbolic snake coiled up at the bottom of the spine, which is raised through meditation and then passes through nerve centers (*cakra*) until it reaches the top of the head (plate 10b). Correlations are drawn between such centers and definite sounds, colors, cosmic principles, Gods (in Hinduism) and bodhisattvas (in Buddhism) (see, e.g., Pott 1966, table II). In a late picture from Tanjore, South India, the corresponding portions of the spinal column are also drawn (see Rawson 1973, pl. 55). Throughout the centuries, Indian yogins have been aware of some of the physical and physiological correlates of the stages of Yoga. Such insights derive from a combination of observation and speculation, but they also reflect the subjective experiences of the meditator.

3. *Contemporary Psychologists on Yoga*

We are now in a better position to turn to modern psychologists. We find that most contemporary psychologists have confined themselves either to selecting data from mysticism in support of some view or other, or to comparing psychology or psychotherapy with mysticism in a general way. In both respects the light generated, though suggestive at times, has remained hazy.

The pioneering work of Freud can certainly be used in the study of mysticism (an example will follow in chap. 9): but his explicit statements on mysticism are heavily colored by his conviction that all religion is an illusion. Not that this might not turn out in some sense or other to be the case, nor that many of his observations are not refreshing and penetrating. But Freud's theory, in the form in which it was formulated, and with the arguments offered, can no longer be taken seriously. Freud was not very open-minded with regard to "dark" phenomena such as mysticism and Yoga; he disliked them. This is obvious, for example, from a paragraph in *Das Unbehagen in der Kultur* (*Civilization and Its Discontents*) (1930), in which he refers to a friend "whose insatiable scientific curiosity has impelled him to the most out-of-the-way researches," and who considered Yoga as conducive to "regressions leading to primordial, deeply-buried mental states. He sees in them a physiological foundation, so to speak, of much of the wisdom of mysticism." Freud adds: "There would be connections to be made here with many obscure modifications of mental life, such as trance and ecstasy. But I am moved to exclaim, in the words of Schiller's diver: 'Who breathes overhead in the rose-tinted light may be glad!' " (Freud 1957, p. 22). A strange admission, to be sure, by the greatest explorer in modern times of the darker and more obscure recesses of the mind.

Unlike Freud, Jung was very kindly disposed toward religion (cf. Conze 1956, p. 39). He approaches it, however, from two very different points of view. On the one hand he stresses that he does nothing but describe what he found as a doctor and scientist: he found that his Western patients spontaneously drew figures resembling oriental mandalas, and so he turned to the study of mandalas and postulated a realm of "archetypes." But on the other hand he speaks as a preacher, if not a prophet: the collective unconsciousness in which these archetypes are housed becomes an established fact, and religious realization is an integral part of the full development of every normal person. The Jungian system of metaphysics, erected on such slender foundations, with its individual and collective unconscious, amina, animus, archetypes, and other concepts, is so flexible, all-encompassing, and hazy that by explaining everything it explains nothing. What it does do, apart from providing an ever-elusive framework, is to provide a general terminology in terms of which a variety of mystical (and other) phenomena can be summarily classified. But almost any of the existing terminologies—e.g., those used in Oriental systems of philosophical mysticism—could, by similar stretching, perform such a function, and some could do it better. Though it is often unclear which particular thesis Jung wishes to argue for on the basis of the evidence he adduces, what is mainly of interest in reading him is the variety of material that is presented.

Jung's followers, even when more intent on doing so, fare less well when explaining mysticism. H. Schär, author of a book on religion and the soul in Jung's psychology (Schär 1946), provided his own doctrine in *Erlösungsvorstellungen und ihre psychologischen Aspekte* (*Ideas of Liberation and Their Psychological Aspects*) (1950). After more than six hundred pages of typology, the author notes that "eine wichtige Grundfrage, die nach *der Struktur der menschlichen Persönlichkeit,* für uns heute noch ganz im Dunkeln liegt" ("an important fundamental problem [sic], that of *the structure of the human person,* lies for us today still entirely in the dark") (Schär 1950, p. 617). This statement is followed by a vaguely existentialist expression of methodological defeat, based upon no arguments but apparently linked with the author's failure to produce anything that could be described as a theory: "a final evaluation of objective validity, going beyond the individual, is impossible" (Schär 1950, p. 628).

Another of Jung's followers, E. Neumann, stresses at the outset of his gigantic *Ursprungsgeschichte des Bewusstseins (Origin and History of Consciousness)* (1949) that his point of departure, too, is that of the practicing psychotherapist. Jung in his Preface, with similar if not cognate modesty, expresses resentment that he himself, absorbed by his own pioneering investigations, could not engage upon such a monumental enterprise. Neumann's central mythological image, familiar to readers of Jung, is that of the *οὐρόβορος*, the snake which eats its own tail and kills, marries, and impregnates itself. Neumann then introduces the concept of "Uroboros-incest," through which the emerging ego of mankind seeks to lose itself in the womb of unconsciousness. This is what happens in mysticism. Again, the explanatory value of such constructions is zero, though the connections traced in the lengthy descriptions that surround them provide material that is of some independent interest (though generally available elsewhere).

At this point let me briefly turn to allegedly psychological literature more directly concerned with the study of particular types of mysticism. The book of R. Rösel, *Die psychologischen Grundlagen der Yogapraxis* (1928), consists largely of interpretations and translations of passages from the Sanskrit literature on Yoga, followed by an appendix which briefly refers to some modern movements with similar methods and aims. The overall orientation is philological and interpretative, and psychological concepts and methods are hardly used. The expression "psychological foundations" in the title does not refer to Western psychology, but reflects what the Yoga itself offers as its foundation.

An early attempt in the psychoanalytical tradition is contained in the booklet of Geraldine Coster, *Yoga and Western Psychology: A Comparison* (1934). This must unfortunately be pronounced unsuccessful. The reason is the incredibly slipshod interpretations of the Yoga, and in particular of Patañjali's *Yogasūtra*, which pervade the entire discussion. These interpretations affect not only points of detail, but fundamental issues. Let me give an example of each. If *cittavṛtti* in *Yogasūtra* 1.2 is translated as "mind and emotions"

(p. 100) instead of "fluctuations of the mind," the *vṛttis* of *Yogasūtra* 1.5 and following, which obviously refer to the same things, must be translated differently (Coster: "activities or states of the personal consciousness," p. 101); otherwise sleep and memory (not to mention the other three states [means of knowledge, misconceptions, and imagination], which are wrongly translated and interpreted) have to be regarded as "emotions."

A more basic misunderstanding concerns the final goal of Yoga, namely *kaivalya*, "isolation." Coster, who illustrates this state in a diagram, writes as follows (p. 242):

> The further stage of kaivalya is not susceptible of description in intelligible terms. Much has been written about it by eastern and western mystics, but all are agreed that it can only be indicated, never defined. In our diagram it is shown as a state of unification and awareness at all levels.

Patañjali in his *Yogasūtra* does make an attempt at meaningful description, not eschewing definitions, and whenever he is very explicit he is in direct contradiction with Coster's characterization. According to the *Yogasūtra, kaivalya* is neither a state of unification nor a state of awareness at all levels. In accordance with the customary affirmation of the Yoga treatises that *yoga* is derived from the root *yuj-* in the sense of concentration (*samādhau*), not in the sense of connection (*yoge*), the final state of *kaivalya* is not the identity of the mind with the *puruṣa* or spirit, but its isolation—a state in which the purity of the mind equals that of the *puruṣa*, without the two ever becoming identical (*Yogasūtra* 3.54, 4.26). It would be correct to say that *samādhi*, not *kaivalya*, obtains at all levels (see below, page 119). But the highest state of *samādhi* is explicitly called *asamprajñāta*, which Mrs. Coster herself interprets as "unconscious samādhi" (1934, p. 105)—hardly an awareness at all levels. It would not be difficult to point out many other inconsistencies and instances of misinterpretation.

There are several other books with promising but misleading titles which claim to study mysticism with the help of psychological concepts or methods.[4] The most valuable is perhaps *Zen Buddhism*

4. For example, H. Benoît, *The Supreme Doctrine: Psychological Studies in Zen Thought* (1955, from the French original of 1951) which is a description of Zen as the author understands, admires, and advocates it, and which is entirely uncritical. H. Jacobs' *Western Psychotherapy and Hindu*

and Psychoanalysis (1960), in which D. T. Suzuki, Erich Fromm, and Richard de Martino volunteer mainly general impressions, comparisons, and evaluations. Suzuki, though writing with the authority apparently derived from his own experience, uses a language replete with such terms as "the unconscious," which cannot be directly derived from one's experience and which seem to beg the question. Fromm, apart from pointing at some general parallels, defends so many pet theories of his own and engages in so much controversy with other psychologists (such as Jung) that it becomes extremely hazardous to find out whether he might be in a position to contribute to the study of mysticism, and if so, what.

With such books as A. W. Watts's *Psychotherapy East and West* (1961) we enter the realm of avowed popularization and bestsellerdom. Not that Alan Watts, in this and other books, does not provide some entertainment, much needed common sense, and several shrewd observations. But he has too many axes to grind for his book to be regarded as a contribution to the study of mysticism.

To sum up, the psychological study of mysticism seems to be mostly impressionistic and in an even more unsatisfactory state than its physiological study. The physiological study of meditation has at least led to the establishment of certain facts which are suggestive, though nobody seems to know what they mean. The psychological studies mainly reveal the limitations of present-day psychology.

4. Deikman on the Psychology of Meditation

Is the outlook for the psychological study of mysticism therefore bleak? On the contrary, it seems very promising. I would not be surprised if the study of mysticism would one day be regarded as a branch of psychology. This does not mean that mysticism would be reduced to what most present-day psychologists seem to spend most of their time on. Rather, it means that psychology would be deepened and widened so as to be in a position to take account of these particular aspects of the mind.

There is a danger of confusion here, since some contemporary

Sâdhanâ: A Contribution to Comparative Studies in Psychology and Metaphysics (1961) is a jumble which combines interesting bits of information with platitudes, hobbyhorses, and case histories of patients.

psychologists do attempt to broaden the study of psychology. But they adopt the irrationalism and get entangled in the difficulties that I have been concerned with in Part I of this essay. R. E. Ornstein, for example, regards as a complement to existing science and psychology "a second stream of knowledge directed toward methods of answering these questions which scientific method excludes, the esoteric traditions of the Middle and Far East" (Ornstein 1972, Preface, p. x). About this he says the following:

As Roger Bacon wrote 700 years ago, "There are two modes of knowing, those of argument and experience." They are complementary to one another; neither is reducible to the other; and their simultaneous working may be incompatible. One mode is verbal and rational, sequential in operation, orderly; the other is intuitive, tacit, diffuse in operation, less logical and neat, a mode we often devalue, culturally, personally, and even physiologically.

What Roger Bacon meant (and said) is that nothing can be known with certainty without experience. Experience, according to him, is twofold, and includes inner experience, which covers mathematical as well as mystical intuitions. Argument or "logic" is separate from these. What Ornstein suggests in addition is that argument or logic is not applicable to experience. So what are we to do—leave our experiences out in the cold and not try to understand them? And what if our "rational" knowledge tells us something, and our "intuitive" knowledge tells us something different?

What I have been arguing is quite different, namely, that there is a need for a rational investigation into this "second stream of knowledge." If we find that our insight greatly increases through the study of this "stream," it will not be surprising. But to assume at the outset that we have here a complement to rational knowledge is begging the question: this is one of the many problems we are investigating.

In the beginning stages, the study of mysticism will be similar to Freud's investigation of dreams. What will happen afterwards we do not know. It should be remembered that Freud, unlike Ornstein, did not advocate that we should dream in order to complement our waking; we do that already. What Freud did do was to take dreams seriously and make them the object of rational investigation.

The one promising kind of experimental psychological work with which I am familiar is the research of A. J. Deikman on experiential aspects of meditation (Deikman 1963, 1966; Tart 1969, pp. 23–43, 199–218 = Deikman 1963).

Deikman (1963) describes the results of eight subjects meditating on a blue vase during twelve sessions. Two of these subjects. who meditated during more than seventy sessions, provided additional data, as reported in Deikman 1966. Deikman observed that meditation resulted in what he calls de-automatization; that is, sensations are more intense and direct and less organized; there is, for example, loss of the third dimension in visual perception, there is less differentiation between the ego and the object, and there is less affect control. At the same time, outside stimuli, though recognized, are barred from attention. "A most striking finding" of the experiment was "the ease and rapidity with which the phenomena were produced . . . In less than half an hour, phenomena occurred that in other contexts have been described as 'depersonalization,' 'hallucination,' 'delusion,' or 'visual distortion' . . ." (Deikman 1963, p. 342).

In his second study Deikman goes deeper into the problems to which these experiments draw attention. He reanalyzes de-automatization as "reinvesting aims and percepts with attention" (Deikman 1966, p. 111). But he also discusses the possibility of a perceptual expansion, on account of which external stimuli ordinarily excluded or ignored are perceived.

> Some of the visual phenomena of the meditation experience . . . appear to be a result of a de-automatization leading to a breakdown of the percepts in the direction of a primitive visual experience. However, the more striking perceptions of force, movement and light . . . may possibly be the product of a de-automatization that permits the awareness of new dimensions of the total stimulus array (Deikman 1966, p. 111).

Deikman's results, and his use of the term "attention" to characterize them, throw some light on the concept of *samādhi* in Yoga. Although it is widely believed that the term *samādhi* is reserved for the higher states of absorption which are the culmination of the practice of Yoga, the commentator Vyāsa on the first *sūtra* of Patañjali's *Yogasūtra* gives the term a much wider application. In providing a preliminary answer to the question "What is Yoga?" Vyāsa says:

Yoga is *samādhi*. And *samādhi* is a property of the mind which exists on all levels (*sārvabhaumaś cittasya dharmaḥ*). The levels of the mind (*cittabhūmayaḥ*) are: the scattered (*kṣipta*), the confused (*mūḍha*), the distracted (*vikṣipta*), the one-pointed (*ekāgra*) and the restricted (*niruddha*).

Vyāsa goes on to explain that the first three do not really belong to Yoga. The fourth is a state of Yoga where there is consciousness of external objects (*saṃprajñāta-samādhi*); in the fourth there is no such consciousness (*asaṃprajñāta-samādhi*). In this passage, the term *samādhi* must therefore be interpreted in such a way that it can refer to a variety of states. Professor T. R. V. Murti suggested (personal communication) "attention," the term Deikman uses to characterize meditation.

The limitations of Deikman's work derive from its psychoanalytic background. Deikman gave minimal instructions about concentration and was very much concerned about avoiding direct verbal suggestions or even covert cues pertaining to expected phenomena. Though this may minimize certain forms of suggestion, projection, and transfer that are undesirable in the treatment of neuroses, and in doing so may also convince some skeptics who think that the whole thing is a put-on, the underlying assumption seems to be that mystical experiences are largely spontaneous or simply induced occurrences, and are not learned or improved by practice. But mysticism is, at least in part, learned, just like French, and is not for that reason imaginary. If one wishes to find out how people learn a language and what is going on when one learns a language, it would not do to give minimum instruction, such as a small vocabulary, and then study what happens, for that would be a study of someone learning a small list of French words, rather than French. What would be required first of all, for such exploration to be fruitful, is a theory of language. Moreover, instead of experimenting with subjects who have been given a minimum of instruction, formulated in terms which reflect what happens to be the experimenter's understanding of the topic, it is necessary to study what happens to subjects who are being trained by recognized masters. Of course, the forms and content of the mystic experience may then be found to be congruent "with the mystics' cultural and religious background" (Deikman 1963, p. 340, referring to Coe). But what is wrong with that? It would be greatly surprising if mystical experiences remained unaffected by the beliefs surrounding them; even ordinary experiences are affected by our expectations. But while mystical experiences may be thus affected whenever they occur, it does not follow that such experiences are not at the same time experiences of something else. Similarly, it makes sense to talk about the general properties of language, and linguists can undertake its study provided they don't neglect the richness and detail of particular languages, including their "congruence with a cultural background." The data of mysticism are not less abundant and varied, and have to be studied closely and systematically before it will be possible to arrive at any general theory.

As we shall see in chapter 11, the need for a qualified teacher is stressed in almost all the traditions of mysticism. In the exploration of mysticism, the importance of the teacher is that he teaches how to meditate. It does not follow that the investigator should accept uncritically what the teacher says about it. Deikman recognizes the importance of the *guru* in the classical literature on meditation, but the mere conclusion he draws from this is that "*E*" (the experimenter) "should not be removed from the situation" (Deikman 1963, p. 331). That under such limitations the results were so spectacular is remarkable. One can only imagine what discoveries are in store when subjects who undergo intensive training at the hands of an expert are studied and become themselves students. The results will undoubtedly go well beyond Deikman's findings, which he characterizes himself, modestly but gratuitously, as follows: "What I have described are analogs of mystic experiences, not true mystic experiences" (Deikman 1963, p. 338). Who knows?

PART III

How to Study Mysticism

We are men and our lot is to learn and to be hurled into inconceivable new worlds.

Don Juan, in CASTANEDA (1971), p. 187

9

Effort, Doubt, and Criticism

> Doubts about doubt.—"To a strong mind, doubt is the best pillow." This saying by Montaigne continued to annoy Pascal, for no one wanted a good pillow as much as he did. What then was wanting?
>
> NIETZSCHE (1954) I, p. 1045

If mysticism is to be studied seriously, it should not merely be studied indirectly and from without, but also directly and from within. Mysticism can at least in part be regarded as something affecting the human mind, and it is therefore quite unreasonable to expect that it could be fruitfully explored by confining oneself to literature about or contributed by mystics, or to the behavior and physiological characteristics of mystics and their bodies. No one would willingly impose upon himself such artificial constraints when exploring other phenomena affecting or pertaining to the mind; he would not study perception only by analyzing reports of those who describe what they perceive, or by looking at what happens to people and their bodies when they are engaged in perceiving. What one would do when studying perception, in addition, if not first of all, is to observe and analyze one's own perceptions.

Comparing the study of mysticism with the study of perception is instructive also because of a specific difference between the two: while most of us have little personal experience of mystical states of mind, our personal knowledge of perception is vast and is taken for granted. When we study reports on perception or theories of perception, we make constant use of this repository.

In 1968 M. Hattori published a study and translation of the theory of perception of Dignāga, a Buddhist logician who lived around A.D. 500. Everybody who evaluates Hattori's work rightly attributes its achievements to the author's knowledge of Sanskrit and of Buddhist logic. But without the vast experience of perception which we all have accumulated from early childhood, such a study could not have been written, nor would it be intelligible. The case of mysticism is different because we do not possess a large storehouse of knowledge in this area which we can personally draw upon. But surely it makes little sense to try to understand mysticism without at least some such knowledge. As is commonly, but also correctly, said, it would be like a blind man studying vision.

Lack of experience is one of the main reasons that the study of mysticism is never undertaken in a simple and straightforward fashion, directly and from within. Its roundabout study is not deplored, but is defended in principle as being more scientific, as if we were to say: "We ought to study Dignāga's theory of perception, but it would be unscientific to make any use of our familiarity with the fact of perception." There are, however, other reasons why mysticism is not studied directly and from within: (1) because it is not so simple; (2) because of the general prejudice already mentioned, that is, that mysticism by its very nature is mysterious and cannot be studied; (3) because of the general mistrust on the part of many contemporary philosophers, psychologists, and behavioral scientists generally, of anything that is not either an aspect of behavior or a fact of physiology; and (4) because of particular beliefs concerning mysticism, to which I shall now turn.

Let us again consider an apparently quite reasonable observation, already referred to (cf. chap. 5, n. 1), that one need not be a mystic to study mysticism. This of course applies to the external (e.g., behavioristic or physiological) study of mysticism. But it does not so clearly apply to the exploration of the subjective aspects of mysticism, to which there is by definition no direct access other than through subjective experience.

Some of the confusion here is semantic: it depends on our notion of what constitutes a mystic. Does a mystic have to be a born mystic, so that one either is or is not a mystic? Or can one become a mystic? In other domain, we can become speakers, though not native speakers, of a foreign language. In respect to language ability, we can become in no way different from a native speaker; but we cannot become native speakers by definition.

As for mystics, some are not born that way; in fact, there are quite a few spectacular conversions from the non-mystic to the mystic life (e.g., plates 14a–b). We call a mystic anyone who for a certain length of time has mystical experiences. Hence, if the investigator of the subjective aspects of mysticism has such regular experiences, he becomes a mystic by definition. Therefore one need not be a mystic in order to study mysticism; but one might have to become one, at least in one of the natural uses of the term. The analogy with the elephant (see chap. 5, n. 1) collapses here. We can photograph the world through an elephant's eye lens on a plate made like an elephant's retina; we can plant electrodes in an elephant's brain; etc. But we need not be elephants in order to study elephants; the fact is that we cannot be elephants.

A formidable objection to the study of mysticism is the religious, and especially the Western monotheistic, belief that a mystical experience or state is the product of a special state of divine grace. Similar in some respects is the conviction on the part of such Indian systems as the Advaita Vedānta that the state of *mokṣa* cannot be obtained by any effort on our part, because an unconditional and infinite effect can never be conditioned by a finite cause (*mokṣa*, therefore, is beyond the pale of *karman*). Such beliefs seem to place the mystical experience in a realm beyond the reach of rational investigation and experimentation. This would not necessarily be the case if only such events were predictable; solar eclipses, for example, though they cannot be caused by human effort, can be predicted, and therefore studied when they occur. But at the present state of our knowledge, neither grace nor *mokṣa* are predictable.

Even these objections, as they stand, are not insurmountable. Revolutions cannot be predicted by present-day sociology, but that does not mean that they never will be (Wertheim 1974, pp. 88–89). Moreover, even if mystical experiences can neither be obtained by any effort nor predicted, the study of such experiences would merely be awkward, not impossible. Volcanic eruptions or earthquakes fall within the same category; they cannot ordinarily be brought about or predicted. But all that is demanded in such a situation is that the investigator be prepared and be at hand when the event takes place.

Actually, several kinds of mystical experience are not even that inaccessible. There are other notions of mysticism than the ones just mentioned. In the Yoga system, in Taoism, and in various forms of Buddhism, a mystical state can be reached by discipline and training. The commentator Vyāsa, introducing *Yogasūtra* 1.12, asks: "Now by what means (*upāya*) can the fluctuations [of the mind] be restrained [the goal of Yoga be reached]?" The answer is provided by the *sūtra*: "They are restrained by detachment (*vairāgya*) and practice (*abhyāsa*)." I shall return to *vairāgya* in the next chapter. What *abhyāsa* means is explained by the next *sūtra* of the *Yogasūtra*: it is "an effort at constancy" (*sthitau yatnaḥ*). And the commentator elucidates: "Constancy is the calm flow of the non-fluctuating mind." Elsewhere the *Yogasūtra* advocates such methods as meditation, breathing exercises, and special postures. Very similar ones are met with in Buddhism and in Taoism.

A simple conclusion follows from this. If mysticism can from one point of view be said to consist of two domains—a domain of phenomena that can be caused by human effort, and a domain of phenomena that cannot be caused by human effort—the experiential study of mysticism should obviously begin with the study of the former. Whether the results of such an exploration will also be valid for the latter domain can only be determined after that domain has come within reach too. But this step need not cause anxiety just now, when we have not well begun.

It is quite possible that most of the monotheistic and Vedāntic forms of mysticism, which purportedly cannot be induced, are quite different from the yogic, Buddhist, and Taoist forms, which purportedly can. In fact, all of these might be found to be different from each other in some respect or other. But it would certainly be unwarranted to exclude the latter forms of mysticism from our investigation, merely because there are also other kinds. After all, the same or similar results are sometimes reached by different methods. A house might burn down because of a willful act of arson or because of an adventitious short circuit. The methodological situation, then, is quite similar to that found in many other domains of rational inquiry, for instance, linguistics. Though we cannot at present look into the brain of a person who is engaged in uttering sentences, we can embark upon the linguistic and psycholinguistic study of sentences by other means. Whether the two domains of inquiry, one accessible, the other inaccessible, are identical, or how they are related if not identical, are problems that can only be dealt with when both domains have become accessible. Yet no linguist would refuse to study sentences because we cannot perceive how they are internally produced. Nor would a physicist be content with mere speculation and refuse to devise experiments to test some part of a hypothesis, on the grounds that such experiments might be difficult to carry out, might be of uncertain outcome, or might be time-consuming or expensive. And neither would a person interested in reaching the South Pole, out of fear that he might not be able to get there, stay at home and refuse even to move in a southerly direction. Yet students of mysticism have, in their field, left all such things undone. Content with mere speculation and talking, they have not even considered the possibility of traveling themselves that part of the road that appears to be within reach—even though not very well paved. This can only be understood if it is the outcome of a deep-seated prejudice, for such a negative attitude has in no domain of knowledge been taken seriously or been expected to lead to results.

The fact that Yoga, Taoism, and many schools of Buddhism regard mystical experience as dependent on human effort is related to their anthropocentrism, rationalism, and relative independence of philosophical evaluation and religious contexts—for example, of particular doctrines and rituals. Massignon, looking at the Yoga system of Patañjali from the perspective of Muslim mysticism, has characterized this independent character of the Yoga as follows: "In Patañjali, the method of mysticism, detached from the background of metaphysics or cult, confines itself to the establishment of an admirably balanced and precise introspective system of liberation, which frees the natural spirit from the body and produces the perfect detachment of consciousness" (Massignon 1954, p. 93).

I shall return to this absence from the Yoga of specific religious or metaphysical superstructures in chapter 13.

A scholar willing to study mystical experience by making an attempt to obtain at least certain kinds of mystical experience for himself will encounter still other objections. I shall refer to the principal one: Is the attitude of mind required of an adept of Yoga not incompatible with a critical, "scientific" outlook? Does not the Yoga, and similarly parallel forms of mysticism in Buddhism and Taoism, demand total submission of the intellect and blind adherence to the teacher's instructions?

The first answer to this objection is, of course, that it would be rational to at least attempt to embark upon such a path without giving up one's critical outlook. How far this approach can be successful may only be determined afterwards, if not by the investigator himself, then by others. However, this expectation of a certain incompatibility is again largely the outcome of the prejudice that mysticism cannot be studied rationally. Let us therefore look more closely at how the *Yogasūtra* itself addresses this issue.

Patañjali, like many other teachers of mysticism, does require *śraddhā* "confidence, trust" (*Yogasūtra* 1.20) as a prerequisite for meditation, and warns against *vitarka* "doubt, uncertainty" (*Yogasūtra* 2.33–34), signs, apparently, of dogmatism.[1] But the context makes it clear that what is here required is not the uncritical acceptance of certain doctrinal interpretations and evaluations, but the *initial* acceptance of the prescribed methods without questioning their rationale. First we should know; then we can judge. Moreover, this is also a matter of efficiency and expedience. Such requirements are known in other domains and are quite compatible with *subsequent* rational analysis. In chemistry, for example, one starts out accepting certain results from physics, which are only later understood and can then be scrutinized and questioned. Similarly, one has to have a certain confidence in the car of the driving instructor, even though one may not know how a car engine works, or not yet be aware that the car is going to break down. To require

1. The term *vitarka* has to be understood in the context of another passage too (*Yogasūtra* 1.17–18). I shall return to this (see also Dasgupta 1922, p. 271.) The translation adopted here is given in Eliade (1954, p. 64 = 1969, p. 51). Different interpreters have offered extraordinary variety, beginning with al-Bīrūnī (Pines and Gelblum 1966, p. 306) and culminating in Woods' "perverse consideration" (Woods 1927, p. 183).

such kinds of knowledge beforehand would indefinitely postpone the acquisition of the desired results.

The term *vitarka*, which in the above context means "doubt, uncertainty," suggests the deliberation of a mind engaged in analysis or inquiry. As such, it is an essential component of a scholarly or scientific investigation. In the process of meditation, such deliberation initially assists in directing the attention of the mind to its own movements. But before these movements can be effectively checked, the activity of *vitarka* has to cease. And so we find in the *Yogasūtra* first a description of consciousness which is accompanied by *vitarka* "deliberation," *vicāra* "analysis," *ānanda* "joy," and *asmitā* "awareness of the ego"; and following it, a description of a state of mind which is without all these (*Yogasūtra* 1.17–18).

The Buddhist descriptions of meditation are similar though not identical, and provide valuable detail. Lamotte has translated a *Dhyānasūtra* from the Chinese (and I have retranslated it from the French), where the first two stages of *dhyāna* "meditation" are described as follows:

> Abandoning desires and bad *dharma*
> Man enters into the first *dhyāna*,
> With inquiry (*savitarka*) and with judgment (*savicāra*),
> Produced by discrimination which is pleasant and sweet.
>
> Abandoning the fire of lust,
> He gains reflection, clear and refreshing,
> Happy as a man, tortured by heat,
> Who enters into a cool lake.
>
> Like a poor man who has hit upon a treasure:
> The *vitarka* of joy excites his mind.
> He analyzes it: that is *vicāra*.
> Thus he enters into the first *dhyāna*.
>
> He knows that *vitarka* and *vicāra* trouble his mind;
> They have to be abandoned, also when good,
> Because only when the sea is calm
> It is possible not to perceive the waves.
>
> When a person utterly exhausted
> Goes to bed for a sound sleep,

Any call addressed to him,
Greatly upsets his mind.

Similarly to a person who in reflection enters *dhyāna*
Vitarka and *vicāra* are a constant annoyance.
(LAMOTTE 1949, pp. 1025–1026)

Elsewhere in the *Mahāprajñāpāramitāśāstra* ("Treatise on the Perfection of Wisdom"), *vitarka* and *vicāra* are said to disturb concentration:

Even if good, they are enemies of concentration, and it is difficult to get rid of them. Some even say that a mind endowed with *vitarka* and *vicāra* is not concentrated. That is why the Buddha declared that concentration with *vitarka* and *vicāra* lacks firmness (LAMOTTE 1970, p. 1488).

Like the great *Prajñāpāramitā* treatise itself, the present exploration of mysticism is not an exercise in meditation: it is an analytic essay, using *vitarka* and *vicāra*. But when the investigator of mysticism has found a *guru* and starts the practice of meditation, he has to abandon intellectual deliberation—of course, only temporarily, as otherwise the investigation would come to a full stop. The difference between a student of mysticism and a person in search of *nirvāṇa*, *mokṣa*, or salvation, lies here. While both have to share certain attitudes, the student has sooner or later to resume a critical outlook so that he can obtain understanding and make it available to others. It is pointless to ask how and when this should be done when we have not even begun. Such a question hardly makes sense. And yet such questions are often raised, mainly because people are deeply convinced that one cannot indulge in a meaningful experiment of this kind without abandoning one's critical faculties.

The problem is not dissimilar to the situation elsewhere in the domain of scholarship. A fieldworker engaged in learning a tribal language has to decide when to stop listening, collecting information, asking questions, and interviewing informants in order to go home, report on his results, and postulate grammatical rules. But nobody asks beforehand exactly when such decisions have to be made, because nobody doubts that it can be done. Obviously, the investigator has to become familiar with the domain of his investigation, take his knowledge and experience into account, and use his judgment and good sense. People who do such work for the first time may make mistakes. Some people return too soon, to find out afterwards that they lack essential information which is not obtainable elsewhere. Others stay too long or go native. Similar things are bound to happen when one starts to explore mysticism seriously. But it would be shortsighted to insist that one should not start because one does not know exactly when to stop or when certain decisions will have to be made.

A good example of the rational acceptance of prescribed methods without questioning their rationale is provided by Carlos Castaneda's experiences with drugs under the guidance of Don Juan, a pseudonym for a Yaqui Indian (Castaneda 1968, 1971, and 1972). The Indian expert prescribed specific doses of drugs and gave instructions on how his pupil was to act and react when the drugs took effect. Castaneda followed these instructions painstakingly, without questioning them, even when they seemed, within his own world view, totally unintelligible. By saying that he did not question them, I mean that he carried them out; but later he did ask questions about their interpretation—in fact, rather excessively so. The resulting descriptions are of considerable value and are certainly susceptible to rational analysis (though no one knows at present what rational hypothesis could account for all of them); in fact, they will be the more valuable, the more thoroughly they are analyzed.

Castaneda has embarked upon a first analysis of the materials he has so magnificently provided and described (Castaneda 1968: "Part II: A Structural Analysis"). But what this analysis establishes most clearly is the inadequacy, in this domain, of the tools provided by the social sciences. In his second book, Castaneda, with a small bow to fashion, calls his method phenomenological, though its range is clearly not confined to what Husserl or Merleau-Ponty would call *Lebenswelt* or *monde vécu* (cf. chap. 4, n. 1, above):

> This work is, therefore, a reportage and should be read as a reportage. The system I recorded was incomprehensible to me, thus the pretense to anything other than reporting about it would be misleading and impertinent. In this respect I have adopted the phenomenological method and have striven to deal with sorcery solely as phenomena that were presented to me. I, as the perceiver, recorded what I perceived, and at the moment of recording I endeavored to suspend judgment (Castaneda 1971, p. 25).

Don Juan repeatedly refers to the fact that the learning process is hampered by "doubting and nagging" (Castaneda 1972, p. 165): "Don't tax yourself trying to figure it out" (p. 167). About himself he says: "I had all the doubts that you have and never followed the instructions I was given"; and to Castaneda: "If you would have followed my instructions and performed all the acts I have taught you, you would by now have enough power to cross that bridge. Enough power to *see* and to stop the world" (p. 168). Much of what Don Juan objects to in doubt is the weakening of one's resolve to carry out instructions.

Another good example of the required kind of unbiased and detached observation of one's own experience is provided by what Freud in his *Traumdeutung* (1900) called *kritiklose Selbstbeobachtung* "uncritical self-observation." What Freud says about the technique patients should adopt when recounting their dreams is of considerable importance for the study of mystical experience. It deserves to be quoted in full:

> We must aim at bringing about two changes in him: an increase in the attention he pays to his own physical perceptions and the elimination of the criticism by which he normally sifts the thoughts that occur to him. In order that he may be able to concentrate his attention on his self-observation it is an advantage for him to lie in a restful attitude and shut his eyes. It is necessary to insist explicitly on his renouncing all criticism of the thoughts that he perceives. We therefore tell him that the success of the psycho-analysis depends on his noticing and reporting whatever comes into his head and not being misled, for instance, into suppressing an idea because it strikes him as unimportant or irrelevant or because it seems to him meaningless. He must adopt a completely impartial attitude to what occurs to him, since it is precisely his critical attitude which is responsible for his being unable, in the ordinary course of things, to achieve the desired unravelling of his dreams or obsessional idea or whatever it may be.
>
> I have noticed in my psycho-analytical work that the whole frame of mind of a man who is reflecting is totally different from that of a man who is observing his own psychical processes. In reflection there is one more psychical activity at work than in the most attentive self-observation, and this is shown amongst other things by the tense looks and wrinkled forehead of a person pursuing his reflections as compared with the restful expression of a self-observer. In both cases attention must be concentrated, but the man who is reflecting is also exercising his *critical* faculty; this leads him to reject some of the ideas that occur

to him after perceiving them, to cut short others without following the trains of thought which they would open up to him, and to behave in such a way towards still others that they never become conscious at all and are accordingly suppressed before being perceived. The self-observer on the other hand need only take the trouble to suppress his critical faculty. If he succeeds in doing that, innumerable ideas come into his consciousness of which he could otherwise never have got hold. The material which is in this way freshly obtained for his self-perception makes it possible to interpret both his pathological ideas and his dream structures (Freud 1953, pp. 101–102).

Since the mere mention of Freud often works as a strong stimulant and evokes unpredictable responses, I want to make it as clear as I can why I regard this observation as so relevant for the study of mysticism. I am not advocating Freud's theories of neurosis, repression, ego, and id, or his pansexism. I am not claiming that the Freudian method of psychoanalysis, or indeed any method of psychoanalysis, is good. But in the above passage, Freud draws attention to something which pertains not only to pathological but also to normal ideas, and not only to neurotics, patients, and analysts, but also to others—a fact of which he was undoubtedly aware. His statement applies in general to anyone who wishes to observe the movements of his own mind, and therefore to students of the subjective states of mystical experience, that is (as I have been arguing), to all serious students of mysticism.

The alleged similarities between mystical and pathological states, here alluded to, rest on very flimsy grounds. What mystical and pathological states have in common, of course, is that both are distinct from the normal state. Beyond that, we know little. It has been argued that particular exercises and the nonordinary states of mind to which they give access must *eo ipso* be pathological. But a gymnast may also acquire nonordinary skill: by the same argument many sports must be pronounced pathological.

The attitude Freud describes requires impartiality and the initial absence of criticism, in brief, receptivity. If on account of such an attitude certain observations have been made, they can be remembered. This becomes easier with a little practice, as in the case of the remembrance of dreams (one keeps paper and pencil at hand). However, the expectation that such future remembrance will be used should not interfere with the observation itself; that would introduce what Freud called reflecting. Subsequently, such remembered observations can be related to each other, analyzed, and evaluated critically. For neurotics and patients, such a process might take time, and the analyst might have to assist or interfere. But for students of mysticism such rational evaluation can begin as soon as sufficient material has been collected. What is important is that the analysis should not interfere with the observation, and that both should be kept carefully distinct. This is by no means impossible, as the irrationalist claims; but it may take some practice. And as in all things, some people will be better at it than others.

That Patañjali, Don Juan, and Freud all demand a certain trust and a certain absence of doubt and criticism may seem to constitute a formidable obstacle to the rational study of mysticism. For we have since Descartes been led to suppose that methodical doubt is the hallmark of the unprejudiced search for truth. Many people assume that such doubt should be resorted to as early as possible, if not immediately. But doubts and suspicions can also mark prejudices that we should try to get rid of. That may take time. A villager who for the first time visits a fashionable restaurant in the city is suspicious of everything new and exotic that he is offered; and he may refuse to eat. The attitude of most people with regard to mysticism is very similar. The doubts which we entertain with respect to very unfamiliar events are largely the outcome of prejudices shaped by our experiences with more familiar events. Too much doubt at the outset will accordingly hold us back and prevent us from entering a new domain. Therefore we should suspend doubt if we wish to learn something new. But if we do not resort to analysis and critical evaluation at a later stage, we move into the new domain like sleepwalkers, without gaining any knowledge or understanding.

Philosophers are especially bad at suspending doubt, perhaps because of the Cartesian tradition. As every teacher of logic knows, it is very difficult to teach mathematical logic to students of philosophy. They keep asking questions: "Why should I write this down this way?" "What does 'assume' mean?" "What is a proposition?" and so forth. Logic can only be learned by those who are willing to start by doing certain technical jobs. Questions can be meaningfully asked when one knows one's way around.

10

Prerequisites and Methods

> Stretch a bow to the very full,
> And you will wish you had stopped in time.
>
> *Tao Tê Ching*, in WALEY (no date), p. 152

It would be nice if open-mindedness and the right frame of mind were all that were required of a student of mysticism. But the training of a mystic generally demands more strenuous and specific discipline and exercises, and it is unlikely that a rational mystic could obtain results without them. Many of the required or recommended methods are likely to be irrelevant, because they are religious or moral paraphernalia belonging to what may be described as a superstructure. The number of these methods increases with the extent to which mystical experiences have been integrated into a religious cult or a philosophical or ethical tradition; I shall discuss some of these superstructures in chapter 13.

Mystical experiences are often seen to follow events which cannot be described as prerequisites or methods. Such events are often dramatic and tragic, and they help to shape a mystic's life. Kalmu, for example, an ordinary Himalayan goatherd, lost his wife and children before he turned into a shaman (cf. plates 14a–b). Venkataraman enacted his own death before he became Śrī Ramaṇa Maharṣi (plate 16). And Prince Siddhārtha left his wife, his home and his kingdom before he became the Buddha (plate 8).

Secular justification exists for many of the methods which mystics have adopted. An example is fasting. At first sight this may seem to be primarily a meritorious form of suffering or self-sacrifice. But apart from its none too elusive effects on the mind, fasting has very definite effects on the body. Many medical experiments require an empty stomach on the part of the patient. So do experiments with drugs. The difference in the effects of drugs on a full and on an empty stomach can be measured, and has been measured fairly precisely at least for animals. Specific effects have also been observed. For example, mescaline produces *bradycardia* (lowering of the heartbeat) and *hypoglycemia* (decline in the concentration of blood glucose) in rats (Fischer 1958, p. 390). Transcendental meditation has the same effects on men, which may explain the relaxed state of the meditator (Wallace and Benson 1972, p. 87–88; but see above, chap. 8, sec. 1). Fischer reports that Speck has shown that fasting significantly reduces the degree of mescaline-induced bradycardia and hypoglycemia in rats, possibly because it encourages the production of endogenous epinephrine (adrenalin). In other words, fasting may have a protective effect, which may in turn explain the fasting that is practiced before peyote ceremonies, for instance (Fischer 1958, p. 401; Castaneda 1968, pp. 107, 135 and 1971, pp. 139ff.; see also Huxley 1963, pp. 150–152, for suggestive speculation along these lines).

Once we abandon the armchair approach, we need not be surprised if we have to prepare an investigator of mysticism by means of an appropriate course of fasting, just as we prepare an astronaut by an appropriate course of eating.

Another prerequisite mentioned in the *Yogasūtra* is *pratyāhāra* "withdrawal of the senses." This is likely to be associated with asceticism and otherworldliness. But we shall see in the beginning of chapter 12 what remarkable effects sensory deprivation has on subjects who undergo a simple experiment. Again, the justification for such a practice is based upon direct experience and has little to do with particular religious or ethical superstructures.

Among the most significant methods used by mystics in the traditions of Yoga, Buddhism, and Taoism are meditation and breathing exercises. Though meditation is of basic importance especially in the religions of India, it is also found elsewhere, and related phenomena, ranging from trance to prayer, are found in all religions. In Christianity, breathing exercises were developed in the spiritual tradition of Hesychasm, but not before Nicephoros the Solitary in the thirteenth century (see Eliade 1969, pp. 63–65, and Monchanin 1956, pp. 7–10). Though there are historical relations between Indian religious ideas and early Christian theology (see Benz 1951), there seems to be no actual link between these Christian breathing exercises and the Yoga system.

Breathing exercises resemble meditation in that they help first to increase the awareness of what is going on inside the mind, and subsequently to reduce the movement of mental fluctuations. We have seen that the physiological and behavioral study of these phenomena has to some extent been undertaken. What is now needed is their subjective or experiential exploration. This holds for the study of fasting too. But while fasting has in the course of time been provided with a moralistic superstructure, partly due to the inverse proportion between wealth and hunger, meditation and breathing exercises illustrate more clearly and directly that these mystical disciplines are specific kinds of training of the body-mind complex.

I shall return to meditation, which is a central topic in the exploration of mysticism. In the study of breathing, it is suggestive that neurotics and psychotics appear to have a faster rate of respiration than normal persons (Clausen 1951). Beyond that, little appears to be known about the relationships between breathing and the mind. Even the effects of smoking do not seem to have been studied from this point of view. And yet it is well known that since ancient times, connections have been felt to exist. The Sanskrit term *prāṇa* means "breath" and "life" as well as "spirit" (itself ambiguous in English), whereas Sanskrit *ātman* "self" is etymologically related to German *Atem* "breath."

Breathing exercises are closely related to recitation, a practice almost universal among the religions of mankind. In India, the Vedas have been transmitted orally through recitation for almost three thousand years (cf. plate 6). For parallels in Islam, especially *dhikr*, see the literature quoted in Eliade 1969, pp. 62–63 and 216–219. While Yoga is often considered of non-Vedic origin (but see chap. 6, sec. 1), the recitation of sacred syllables such as *om* in what has been called "mantra Yoga" resembles certain forms of ritual Vedic recitation (in particular, the *śastra* recitation of the *Ṛgveda* during Soma sacrifices).

Even at present, the lengthening of certain syllables in the Veda recitation of Nambudiri Brahmans in Kerala is quite extraordinary. In *Sāmaveda* chant, I noted syllables such as *o, bā,* chanted with a single breath lasting for eighteen seconds (Staal 1961a, p. 83). This type of chanting requires rigorous training and can certainly be described as at least in part a breathing exercise. The breathing patterns brought about by the chant and possibly the temporary increase of carbon dioxide in the lungs and blood have a greater effect on the mind than the content, generally unknown, of what is recited (cf. Huxley 1963, pp. 143–145). In the case of monosyllabic mantras or mantras consisting of a few syllables, a more physical than mental effect is even more likely. After all, many mantras of this kind are literally devoid of meaning.

Fasting, withdrawal of the senses, breathing exercises, and meditation are closely related to what in Indian religions is called *vairāgya* or *tyāga* "detachment." Here again we have a concept that in the context of Western religion smacks of morality. Detachment seems to imply that the adept forgoes worldly pleasures, selfishness, and ambition. The notion of *tyāga* undoubtedly has such overtones in the *Bhagavad Gītā,* where it indicates that the doer should renounce the fruits of his deeds (*karma-phala-tyāga*). Originally, *tyāga* was used in the Vedic ritual for a formula recited by the main sacrificer at the time of an oblation, as he offered its fruits to the presiding deity and renounced his own claims: "This is for Agni (Indra, Prajāpati, . . .), not for me" (*agnaye/indrāya/prajāpataye . . . idam—na mama*).

The mystical significance of detachment does not lie in the realm of ethics. It is an aspect of most of the techniques for training the mind. Before the fluctuations of the mind can be brought to a standstill, they have to be examined, as we have seen. But when examined, they are naturally found to exhibit a person's preoccupations in life, his plans, expectations, desires, tensions, memories, and so on. For a mystical experience to come about in the mind, all these fluctuations have to be shelved—at least temporarily. Since struggling against them would only introduce new waves of motion, the natural method to bring about this cessation is detachment.

9. Bhakti: loving devotion (the saint Sundaramūrti).

10a. Horned deity with animals from Harappā.

10b. The six cakras in *kuṇḍalinī* Yoga.

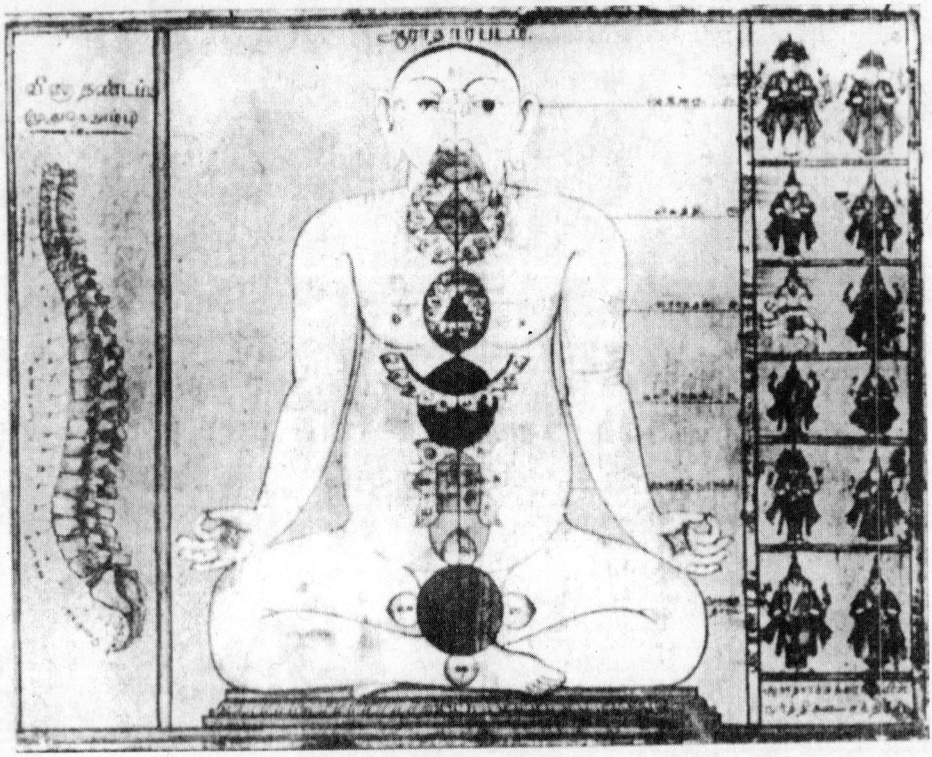

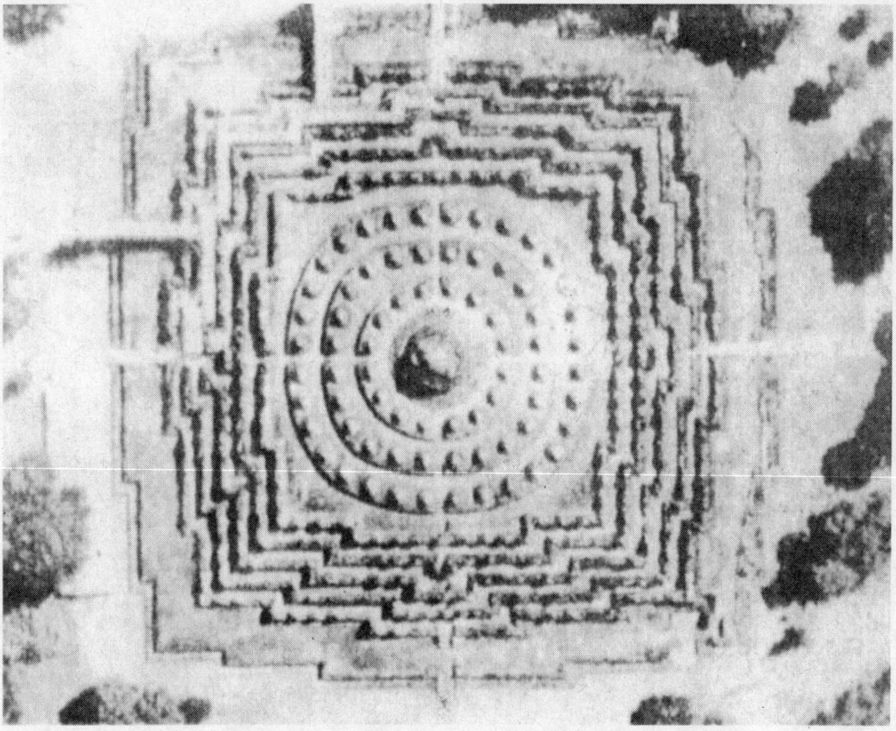

11a. Yantra or maṇḍala: aerial view of Borobudur on Java.

11b. Ritual preparation of a maṇḍala.

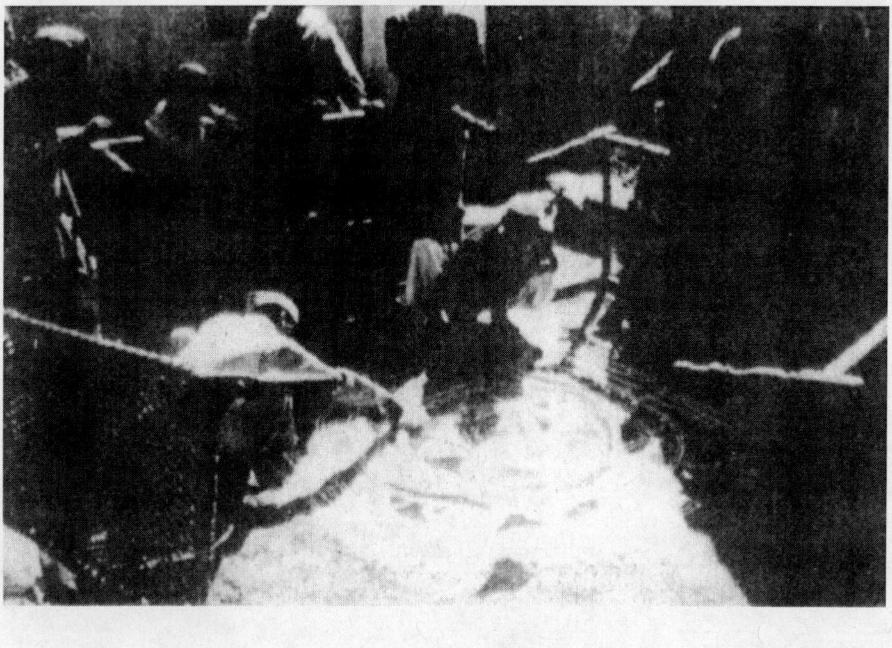

12. Muhammad's heavenly ascent (*mi°rāj*).

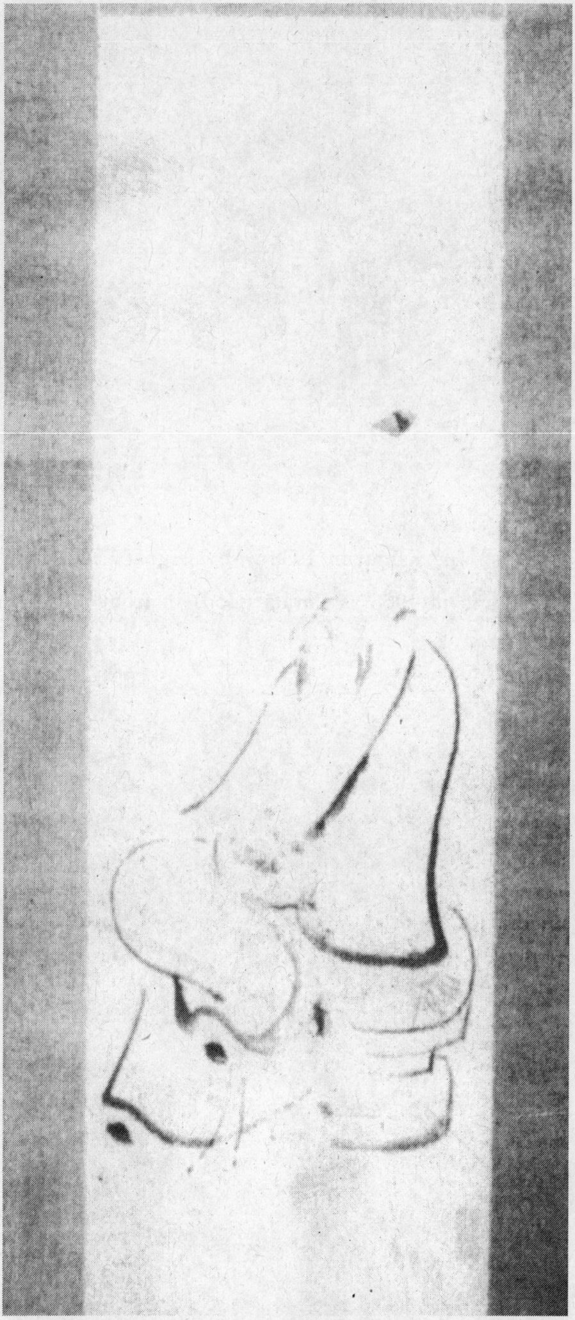

13. Chuang Tzu's dream of the butterfly.

14a. Kalmu in 1958 with his goat herd.

14b. Kalmu in 1968 as Devatā (God) in front of his temple.

15. Hanumān, the Monkey God, in meditation.

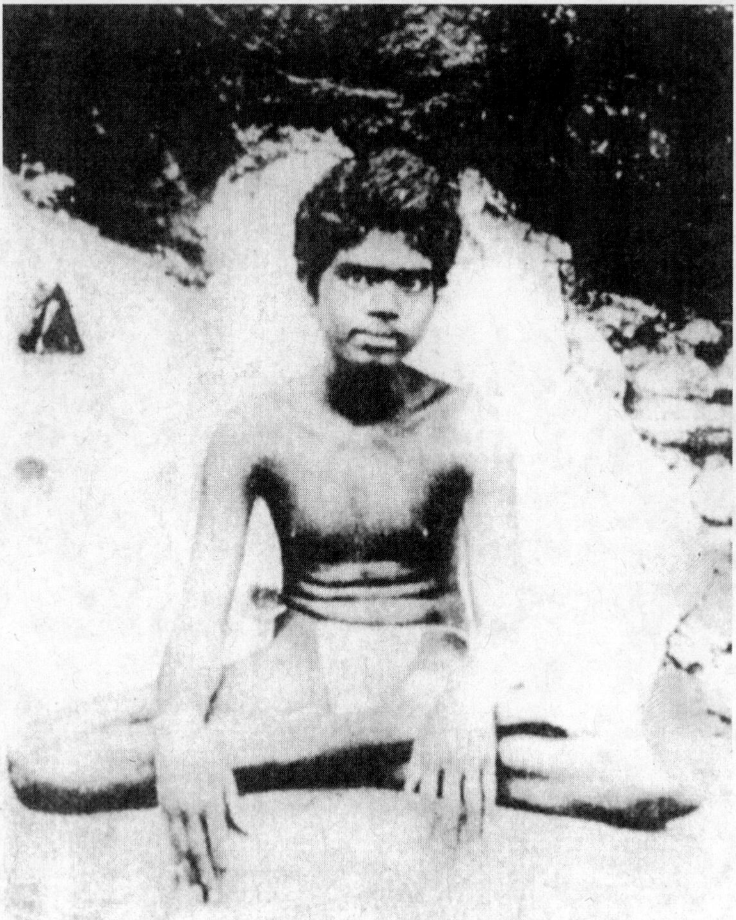

16. Jñāna: Śri Ramaṇa Maharṣi at age 21.

Detachment is to some extent a prerequisite for the other methods, but it is in turn increased by their practice. Fasting, of course, weakens a person and thus paves the way for detachment in a purely physical manner. But any device that diverts the mind's attention from its habitual content is helpful. Recitation or meditation on a mantra has to be primarily undertstood in this context. When the mind follows a mantra, it does not get caught in its usual preoccupations. This is the more easy, the more the mantra is believed to be unique, divine, uniquely valuable and uniquely powerful. Such beliefs are intensified when the mantra is kept secret. The mantra functions like a deity upon whom one concentrates, and it is not surprising that in Indian religions, mantras are often considered the bodies of deities (see, for example, Gonda 1970, p. 65). When the mantra is felt to exercise its influence, the belief in its supernatural nature increases. It seems reasonable to suppose that this is one of the origins for the belief in deities and in their divine grace.

Strong faith in a mantra or in a forgiving deity facilitates meditation. Such meditation, however, tends to strengthen theistic tendencies, and what results is strong devotion rather than a cessation of the fluctuations of the mind. When faith in the mantra, or in the deity it is thought to represent, is lacking, detachment assumes greater importance. A person who regards his mantra as a mere device consisting of meaningless sound can meditate, provided he has enough detachment from his daily preoccupations to be able to pursue the mantra and forget about his affairs. In his meditation, the simple repetition of the mantra then prevails over the customary fluctuations of his mind. It is likely that the enjoyment of music is related to this stilling of the mind. Art contributes in general to what Deikman called de-automatization.

A general difference between the religions of India and the monotheistic religions of the West is that religious practice in the former is generally related to mystical experience, while in the latter, even when mysticism is recognized, it is subject to moral strictures. "The mystical approach does not come naturally to anyone schooled in a monotheistic creed. It is, on the other hand, the very stuff and substance of the religions that have grown up in India" (Zaehner 1960, p. 3). The detachment of mysticism from morality is in the West advocated only by a minority, and is strongly disapproved of. The Muslim mystic Ibn Dāwūd disapproved of sex, which most mystics fear. But he made a distinction between sexual relations and looking, which he regarded as harmless. But Massignon interjects: "on the contrary, *illicit*, according to Sufism and to reason!" (Massignon 1922, n. 175; see similar moralizing on pp. 796–799).

In Tantrism or Taoism, on the other hand, sexual practices are judged only in terms of their efficacy in relation to mystical experience. If they assist, they are welcome; if they interfere, they are not; and if neither, they are neutral. In Islam or Christianity their effectiveness is not even in question, since they are rejected on moral grounds. In Hinduism there is a certain ambivalence between the extremes of Tantrism and modern puritanism as exemplified, for instance, by the Ramakrishna Mission, by Gandhi, or by what is sometimes called the Hindu Renaissance. Gandhi's sexual asceticism, however, was rather atypical, and has been shown to be closely related to his specific personality structure.

Mystical detachment assumes forms in Indian civilization which are quite unheard of in the West. In Tantrism, sexual practices which would be rejected if they were held to be conducive to an increase in mental tension are on the contrary utilized in order to bring about greater detachment from the rules of morality. This sounds suspect in the context of modern Western civilization, where there is already a strong tendency to relax sexual restrictions. But the Tantric detachment has to be understood within the perspective of Indian civilization. In Indian society, high status is in the first place related to high caste; but prestige, and even a high status, can also be derived from conformity to the rules of morality which the high caste members observe. Thus the lower castes adopt vegetarianism from the higher castes. This is one aspect of what has been called Sanskritization (see Srinivas 1952 and cf. Staal 1963). The rules of morality observed by the higher castes surround sexual activity, as well as eating and drinking, with numerous taboos and restrictions. But such restraints (like the obsession with impurity) are gladly accepted when they provide status and prestige—much more highly valued goods than sexual gratification. Given the strong nature of our sexual instincts, the result is both a high status and a fair amount of tension and repression, as such tensions are repressed rather than resolved (cf. Carstairs 1957, pp.

168–169). Neither is conducive to a lessening of the fluctuations of the mind.

By introducing sexual practices, Tantrism undermines in the first place the value system of the caste hierarchy, and thus frees the mind from numerous fluctuations. But if these were to be replaced by the fluctuations that sometimes accompany sexual activity (*maithuna*), the goal would not be reached. The same holds for the other "M's," which are forbidden in orthodox society: *madya* "wine," *māṃsa* "meat," *matsya* "fish," and *mudrā* "parched grain; gesture" (also: the woman who participates in the Tantric ceremonies). As a mystical method, Tantrism is therefore risky. At the same time, its possible efficacy is intelligible only within the perspective of Indian society.

The Tantric attitude has been related to Indian ritualism and to the supposed fact that Indian civilization is a "shame" culture rather than a "guilt" culture. It would be more appropriate to say that in both ritualism and Tantrism, particular devices are regarded strictly as techniques and are evaluated only in terms of their efficacy.

The practice of detachment for the sake of meditation need be no more than a stage in the training of the mystic; it does not imply that mysticism is quietism. One need not suppose that such detachment, or meditational practices in general, have an adverse effect on the other activities a person engages in. But the opposite need not be true either—that meditation improves one's performance in other respects (a piece of advertisement sometimes invoked in contemporary commercials in support of the practice of meditation). Of course, sitting quiet is always healthy in a society based upon strife, competition, and warfare. But at a deeper level, all such questions can only be dealt with at a later stage of the exploration of mysticism. I mention them here because the view that mysticism is connected with passivity and/or irresponsibility is pure prejudice.

A typical expression of this prejudice occurs in a recent book by a Western philosopher (Danto 1972, pp. 89–90): "The yoga" (read: yogins) "go into increasingly protracted periods of inanition. And there is in general an almost overwhelming propensity, as the underside of Indian practice, to attain a state of apathy, or actionlessness, in such a way that one passes a lifetime without doing anything."

Alas, this is pure nonsense, like many other claims by the same author (see my review: Staal 1974).

It is difficult to defend such a view when one reads, for example, the following verse attributed to Nāgārjuna:

> He who observes the rules of ethics
> Is called a monk (*bhikṣu*).
> He who contemplates the void (*śūnyatā*)
> Is called an ecstatic (*dhyāyin*).
> He who is alert, vigorous, and energetic
> Is called a real yogin.
> (LAMOTTE 1944, p. 325; 1970, pp. 1220–1221)

Buddha's life provides an illustration, for it seems to have been filled with activity, mental as well as physical. Kosambi (1965, p. 110) is eloquent on this point:

> The peripatetic life with its simple and spare diet kept him healthy through a long life, with little recorded illness. Though he spoke jestingly of his aged body, "held together somehow like an old worn-out cart," he seems to have swum across the Ganges at Patnā in his seventy-ninth year, while less hardy disciples looked for boats and rafts to ferry them over.

The distinction between Yoga and passivity is nowhere clearer than in the realm of the Gods. Śiva, the divine yogin, is also the creator and is not given to a life of inactivity (plates 3 and 4).

11

The *Guru*

Harmful when too close, useless when far—
They have to be kept at medium distance:
The king, fire, the *guru*, women.

Sanskrit proverb: BOEHTLINGK (1870), p. 33

Of the practices of mysticism, meditation stands most in need of experiential or subjective study. But it is unlikely that meditation can be properly learned without what most traditional mystics consider essential: the guidance of a competent teacher. Here too the experiences of Castaneda are significant. Investigators will have to learn from traditional experts exactly what to do, how to do it, and, when the effects are beginning to be felt, what to look for and how to react. Again, there is nothing surprising here: we would not know much Sanskrit if Western scholars had not sat at the feet of the traditional experts or pandits. The first British Sanskritists did this quite naturally (though later some of them came to look down upon pandits) and criticized the first German Sanskritists, who had only studied books, for not having obtained their knowledge firsthand in India.[1]

1. The Englishman H. H. Wilson, attempting to show that he was the only deserving condidate for the newly established Boden chair of Sanskrit at Oxford, wrote from Calcutta in a *Memorandum* of 1830: "I should think it is an indispensable requisite in the first Professor of the Sanscrit Language, that he had acquired his knowledge in India. It is true that considerable proficiency has been attained by some learned men on the Continent, but it is evident from their publications that their reading has been very limited, and

The need for a qualified teacher is stressed in almost all the traditions of mysticism. It is widely recognized among the religious orders of the West, in Christianity as well as in Islam. In Islam it is the foundation of the *silsila* or "spiritual lineage." The teacher (*murshid, shaikh, pīr*) does not merely initiate the novice (*murīd, gandūz*) but guides him throughout. He is the real *Kaʿba* to which the pupil turns. More specifically, he interprets what the pupil experiences during his meditations and fasts: "the increasingly transparent colored veils, the divine sayings, etc." (Massignon 1963, p. 405).

In Indian religions the need for a spiritual teacher has been emphasized in almost all mystical writings. It is the foundation of the *guruparamparā*, "the direct lineage of teachers." The most well-known exposition occurs in the *Kaṭhopaniṣad* (2.7–9), where Death is the teacher who addresses the young Naciketas:

> That which not many gain through hearing, not many
> know even when they hear it—
> Marvelous is the teacher, skillful the receiver,
> marvelous the knower, skillfully instructed.
> When taught by an inferior person it cannot be
> understood even though reflected upon.
> Unless taught by another, there is no way, for it is
> inconceivably more subtle than the most subtle.
> It is not obtainable by reasoning but taught by some-
> one else it may be easily known, my dear.
> You have obtained it, resolve come true. May we
> find an inquirer like you, O Naciketas! [2]

---

that they are far from possessing any degree of conversancy with the great body of Sanscrit Literature. Their knowledge is, in fact, of the most elementary kind, and restricted to the grammar of the language" (cited in Staal 1972, p. 57). A. W. von Schlegel retorted in 1832 with a warning, should Wilson be appointed at Oxford: "If you publish nothing, people will say that when leaving Calcutta, you forgot to ship your knowledge"—an obvious reference to Wilson's Indian pandits and teachers. And twenty years later, A. Weber confirmed this: "It is certainly very discouraging to see that Professor Wilson during all the time since he got his one professorship in Oxford, has not succeeded in bringing up even one Sanskrit scholar who might claim to be regarded as one who has done at least some little service to our Sanskrit philology" (Staal 1972, p. 58).

2. *śravaṇāyāpi bahubhir yo na labhyaḥ*
śṛṇvanto'pi bahavo yaṃ na vidyuḥ /
āścaryo vaktā kuśalo'sya labdhā

In early Hinduism, the teacher of the gods was called Bṛhaspati. As Agni-bṛhaspati he was also the divine ritualist. Though he was Indra's spiritual adviser, he also composed treatises on government and on "the polity and stratagems of married love" (Zimmer 1946, pp. 10–11). Zimmer rightly calls him "Lord of Magic Wisdom."

In later times, the notion of the *guru* is best illustrated by Śiva as the divine preceptor (plate 5). In this form, Śiva is called *dakṣiṇāmūrti* and he is represented facing south (*dakṣiṇā*). Images of *dakṣiṇāmūrti* are found, for example, on the southern outer walls of the four gateways (*gopura*) to each of the great South Indian temples. To those familiar with Indian civilization, it stands to reason that the *guru* faces south because the traditional teachings came from the north. In some of the non-Brahman temples of South India, too, vegetarian deities and rites, which came from the north, are on the northern side, while nonvegetarian deities and rites are on the southern side (Dumont 1953, p. 264).

Śiva as *dakṣiṇāmūrti* is often surrounded by an audience consisting of human and animal listeners. Foremost among these are the seers (*ṛṣi*), the sages who received sacred revelations such as the Vedas. The teaching transmitted by Śiva may be described as spiritual and mystical, but in the East that does not exclude what in the West is nowadays disparagingly called "intellectual." Witness the three forms of the divine *guru*: there is a *jñāna-dakṣiṇāmūrti*, a *yoga-dakṣiṇāmūrti* and a *vyākhyāna-dakṣiṇāmūrti*. The latter expounds a commentary (*vyākhyāna*) and holds a book in his left hand. He transmits the intellectual tradition.

What was said before about the need for "trust, confidence" applies equally well to the need for a competent teacher. In Indian religions, *śraddhā* "trust" was originally understood as confidence in the efficacy of the sacrifice, not as faith in the truth of some corpus or doctrine. The concept of *śraddhā* originated in a ritual context

---

āścaryo jñātā kuśalānuśiṣṭaḥ //
na nareṇāvareṇa prokta eṣa
suvijñeyo bahudhā cintyamānaḥ /
ananyaprokte gatir atra nāsti
aṇīyān hy atarkyam aṇupramāṇāt //
naiṣā tarkeṇa matir āpaneyā
proktā'nyenaiva sujñānāya preṣṭha /
yāṃ tvam āpaḥ satyadhṛtir batāsi
tvādṛk no bhūyāt naciketaḥ praṣṭā //

and is directed toward impersonal objects. Hara (1963–1964), who has collected and analyzed many occurrences of this term, has also shown that the concept of *bhakti*, though in some respects similar, denotes a less fundamental trust, which is, however, personal and emotional. *Bhakti* may be directed toward the members of one's family, one's teacher, or God (plate 9). Such trust in the teacher may develop into devotion and love, but it does not demand submission of one's critical faculties. And so it is quite proper for a student of mysticism, after the teacher has taught him how to meditate, breathe, or sit, and after he has acquired a certain proficiency, to make critical evaluations of his own abilities and to introduce experimental variations. This step is not inconsistent with Yoga or Taoism, which do not require the acceptance of certain dogmas or a specific act of religious allegiance, and are by their very nature oriented toward experience and experimentation. Unfortunately, some Western students tend to take *śraddhā* and *bhakti* in the wrong sense and follow their *guru*'s teachings with zealous bigotry.

The need for a qualified teacher is paramount in the study of mysticism. It is precisely here that the most promising psychological work, that of Deikman, was found most lacking. But despite the initial need for the uncritical acceptance of certain methods of training, it is equally important that the student of mysticism does not turn into a follower of the *guru*, or into an adherent of a particular sect. Having learnt what he can learn, he should be prepared to question and check what the teacher says, and introduce new variables and experimental variation.

Some teachers encourage criticism, or at least a critical attitude, to a certain extent. The Buddha may have been one of them. It is often the followers who wish to follow slavishly. Nakamura (1973, p. 33) quotes the following dialogue from the Pāli Canon (*Dīgha-nikāya* I, p. 61):

> The venerable Sāriputta came to the place where the Exalted One was, and having saluted him, took his seat respectfully at his side, and said: "Lord, such faith have I in the Exalted One that methinks there never has been, nor will be, nor is there now, any other, whether Wanderer or Brahmin, one who is greater and wiser than the Exalted One . . . as regards the higher wisdom." "Grand and bold are the words of your mouth, Sāriputta," answered the Master: "verily, then, you have burst forth into a song of ecstasy! Of course, then, you have known all the

Exalted Ones of the past . . . comprehending their minds with yours, and aware what their conduct was, what their wisdom . . . and what the emancipation they attained to." "Not so, O Lord!" "Of course, then, you have perceived all the Exalted Ones of the future . . . comprehending their whole minds with yours?" "Not so, O Lord!" "But at least, then, O Sāriputta, you know me . . . and have penetrated my mind?" "Not even that, O Lord." "You see, then, Sāriputta, that you don't know the hearts of the Able, Awakened Ones of the past and of the future. Why, therefore, are your words so grand and bold?"

Most teachers, even when saying so, do not really appreciate deviation. The student of a *guru* who is a student of mysticism should therefore learn to distinguish between the valid instruction into a practice, such as meditation, which cannot be learned in any other way, and the religious or philosophical superstructure which is added and which is often meaningless if not worthless. The question now arises, how are we to distinguish between the practice of meditation or any other mystical practice on the one hand, and philosophical and religious superstructures on the other? And furthermore, what are the criteria for distinguishing a real *guru* from a phony one?

It is difficult to legislate how in general such distinctions are made, and it would be fruitless to insist that such a matter should be entirely settled in advance. But some simple observations may be made. As to the first problem, there is a distinction that is basically simple, between the teacher's telling you something to do, and his telling you something to believe. The first often regards practice; the second is often related to superstructure. If the teacher of Yoga tells you, "Now inhale deeply and hold your breath for one full minute," you try to do what he says without questioning him. But if he says, "At this very moment, the goddess comes up your spine and enters your heart," you may say "Okay" or "Thank you," but you need not believe what he says. Of course, the teacher may be right—we do not know—but we can try to determine that at a later stage. Perhaps we will be able to feel the goddess do these things after sufficient practice. But we have here a clear distinction between an injunction (what the philosophers of the *Mīmāṃsa* called *vidhi*) and an interpretation (what they called *arthavāda*). The first we should accept; the second we may question. Of course, this example is artificial and simplified, and many teachings cannot be evaluated that easily. But there is a general feature in each of the two, and the pupil had better try to grasp it and use his judgment.

An analogy from language learning may clarify this point further. If the French teacher explains the distinction between "je t'aime" and "je ne t'aime pas," try to remember what he says without questioning him, and test it later in concrete situations. But if a teacher says that in the language of the Hopi, for example, space and time are closely related or indistinguishable (as Whorf claimed), shelve that for a much later period; it does at any rate not help when one is beginning to learn the language. Remember at all times a truism from linguistics: that a fluent speaker *of* the language may not be able to make a single correct statement *about* the language.

There is another, quite different reason, that one need not believe what the teacher says even though one has undertaken to do what he says. Like physicians, teachers in the realm of mysticism are apt to use the art of what Doctor Peter Shaw in 1750 called "fine lying": "It is doubtless as well for the Patient to be cured by the working of his Imagination, or a reliance upon the promise of his Doctor, as by repeated Doses of Physic." Claridge, who quotes this passage (1972, p. 25), related remarkable "placebo effects." The most striking is that of an individual who was given a harmless placebo but was told it was LSD, and who produced a classical description of the LSD state; but a week later, when given a normal dose of LSD, reported that the drug had no effect at all. Claridge comments: "Perhaps distilled water, dispensed with appropriate ceremony, is, after all, the answer to man's search for the occult!" (Claridge 1972, pp. 113–114). As we shall see, Claridge was nearer a truth than he imagined.

It is the task of a physician to cure his patient, not merely to make him think that he is cured. But since some diseases are at least in part imaginary, to think that one is cured may be real recovery. The same situation may obtain in all or part of the domain of mysticism. A person in search of salvation may have attained his goal when he thinks he has. But whether this is so is itself one of the interesting problems a student of mysticism, as distinct from a seeker of salvation, needs to explore. Hence the distinction between what a *guru* tells you to do and what to believe is a relevant one, at least initially. Later we shall also need to explain why a *guru* attaches importance to certain doctrines or beliefs.

Like ceremonies or ritual (to which I shall return), imagination undoubtedly plays an important part in mysticism. The expression "creative imagination" has in fact been used to characterize (though not very perspicuously) the Sufism of the Muslim monistic mystic Ibn 'Arabī (Corbin 1969). Oriental scholars like Corbin come dangerously close to adopting what I have called the dogmatic approach. Scientists, on the other hand, are apt to forget that, while what is imagined is by definition imaginary, imagination itself is not imaginary. It is only the object of imagination that is empty, as the *Yogasūtra* says (I.9: *vastu-śūnyo vikalpaḥ*).

As I mentioned before, Yoga as a method of discipline (not as a theory expounded, for example, in some of the more speculative parts of the *Yogasūtra*) seems to be especially appropriate as an area of research in the study of mysticism because it has little of a religious or philosophical superstructure. Perhaps the teacher will ask the student to perform a simple ritual, to burn incense or even to invoke a deity, at the beginning of his instruction. No harm in doing that; neither does one object to taking off his hat or shoes. In general, there are no restrictions on admission: teachers of Yoga accept anyone provided he wishes to learn the practice of Yoga. Therefore we find Yoga in Hinduism as well as in Buddhism. This has nothing to do with syncretism. Hindus, on the whole, believe that there is a self (*ātmavāda*); Buddhists, on the whole, that there is no self (*anātmavāda*) (see page 13). One cannot without strain be both a Hindu and a Buddhist. But Yoga, which makes no assumptions about the self, is practiced by either (and with different results).

I now come to the second question, namely, how to distinguish between a real teacher and a false one. Of course, the question is formulated in exaggerated terms; one should rather ask, how to distinguish a good from a bad teacher. A first criterion is related to the previous point: a good teacher will emphasize practice, a bad teacher will expound theories. In general, the question should be lifted outside the religious realm and placed on a level with the evaluation of teachers in general. If we wish to study a well-established subject—e.g., Sanskrit—some of these choices will have already been made for us by the institutionalization of the field. One would be well advised to go to a good university rather than to a bad one, if one has the choice. Beyond that, we go by the reputation of the individual. One who does not know any Sanskrit cannot tell whether the teacher knows his subject. But one can tell pretty soon whether or not he is a good teacher. More important, we can tell after some time whether we have learned something. Of course, one should be reasonable. If after one year the pupil cannot translate independently the most difficult texts, it does not mean that the teacher is bad. But if after that period he cannot translate anything at all, the teacher is at any rate not very effective. We proceed in the same way when we evaluate a teacher of meditation, or a *guru* in general. There is not much institutionalization in this area (though many *gurus* have their own institution); and reputations are often unreliable. But if the pupil has not obtained *nirvāṇa* after one year, it does not imply that the teacher is bad. If on the other hand after that period he has not learned how to meditate at all, the teacher cannot be very good. Unless of course the pupil himself is no good.

Throughout the Indian tradition it is emphasized that a person in search of a *guru* should use his intelligence and judgment. Śaṅkara, stressing this need at the outset of his *Brahmasūtrabhāṣya* (1.1.2), quotes a passage from the *Chāndogyopaniṣad* (6.16.2), in which such a seeker is compared to a man who has been kidnaped and left blindfolded in a desolate place. Seeking his home, he asks his way from village to village. In this way, becoming informed (*paṇḍita*) and relying on his own judgment (*medhāvin*), he will reach there.

When all is said, it must be admitted that critical exploration under the guidance of a *guru* remains a tricky piece of research. The subjective and experiential study of what happens when one learns meditation or other mystic techniques from a *guru* (or, similarly, when one takes a drug: see next chapter) is not simple and there are numerous pitfalls. Such work will therefore have to be carried out slowly, carefully, and systematically by many investigators, individually and through teamwork, and over a long period of time. We are beginning to explore a domain of the mind that appears to be as vast, varied, and intricate as many of the areas of physics. No wonder that it may be a difficult enterprise, and that at present we cannot answer even the most basic questions. What I have been arguing is only that the objections to the possibility of such an exploration are biased but not unsurmountable, and that without it, the serious study of mysticism is impossible, since only such investigations will provide the experiential and subjective data we require.

That we do need such data in the study of mysticism first became apparent when we tried to evaluate physiological and behavioral investigations (see chap. 8, sec. 1, and cf. Kamiya 1961). Let me try to clarify this point further with the help of an analogy from the study of sleep. This is appropriate if only because it has long been known that sleep is similar to mystical states at least in that it is also a different state of consciousness from the waking state—whatever that may precisely mean. As early as the Upaniṣads we find analogies between the states (*avasthā*) of waking, dreaming, and (dreamless) sleeping, and the "fourth" state (*caturtha, turīya*), the mystical state of final *samādhi*. In the *Māṇḍūkyopaniṣad* and elsewhere we read that the mantra or sacred syllable *om* refers symbolically to these three states. *Om* is analyzed into *a*, *u*, and *m* which stand for waking, dreaming, and sleeping, respectively, whereas the fourth state, which in the written form is symbolized by the dot representing nasalization, is also the silence in which *om* culminates (Mahadevan 1960, pp. 94–113, 174–180).

Throughout the Indian tradition, sleep and dreams are understood as states during which creative energy is stored before its release in the waking state. This is symbolized in legends such as the myth of Viṣṇu which depicts the God as sleeping between creations, until he manifests a new universe through creative meditation (plate 1; see, e.g., Zimmer 1946, pp. 35–53).

In the Upaniṣads and later in the Vedānta, an even more striking claim is made: when we are asleep we are at one with the Absolute; that is, the fourth state is the same as the state of dreamless sleep. The only difference is that we are aware of our state in the first case, but not in the second. Even Indian interpreters have been puzzled by this Upaniṣadic doctrine. Ranade (1926, p. 125), for example, says, "The idea was that in deep sleep the Soul was at one with Brahman, and thus deep sleep was likened to the state of ecstasy. There is, in fact, as much likeness, or as little, between sleep and ecstasy, as there is, as Spinoza would have said, between God and Dog: the same letters, but what an important difference!"

It would seem that Ranade was carried away by the contrast between the sacred overtones of the fourth state and the secular and apparently commonplace character of sleep. Such overtones, however, need not have anything to do with these mental states, and may belong to what in chapter 13 I shall call "superstructures." The Upaniṣadic sages were at any rate not upset by the parallel, and were quite emphatic on this point. The *Chāndogyopaniṣad* (8.3.2.), for example, says: "As people, who do not know a field, walk again and again over a golden treasure that is hidden somewhere in the earth, and yet are not able to discover it, thus do all these creatures day after day become merged in Brahman, and yet do not discover it, because they are carried away by untruth" (transl. Ranade 1926, p. 126). It is my impression that this identification between dreamless sleep and the fourth state should be taken very seriously, and may indeed provide a key to the understanding of mysticism. It is at any rate a view that any satisfactory theory of mysticism would have to account for.

Problems of personal identity, much discussed in contemporary philosophy, acquire special significance through the waking, dreaming, sleeping, and "fourth" states. These problems are hinted at in the parable, already referred to, of Chuang Tzu, who dreamed he was a butterfly and didn't know after waking up whether or not he was a butterfly who dreamed he was Chuang Tzu (plate 13; Watson 1964, p. 45; Graham 1969, p. 159).

In later Taoism the uncertain status of the different states of consciousness is further illustrated with stories about dreams which interfere with the waking state and seem to undermine its apparent preeminence. Such tales seek to illustrate that the distinction between reality and appearance may also be applicable to the waking state, which may in fact be quite different from what it appears to be. In Lieh Tzu (around A.D. 300, according to A. C. Graham) we find the following story:

> There was a man of Cheng who went to gather firewood in the moors, and came on a frightened deer. He stood in its way, struck it and killed it. Fearing that someone would see the deer, he quickly hid it in a ditch and covered it with brushwood. His joy overwhelmed him. But soon afterwards he could not find the place where he had hidden it, and decided that he must have been dreaming.
>
> He came down the road humming to himself about the affair. A

passer-by heard him, acted on his words and took the deer. When this man got home he hold his wife:

"Just now a woodcutter dreamed he caught a deer, but did not know where it was. Now I have found it. His dream was a true one."

"Isn't it rather that you dreamed you saw the woodcutter catch the deer? Why should there by any woodcutter? Since you have really got the deer, isn't it your dream which was true?"

"All I know is that I have got it. What do I care which of us was dreaming?"

When the woodcutter got home, he was not reconciled to his loss. That night he had a true dream of the place where he hid the deer, and also of the man who found it. Next morning, guided by the dream, he sought out the man, and then went to law to contest his right to the deer.

The case was referred to the Chief Justice, who said:

"If in the first place you really did catch the deer, you are wrong to say you were dreaming. If you really dreamed that you caught it, you are wrong to say it actually happened. The other man really did take your deer, yet contests your right to it. His wife also says that he recognised it in his dream as another man's deer, yet denies the existence of the man who caught it. Now all I know is that here we have the deer. I suggest you divide it between you."

It was reported to the lord of Cheng, who said:

"Alas! Is the Chief Justice going to dream that he has divided someone's deer?"

The Prime Minister was consulted. He said:

"It is beyond me to distinguish dreaming and not dreaming. If you want to distinguish dreaming from waking, you will have to call in the Yellow Emperor or Confucius. Now that we have lost the Yellow Emperor and Confucius, who is to distinguish them? For the present we may as well trust the decision of the Chief Justice" (Graham 1960, pp. 69–70).

So let us now see what the difference between the physiological, the behavioral, and the experiential or subjective study of sleep amounts to.

The physiological study of sleep has yielded the rapid eye movement criterion, which was later seen to accompany only a special kind of sleep, so-called paradoxical sleep (e.g., Claridge 1972, p. 76). This seems to correspond at least roughly to "dreaming." A better criterion seemed to be the EEG (electroencephalographic) criterion. But since this criterion also indicates sleep when the subject has been deprived of sleep for a long time but is still awake by behavioral standards (e.g., replies to questions), what is indicated is the "imperfect validity of the physiological indicator" (Kamiya 1961, pp. 155–156; see also page 104, above).

Behavioral criteria do not indicate sleep either. This is obvious from the fact that we can *pretend* to be asleep. We can simulate the behavior of sleep, and with some training, improve our performance. If more behavioral criteria are taken into account, we can learn to simulate those as well. Whatever the behavioral criteria, we can pretend to be asleep under those criteria. Now if we become more and more adept at pretending to be asleep, does it mean that we come closer and closer to being asleep? No, not at all. Let us assume that we are behaviorally asleep: we are lying down with our eyes closed, breathing regularly, not responding to small outside stimuli, etc. Now it is obvious that, if we are pretending and are not asleep, we are not asleep. The subjective and experiential experience is the final authority in these matters and sets aside the behavioral, just as behavioral criteria set aside physiological criteria.

A particular feature of sleep is that one is aware of not being in that state when one is not asleep, but unaware of being in it when one is asleep. Whether or not this features applies to mystical states, and what "awareness" would mean so as to be applicable here, is one of the problems we wish to explore. But the fact that the final criterion in the case of being not asleep is the sleeper's own subjective and experiential awareness also suggests the primacy of the subjective and experiential in the domain of the mystical. A serious student of mysticism therefore has to experience mystical states for himself. And since we cannot learn them from books, or in any other known indirect fashion, we have to learn them directly from someone who knows them and is willing to teach.

12

Drugs and Powers

> "I *have* tasted eggs, certainly," said Alice, who was a very truthful child; "but little girls eat eggs quite as much as serpents do, you know."
> "I don't believe it," said the Pigeon; "but if they do, why then they're a kind of serpent, that's all I can say."
> CARROLL, *Alice's Adventures in Wonderland*, (1963), p. 75

It seems difficult to deny that there are numerous parallels and similarities between mystical and drug-induced states. With regard to this fact the same should be said as with regard to the varieties of mysticism, of which it is claimed that they can or cannot be induced: all of these might be found to be different from each other in some respect. There appears to be a great variety of mystical states and of kinds of meditation or breathing and other preparatory exercises, between different systems or within the same system; a great variety of drugs with different effects; and a great variety of states which the same drug can induce among different people or in the same person at different times.[1] Yet there are at least general

1. That the same drugs affect people very differently is clear from Claridge 1972 (especially chap. 6). Huxley referred mostly to mescaline and LSD, drugs which in general have very different effects. Zaehner complained that Huxley assumed that all forms of mysticism were "essentially one and the same" (Zaehner 1961, p. x); but he himself seems to assume that the effects

similarities on the physiological, the behavioral, and the experiential levels which it would be arbitrary to deny. Let me mention a few examples of each. On the physiological level, there is often in both mystical and drug-induced states a decline in the pulse rate, in the concentration of blood lactate, and in the respiratory rate, and an increase in the concentration of carbon dioxide. But drugs may also increase the respiratory rate, or produce an alternation of states in which the respiratory rate is increased and decreased. On the behavioral level, there is in both states insensitivity to outside stimuli (e.g., an increased electrical resistance of the skin), introversion, and trance-like behavior. On the experiential level, there are many similarities, some of which seem straightforward (the experience of light, movement, sounds), but others very difficult to describe precisely. Huxley has drawn attention to several of these similarities in *The Doors of Perception* and *Heaven and Hell* (I refer to the combined edition of 1963); he was criticized by Zaehner in *Mysticism Sacred and Profane* (1961), to which I shall return. Several others, such as H. Smith (1964), have adduced and discussed similar evidence.[2]

Some scientists, apparently unfamiliar with meditation, have observed parallels between the effects of certain drugs and the effects of so-called "sensory deprivation," a state in which the input of

---

of drugs are essentially one and the same. Even if one confines oneself to mushrooms, the effects are astonishingly diverse (Heim 1963). Zaehner himself considered two or three kinds of mysticism. Not so the later Buddhists. In Chinese Mahāyāna texts the list of *samādhis* or yogic states, contains 156 entries. But other texts tell us that these are but a few of the 60,000 or 77,000,000 millions of *koṭis* (each ten million) which can be experienced (Lancaster 1975). In Taoism, special states have (at least in Watson's translation of Chuang Tzu) colorful names: Pattern of Earth, Workings of Virtue Closed Off, Heaven and Earth, Workings of the Good One, Great Vastness Where Nothing Wins Out, Workings of the Balanced Breaths, Not Yet Emerged from My Source (Watson 1964, pp. 93–94). Some of these names suggest the kind of pranks Don Juan played on Castaneda (e.g., Castaneda 1972, pp. 247–250).

2. Smith (1964, p. 522) carried out a small experiment which established that many subjects could not distinguish between an account of a religious experience under the influence of drugs, and one without their influence. Of course, as Smith points out, this descriptive similarity does not preclude the possibility that the two kinds of experience are basically different. Similar experiments show the indistinguishability of some of the descriptions given by schizophrenics and by people who have taken a hallucinogenic drug (Claridge 1972, pp. 119–120). Again, indistinguishability does not establish nondifference.

external stimuli is drastically reduced and which offers parallels to some kinds of meditation. In the *Yogasūtra*, for example, *pratyāhāra* "withdrawal of the senses" is enjoined. In *Zen*, on the other hand, external stimuli are not excluded: not only is there often a fair amount of noise, sometimes structured (e.g., gongs and bells), but adepts are likely to be beaten with a stick.

Claridge describes psychological tests in which sensory deprivation is experimentally produced "by putting subjects in a sound-proofed room cut off from human contact and getting them to wear goggles on their eyes and cuffs on their arms, all of which combine to isolate the brain from a good deal of the information that is necessary for its proper functioning. The normal effects of sensory deprivation are very like those of LSD. The individual loses track of time, shows poor concentration and mental control, and experiences visual illusions of various kinds" (Claridge 1972, p. 114).

The parallel with a mystic who isolates himself in a dark cave (a practice not rare in Himalayan regions) is striking. Even the relative isolation of a goatherd can pave the way for mystical vision. The characteristics of "poor concentration and mental control," mentioned by Claridge, seem to conflict with the fact that in systems like the Yoga, "withdrawal of the senses" is held to be conducive to concentration. Strange as it may seem, this difference is only apparent and may be entirely due to cultural evaluations: to a Western scientist, concentration is related, for example, to puzzle-solving, which the commentary on the *Yogasūtra* would regard as *vikṣipta* "distracted"; it is such concentration which may be affected by sensory deprivation.

While some of the similarities that have been discussed here are very general and appear vague, given the present state of our knowledge and formulated within our present frameworks (which admittedly are not very well suited to such a task), other similarities are fairly definite and precise. Most stand in need of further elucidation. There are similarities, moreover, not only between descriptions of experience but also between interpretations or doctrines provided by traditional experts. It is important to bear in mind that interpretations and doctrines are never simply "drug-induced" or merely based on experience; they are also related to other traditional concepts of a civilization. Perception does not take place in a vacuum but is always interpreted in terms of preconceived notions.

It is instructive to compare in this light Don Juan's doctrines of *seeing* and *stopping the world* and the Buddhist doctrine of *śūnyatā* "emptiness," which are in turn similar to the speculations on "nonbeing" referred to above (chap. 5; cf. also Deikman 1963, p. 337). We cannot at the present state of our knowledge determine whether the underlying experiences are the same or not. But the parallels which I shall quote without further analysis may show that there is at least the possibility that the differences are largely cultural, or "superstructural."

That Don Juan's teachings are not simply "drug-induced" becomes increasingly clear in Castaneda's publications. Don Juan's teachings are concerned with a state of mind which is reached through specific teachings and exercises, such as hunts. Drugs may be used as additional aids, when necessary. Although the use of drugs seems fairly important in Castaneda's first two books, he says in his third book (Castaneda 1972, p. 13), "it was simply my lack of sensitivity which had fostered their use." So drugs have a place in the doctrine, albeit a subordinate one.

The Buddhist Mādhyamika system holds that reality is ultimately *śūnya* "empty, void," a doctrine that by its nature is difficult to express adequately or interpret meaningfully, but that has given rise to a voluminous literature, ancient as well as modern. Now the nature of *śūnyatā* is not a matter of pure speculation; it is grasped in and through meditation. "It would be a mistake," says Conze (1962, p. 244), "to treat the views of the Mādhyamikas as though they were the result of philosophical reasoning, when in fact they derive from age-old meditational processes by which the intuition of the Absolute is actually realized." *Śūnyatā*, accordingly, is not a theory; in fact, it is regarded as the end of all theories (Murti 1955, pp. 160–164, and cf. page 45, above).

Two quotations may illustrate how these ideas are held to be derived from experience. The first consists of the first two *sūtras* of the *Prajñāpāramitāhṛdayasūtra*, popular in Japan under the name *Shingyo* (after Suzuki 1960, p. 26):

> When the Bodhisattva Avalokiteśvara was engaged in the practice of the deep *Prajñāpāramitā*, he saw that there are the five Skandhas: and these he saw in their self-nature to be empty.
>
> O Śāriputra, form is here emptiness, emptiness is form; form is no other than emptiness, emptiness is no other than form; that which is

form is emptiness, that which is emptiness is form. The same can be said of sensation, thought, volition,[3] and consciousness.

The other quotation is from a Chinese Ch'an master, Yung-chia Ta-shih (in Japanese, Yoka Daishi), who died in A.D. 713. It is taken from his *Cheng-tao Ke* "realization-way song" (Suzuki 1960, p. 90):

> While in a world of dreams, the six paths
> of existence are vividly traced,
> But after the wakening there is vast
> Emptiness only . . .

Don Juan in his teachings often refers to *seeing*, a mode of experiencing which may be facilitated by the use of drugs as he prescribes it, but which also reflects his traditional way of looking at things, which may well be characterized as mystical. Castaneda tries to learn to *see*, and repeatedly asks Don Juan to explain what *seeing* means. Though a verbal explanation is obviously not very helpful, Don Juan answers these questions with considerable patience. In one passage, in *The Teachings of Don Juan*, where he becomes rather explicit, he says:

"When you *see* there are no longer familiar features in the world. Everything is new. Everything has never happened before. The world is incredible!"

"Why do you say incredible, Don Juan? What makes it incredible?"

"Nothing is any longer familiar. Everything you gaze at becomes nothing! Yesterday you didn't *see*. You gazed at my face and, since you like me, you noticed my glow. I was not monstrous, like the guardian, but beautiful and interesting. But you did not *see* me. I didn't become nothing in front of you. And yet you did well. You took the first real step toward *seeing*. The only drawback was that you focused on me, and in that case I'm no better than the guardian for you. You succumbed in both instances and didn't *see*."

"Do things disappear? How do they become nothing?"

"Things don't disappear. They don't vanish, if that's what you mean; they simply become nothing and yet they are still there."

"How can that be possible, Don Juan?"

"You have the damnedest insistence on talking," Don Juan exclaimed with a serious face. "I think we didn't hit it right about your promise.

3. Suzuki translated the fourth *skandha*, *saṃskāra* "volition, impulse" as "confection," which is literal (from *sam* "together" and *kr* "make") but is in English nowadays a term mainly used of sweets.

Perhaps what you really promised was to never, ever stop talking" (Castaneda 1971, pp. 194–195).

In Castaneda's later book, *The Journey to Ixtlan* (1972), it becomes clear that one of the main tenets of Don Juan's knowledge is the idea of "stopping the world." In fact, Don Juan says, "Everything I have told you to do was a technique for *stopping the world*" (Castaneda 1972, p. 13). Finally, Castaneda does himself "stop the world": He sees the "lines of the world"—an extraordinarily new world that cannot be put into words. But just before this happens, Castaneda describes his state as follows: "I had no thoughts or feelings. Everything had been turned off and I was floating freely" (Castaneda 1972, p. 298). Again, this seems to be similar to the Buddhist experience of emptiness. There may also be similarities with the "dark night of the soul" of Christian mystics.

The Buddhist concentration on emptiness (*śūnyatāsamādhi*) is not the same as nihilism (*śūnyatādṛṣṭi*), the philosophical view that "nothing exists." The latter is similar to Nietzschean, Heideggerian, or existentialist nihilisms, which try to express that "nothing" "exists" and which are sometimes erroneously compared to Buddhist doctrines. The Buddhist literature is very explicit in making this distinction. Another Chinese text, translated by Lamotte (1970, pp. 1227–1228), has the Buddha say to Ānanda:

> I regard a person who adheres to the doctrine of emptiness (*śūnyatādṛṣṭi*) as incurable. If someone believes that there is a personality, be it as big as Mount Sumeru, I am not surprised and I don't blame him. But if some idiot believes in the doctrine of emptiness, be it as small as the sixteenth part of a single hair, I cannot allow it.

The matter is summed up in the following verse of Śāntideva, translated in accordance with de la Vallée Poussin (Lamotte 1970, p. 1229n.):

> When the notion of emptiness is accepted, the notion of existence disappears. Later, through the repetition of "nothing exists," that notion itself also vanishes.
>
> When an existence that has been denied is no longer perceived, how then could a nonexistence that has no further support be conceived?
>
> And when neither existence nor nonexistence are conceived any more, then when there is no other way, the mind achieves peace.

The Tibetan historian Tāranātha reports that Śāntideva, when he had arrived at the middle of the last verse, rose up in the sky and disappeared—but not until his words had reached their audience. These statements are reflected in Buddhist logic in the *catuṣkoṭi*, which I have discussed in chapter 2. Such expressions, which are certainly not easily interpreted, show that terms like "nonexistence" have to be interpreted in the light of experience (*śūnyatāsamādhi*), and not within the perspective of philosophical speculation (as in the case of Heidegger).

There is a great need for detailed studies of such similarities, undertaken in different contexts and from different points of view, and without disregarding the differences. Much of this work has to be done before any analysis or theory construction can be embarked upon. I think that Huxley was quite right when he wrote about this: "However lowly, the work of the collector must be done, before we can proceed to the higher scientific tasks of classification, analysis, experiment and theory making" (Huxley 1963, pp. 83–84).

Though Huxley was the first among contemporary authors to argue for the relatedness of mysticism and drugs, it is now becoming widely known that the religious use of drugs is old and widespread. Also, the types of mysticism with which I have been especially concerned refer to drugs. In the *Yogasūtra*, Patañjali pays much attention to certain supernatural powers called *siddhi* "perfection," or *vibhūti* "power," which accompany a high state of concentration (called *saṃprajñāta samādhi*), though not the highest (*asaṃprajñāta samādhi*). These powers are similar to the supernatural powers (*prabhāva*) we came across in connection with *tapas* in the first section of chapter 6. *Yogasūtra* 4.1 enumerates different possible causes for the emergence of these powers: birth (*janma*), drugs or herbs (*oṣadhi*), mantras, asceticism (*tapas*), and concentration (*samādhi*). That it was attempted to attain *samādhi* with the help of drugs seems to follow indirectly from a passage from the *Siva Samhitā* (V.6) quoted by Lindquist (1932, pp. 193–194). Śiva, the divine ascetic, is also portrayed with the flowers of the hallucinogenic datura plant (*dhurdhura*) in his hair (plates 3 and 5).

The *Yogasūtra* enumerates among these special powers which the yogin acquires: the understanding of the cries of living beings (cf. Castaneda's "conversation" with the coyote, Castaneda 1972, p. 296); the knowledge of previous births; the knowledge of other minds (see chap. 6, sec. 1, above); the power to become invisible; and other powers, which are elsewhere in Indian literature and folklore the subject of fables, fairy tales, legends, and mythologies. In most modern scholarly literature such powers are frowned upon, and it is generally suggested that Patañjali himself also looked down upon them. But Corrado Pensa (1969) has shown that such an evaluation is the outcome of modern prejudice, and that the *siddhis* or *vibhūtis* are in fact an integral part of Yoga. Miracles were also frowned upon, at least initially, in the most modern of the Western monotheistic religions, Islam (see, e.g., Von Grünebaum 1961, pp. 91–97). Disbelief in miracles may itself be a modern prejudice, though it does not follow that miracles therefore must be true.

In Buddhism, these powers are called *abhijñā* or *ṛddhi*. The *Abhidharmakośa* of Vasubandhu (ed. de la Vallée Poussin, 1923–1931, VII, p. 122, quoted in Lamotte 1944, p. 383, n. 1) gives an enumeration of five kinds of *ṛddhi* which is in some respects similar to Patañjali's enumeration in the *Yogasūtra*: those which are produced by meditation (*bhāvanāja*), inborn (*upapattilābhika*), obtained by spells (*vidyā-* or *mantrakṛta*) or by herbs (*oṣadhikṛta*), or produced by activities (*karmaja*). The Buddha prohibited, not the attainment of these powers, but their exhibition to laymen (Eliade 1954, pp. 185–186; 1969, pp. 177–180; cf. the Muslim attitude, above, page 64). The connection that is felt to exist between these powers and certain drugs is further illustrated by the fact that in Bengal, even at present, *Cannabis sativa* is called *siddhi*.

Miraculous powers are of course not confined to the East. Though they were originally disapproved of in Islam, they soon made their appearance. A little over a century after Muhammad's death, legends sprang up: He gave a believer a piece of wood, and it changed into a sword; the hands of an opponent who threw stones at him dried up; a light emanated from his mother when he was born, etc.

Further west, Christianity originally had a fair share of miracles. The Christian apologists (inspiring Pascal: see above, page 24) ridiculed Muhammad for his inability to perform the miracles which Christ performed. Bartholomew of Edessa, for instance, wrote:

> So Mohammed is the equal of the Christ, albeit he never revived the dead, nor like the Christ called back to life Lazarus who had been dead for four days, or opened the eyes of one born blind, or cured every disease and infirmity, or cleaned the lepers. No deaf or mute were healed

by him, never did he stay the force of the winds and the furious billows, nor did he ever walk on water as upon dry land. He never entered unto his disciples through closed doors. He was neither impeccable nor immortal nor a just judge. How then can you declare him the Christ's equal, since he did nothing of this kind nor anything like it? He had no share in truth or justice, but exhibited every kind of injustice ordering everybody executed who would deny that he was the Apostle of God. And still you will impudently assert that Mohammed and Jesus Christ were on the same level! (Von Grünebaum 1961, pp. 94–95).

The early Christians were described as having many miraculous powers, in fact, no less than Tibetan lamas. The influencing of other minds is among the most common; the curing of diseases and even resurrection from the dead are heard of again and again. But there are reports of even more spectacular achievements. When Mucius wanted to visit a dying brother, night fell. As a good Christian unwilling to travel by night, he invoked the sun: "In the name of Our Lord Jesus Christ, interrupt your course for a moment and wait until I reach the village!" And immediately the sun stopped, until the pious man had reached the village (Lucius 1904, p. 389).

We do not know how many of these miracles or which miracles, if any, really took place. There are responsible scholars who accept some, and equally responsible scholars who reject all. Moreover, miracles depend to some extent on the development of science, for a miracle is something that seems to be inconsistent with the laws of science. Though there may be more to it, it would seem to be a reasonably cautious attitude, at the present state of our knowledge, to start from Kosambi's sober judgment regarding the physical reality of yogic powers: "Yoga within limits is a good system of exercise in a hot climate for people who do not live by muscular exertion and hard physical labour. The most that one can attain by it is some measure of control over normally involuntary functions of the body, and good health; but no supernatural powers" (Kosambi 1965, p. 105). Such a statement concerning the physical features of Yoga (it does not deal with the mental) provides a good starting point, beyond which the student needs to proceed with empirical evidence, experience, and an open mind.

While reports of miracles are quite common in the major religions, the attitudes toward them vary a great deal. Going from West to East, the reactions to drugs change as well. In Islam, certain mystics, possibly under Indian influence, began in the thirteenth century to use hashish, coffee, and opium as stimulants (Massignon 1954, p. 106). The orthodox disapproved of this, and also of the contemplation of handsome boys as an aid to mystical contemplation. I have already referred to the *Yogasūtra* and the *Abhidharmakośa*, but it is in addition well known that later the yogins sometimes used *bhang* (*Cannabis sativa*), datura, and other drugs (see, e.g., Lindquist 1932, pp. 194–198; cf. Eliade 1951, pp. 355–61, and 1969, p. 338; and Arbman 1922, pp. 300–302). The Buddhists, who did not encourage the search for miraculous powers which might detract from the quest for *nirvāṇa*, still describe them in detail, as we have seen (e.g., Lamotte 1944, I, pp. 328–333; Lindquist 1935; Lancaster 1975). In Taoism, especially in its later developments, mystics did not feel hampered by religious, moral, or social disapproval, and freely engaged in experiments with drugs and chemical substances, especially cinnabar (see, e.g., Maspero 1950, pp. 96–98; Welch 1966, pp. 97–99; and Kaltenmark 1969, pp. 121–132).

If we want to follow Patañjali's lead in the *Yogasūtra*, and Vasubandhu's in the *Abhidharmakośa*, it would seem safe to conclude that drugs may assist in the bringing about of certain results, which can also be reached by other methods of training, such as meditation. That these results are the only "mystical experiences" that exist does not at all follow, or even seem likely. Moreover, there are cultural and individual factors to be taken into account, and a person who has a *nirvāṇa*-like experience *after* taking a drug need not have that experience *only because* he took the drug. Here, as elsewhere, the transition from *post hoc* to *propter hoc* is not automatic.

This conclusion is consistent, for example, with Castaneda's views as expressed in his third book (1972). Earlier, Castaneda had assumed that the perception of nonordinary reality which he reached could only be obtained by the ingestion of the three psychotropic plants he used. But in the Introduction to his third book he says about these plants: "They were not the essential feature of the sorcerer's description of the world, but were only an aid to cement, so to speak, parts of the description which I was incapable of perceiving otherwise. My insistence in holding on to my standard version of reality rendered me almost deaf and blind to Don Juan's aims. Therefore, it was simply my lack of sensitivity which had fostered their use" (Castaneda 1972, p. 13).

It is not surprising that the religious use of drugs has not met with the approval of religious establishments. Institutionalized religions are not so much concerned with the religious or mystical experience of individuals, as with society, ethics, morality, and the continuation of the *status quo*. One of the ways to make ethical actions palatable and even desirable is to show that they are meritorious. By extrapolation, they are claimed to contribute to the highest realization of the religious life, which is often regarded as a mystical vision. But the mere ingestion of a drug can hardly be considered meritorious, so how could it lead to such an exalted state? That would seem unfair, to say the least. Hence the moralist's distinction between "easy" and "difficult" ways (as we found in Eliade's work).

Moralizing of this kind comes not only from institutionalized religions. Examples are abundant. Kant's ethics adopts the Christian position, that a virtuous action is one done against inclination. I. F. Stone of the *Weekly* intoned a logical equivalent: "I really have so much fun, I ought to be arrested." Fellini, when asked whether he thought that drugs could enrich the creative process, said: "It would be too easy if all you had to do was to take LSD to become a visionary or a prophet" (Claridge 1972, p. 111). And Huxley wrote: "I am not so foolish as to equate what happens under the influence of mescaline or of any other drug, prepared or in the future preparable, with the realization of the end and ultimate purpose of human life: Enlightenment, the Beatific Vision" (Huxley 1963, p. 73). Zaehner should have been pleased by that.

Despite these strictures, some clarification seems to be in order here. An analogy may suggest a direction in which it might be sought. In many religions, pilgrimages are considered meritorious, partly because they require a certain amount of sacrifice or at least discomfort. But they also lead to a certain place, generally an inaccessible spot where a temple or other sacred structure or object exists. With the improvement of roads and the advent of modern means of transportation, most inaccessible places have become quite accessible. And so we find the pilgrims of old turned into members of the jet set. The difficult way has become an easy way. Nowadays people fly to see their *guru* or to witness the miracles of Sai Baba, just as they fly to the beaches of Goa to drop acid. When I visited the Cāmuṇḍā temple on a hilltop near Mysore, the greatest attraction to the pilgrims gathered there was the arrival by limousine of a famous filmstar from Madras. Of course, the physical result, the presence of the worshipper-cum-traveler at a certain place, is just the same, whether he measured the distance by prostrating himself all the way or whether he arrived by plane. But expectations grow and the subjective experience is generally not the same. This analogy indicates that we cannot eliminate the possibility that the physical and brain states of a college boy who has taken a drug are in relevant respects the same as those of a Buddha. Yet their mental states (which may have other physical correlates too) need not for that reason be identical. This suggests that specific physical or brain states may not be sufficient conditions for mystical experiences to arise; preparations and expectations also count. Moreover, the minds of a Buddha and of a contemporary student would have been different even if neither of them had meditated or taken a drug.

In order to evaluate mental states, cultural contexts have to be taken into consideration, and of course psychological ones, which are by no means confined to mystical or religious phenomena. The case of pilgrimages is, for example, analogous to Snellgrove's contrasting descriptions of a journey on foot and an air flight into the Nepal Valley:

> Approaching on foot, one's arrival is the culmination of days of slow travel with ever mounting expectancy, and that feeling of calm satisfaction and happy fulfilment, which pervades one on mounting the pass and seeing the Valley at one's feet, belongs, I am sure, to the very best of human experience . . . By mere speed, expectation is robbed of its substance: this is now no land of promise, whose frontiers have at last been gained by one's own patience and endurance, but rather an illusive dream-country, delightful while the vision lasts, but vanishing as soon as the plane touches land, and life shows itself as prosaic as ever (Snellgrove 1961, p. 1).

In the present context I am not concerned with questions of merit and problems of ethics, though these also affect the mind. But the analogy between a pilgrimage, a hike, and a mystical journey provides at any rate an additional reason for emphasizing the distinction between the physical state of a mystic insofar as it is induced by drugs or meditation, and his mental and subjective state, (which may have other physical correlates as well. It also demonstrates that training and preparation contribute much to the experience itself—a circumstance to be taken into account when one studies with a *guru*. In general, the parallels and differences between drug-induced experiences and the states of mind reached through meditation or other mystical exercises deserve close experiential study. Even if the differences turn out to be fundamental, the known similarities require an explanation. But one should not imagine that significant results will be reached unless psychological and cultural variables are taken into account, and unless we begin to understand these experiences themselves.

13

Superstructures

> In the interest of truth, it would seem better, and indeed necessary, to give up even what is dearest to us.
>
> ARISTOTLE, *Nicomachaean Ethics* I 6, 1096 a 14–15

Earlier we made two distinctions: on the one hand, the distinction between the difficult way of contemplation, and the easy way of drugs; and on the other hand, the distinction between the types of mysticism that can be induced by human effort and may therefore be difficult, and those that cannot be so induced and therefore are not in a position to be difficult. The difference between the latter type and the drug-induced experiences is that what does not depend on human effort can be said to be easy, provided only that it occurs; while the other kind is generally easy because it is brought about by the mere act of ingestion. The effect of a drug still depends on the cultural background, on general psychological factors, and on the individual's receptivity and mental attitude. Some people are unaffected at least by the milder drugs, and others are affected when they merely come close to a drug. In fact, there is much more significant variety (see, e.g., Claridge 1972, chaps. 2 and 6)—the same kind of variety as surrounds other mental experiences.

By definition, the attainment of a mystical experience is easy for a natural mystic, a person who is capable of attaining mystical states because he is born that way. This is what is indicated by the word *janma* "birth" in the *Yogasūtra* and in the *Abhidharmakośa* (pages

161 and 162). The nineteenth-century Indian saint Rāmakṛṣṇa Paramahaṃsa and the twentieth-century sage Ramaṇa Maharṣi (plate 16) were such mystics, and went into trances frequently. But the aim of such difficult and complicated processes of training as we meet with in the Yoga is the same: they produce a yogin who can enter a state of *samādhi* easily and at will.

What is suggested by the parallel between these distinctions of easy and difficult ways? Since a mystical experience is like entering a mental state or like gaining access to a domain of the brain, there are different methods which can bring the experience about, just as a house can be entered by various means: by climbing through a window, by breaking through a wall, by digging a tunnel to reach the cellar, or by opening the front door with a key. Some methods are easier than others, a fact which may be reflected in different evaluations, competing with each other. Someone who has just broken a window to enter his own home is irritated when he afterwards finds in his pocket a key that fits the door. Moreover, the house he has entered is no longer the same; it is now quite drafty and difficult to heat. Of course, entering a house with the help of a key is only easy when one possesses the right key; and obtaining the right key may be as difficult as digging a tunnel.

Such analogies may be helpful, and yet are only valid in some respects. In the realm of mysticism, we do not know whether it is actually the same state which is reached in different ways. Also, a mystical experience is a more mental event than entering a home. Even if it were possible to reach the same state by different methods —effortlessly or after expending great effort—the resulting effect would not be experienced in the same way. The different methods and techniques of mysticism therefore have a much more dissimilar impact on the total personality than the attainment of an allegedly identical physical or brain state might seem to suggest. Hence the tendency to claim that the different mystical methods do lead in different directions. But these differences may in fact result from different religious or moral evaluations and may have little to do with the mystical states themselves. It is therefore important to distinguish between mystical experiences and superstructures.

I have paid some attention to the distinction between easy and difficult methods in mysticism because it is apparent that the distinction is largely a moral one, and the resulting mystical and corresponding brain states need not be different. Let me try to be more precise. Let us assume that there are two methods, α and β, one easy and one difficult, which induce, among other things, an identical brain state C, a state which corresponds in turn to a certain mystical experience. In such a case, the subjective experience not only will be of C but will also reflect the preceding methods α and β. The different results of α and β will also be located in the brain, say through different brain conditions A and B, respectively. Now the resulting experience will in the one case correspond to a condition of the brain which incorporates A and C, and in the other case, B and C. Though the state which incorporates A and C (or respectively, B and C) may present itself as a unified experience, one should distinguish between A on the one hand, which reflects past experience, expectation, degree of satisfaction, confirmation of existing beliefs, etc., and C on the other hand, which reflects the mystical state itself.

In this construction, which is of course simplified, artificial, and schematic, the distinction between "easy" and "difficult" does not play an essential part. The same reasoning would apply to any two different methods α and β. And so we can conclude that different methods may well result in different experiences, and yet incorporate an identical mystical experience.

The same reasoning might apply to the distinction between mystical states that can be induced by conscious effort, and mystical states that cannot be so induced. In the Western monotheistic view, and in several medieval Hindu sects, the latter states are attributed to the workings of grace. Such grace may be attained through loving devotion (*bhakti*) or surrender (*prapatti*) to God (plates 7 and 9). But in Advaita the concept of grace receives a special interpretation. The grace of the semi-personal divinity *īśvara*, who is nothing but a reflection on a lower level of *brahman*, is interpreted as his mere permission that the effects of *karman* be wiped out and the chain of transmigration be interrupted (see Staal 1961b, p. 146). In general, grace is postulated whenever no other source is known or acknowledged. The difference between mystical states that can be induced and those that cannot might therefore be only in degree of awareness. Difference in awareness, it should be remembered, is the only difference between the mystic state and deep sleep according to the Upaniṣads and the Vedānta (see pages 151–152). Whatever the correct interpretation turns out to be, if the subjective experiences in different cases are different, it does not follow that we are dealing with states that are necessarily different from each other.

Before turning to specifics, let me summarize the significance of these observations. I am not claiming here that many different states *must* lead to the same mystical state. They *may* lead to different states. I am only claiming that multiplicity of states is not inconsistent with an alternative possibility, and that the resulting states *may* incorporate one identical mystical state, or at any rate may be more closely related than the different approaches would suggest.

Differences between easy and difficult ways, and between mysticism based upon effort and not so based, are partly related to the level of mystical techniques and methods, but partly they reflect what I have called superstructure. In the case of easy and difficult ways, this difference is fairly well defined: We assign, on moral grounds, greater merit to the performance of a difficult task than to that of an easy one. In Christianity, for example, the Protestant doctrines that salvation can be reached by faith alone (*sola fide*) or by grace alone (*gratia sola*) strike believers in the effectiveness of good works as irresponsible because they seem too easy. It seems a kind but unfair thought that a sinner should be saved without any great effort on his part. The Greek philosopher Diogenes, when told about the Mysteries of Eleusis, said: "What do you mean? Is Pataikion the thief going to have a better lot after death than Epaminondas, just because he was initiated?" (Cornford, 1923, p. 51). Ranade, similarly, was unable to believe that the sleeping state, which we easily enter every night, could really be the same as the "fourth" state of *mokṣa*.

In Hinduism, the medieval *bhakti* cults advocated personal and emotional expressions of affection which offered a simple and popular alternative to ritual or asceticism (plate 9). A feature of some of these cults is the chanting of a divine name (e.g., Hare Kṛṣṇa). In Rāmānuja's *Viśiṣṭādvaita, karman* "(ritual) activity" and *jñāna* "knowledge, insight" are subordinate to *bhakti* "loving devotion" and the grace of God, which will bring about salvation (characterized by Otto in 1930 as *Indiens Gnadenreligion*: "India's religion of grace"). But since Rāmānuja was after all a theologian and moralist, his *bhakti* is not simple or easy. In fact, it is confined to the twice-born castes (which, in South India, means the Brahmans), and one of its prerequisites is that the person who wishes to engage in *bhakti* must first be *jñānaniṣṭha* "firmly established in knowledge" (Muneo Tokunaga, personal communication). Acts are also important when one engages in this kind of *bhakti* (Van Buitenen 1968, p. 23). As the first step in *bhakti* Rāmānuja regards *prapatti* "surrender" (to Viṣṇu; plate 7). This notion is developed in one school of the later *Viśiṣṭādvaita*, where it finally becomes an easy path which is open to all. In popular religion, *bhakti* may be further facilitated by drugs such as *bhang*, about which Carstairs was told by one of his informants: "It is very good for *bhakti*; you get fine concentration with *bhang*" (Carstairs 1957, p. 119). The term *bhaṅga*, literally, "breaking, bursting," is used once of the Soma in *Ṛgveda* 9.61.13. In *Atharvaveda* 11.6.15 it probably means "hemp."

In Japan, in the Jōdo or Amida (Amitābha) Buddhism of Hōnen and his pupil Shinran we have another similar, easy, and popular method. Here, as in some forms of Protestant Christianity, the sufficiency of mere faith is stressed. But now the moralistic superstructure is inverted, and these new doctrines are advocated with slogans intended to shock the piously toiling practitioners of virtue. A saying of Hōnen runs: "Even a bad man will be received in Buddha's land; how much more a good man." Shinran turned this into "Even a good man will be received in Buddha's land; how much more a bad man" (Anesaki 1963, pp. 182–183).

To interpret such passages it should be borne in mind that the Pure Land Buddhism of Shinran was obsessed by a morbid sense of sin, to which only Manicheism and Christianity offer parallels. Nakamura, after quoting statements by Shinran like "There is no end of evil nature; man's mind is as abominable as a viper," characterizes this doctrine as follows: "Man is by nature evil, and because he is evil . . . he is entitled to be saved by the great benevolence of Amitābha" (Nakamura 1964, p. 515; for literary illustrations see Niwa 1966). When Jōdo Buddhism and Christianity came into direct contact on Japanese soil, these similarities were not discussed. This may be so because, as Nakamura has shown, the encounter of the two was primarily a confrontation between political powers, not a confrontation between ways of thinking (Nakamura 1967, I, pp. 111–149).

In all these cases we are concerned with mystical experiences which may have nothing to do with the superstructural distinction between easy and difficult. I shall now survey some other superstructures which may have to be evaluated in a similar manner. Such surveys constitute a necessary part of the exploration of mysticism because superstructures generally express mystical doctrines and offer interpretations of mystical experience. Since they generally involve religious or philosophical considerations, differences between them need not reflect differences in mystical experience. If we wish to isolate mystical experiences, we must disentangle them from such superstructures. We ourselves approach mystical experiences, like any other kinds of experiences, always within existing perspectives and superstructures. We must be aware of these before we can remove them or minimize their impact. Lastly, the theory of mystical experience which the student of mysticism must evolve is itself such a superstructure. In fact, it might turn out to be related to one of the existing superstructures. After all, many philosophers, especially in the Orient, have constructed superstructures in order to make sense of mystical experience. In the present essay, I am trying to pave the way for the same kind of interpretative superstructure.

In Hinduism, the "easy" way of *bhakti* has to be understood within a wide perspective. In Indian religion, *bhakti* appears relatively late (in the *Śvetāśvataropaniṣad* and in the epic). But the controversy on the value and efficacy of *karman* and *jñāna* runs through the centuries. In Vedic ritualism as described in the later Vedic texts, codified in the ritual *sūtras,* and systematized in the ritualistic philosophy of the (Karma- or Pūrva-) Mīmāṃsā, it is claimed that only the correct performance of *karman* "(ritual) activity" (plate 6) will lead to the desired result (e.g., wealth, offspring, heaven). Subsequently the notion of *karman* is developed into a doctrine of retribution; the strict law of cause and effect is extended to all human activity, aims, and ends, in this life and beyond; and the belief in transmigration makes its appearance. This belief, which constitutes the foundation of "orthoprax" Hinduism,[1] does not lead to fatalism, as is sometimes said—at any rate not

1. Orthopraxy, "adherence to right activity," is different from orthodoxy, "adherence to right opinion." It is the former that characterizes the traditional advocates of *karman* and good works; the latter characterizes the attitudes of the Hindu sectarians (cf. Staal 1959). See page 65.

to any greater extent than any other religious notion does. Fatalism occurs all over the world, especially among the uneducated and the poor. In Indian thought, however, human freedom and the law of *karman* presuppose each other. Past activity leads to a particular birth which restricts possibilities in a certain way; but within these restrictions, man is free to do his *karman* as he sees fit. One can influence the forces of *karman,* for example, by performing the austerities of *tapas,* as we have seen (plate 2). Men can do such things because they are free.

That fatalism is a mark of Oriental thought continues to be a Western prejudice. A recent illustration is provided by Danto, who writes that in the East "there is none of the agony over freedom of the will, which is, after all, the paradigmatic philosophical concern in the Western tradition" (Danto 1972, p. 17). Whether there is agony about it I am not sure; but there is a great deal of analysis of the concept of freedom in the Indian systems. Of course, we need not expect to find the exact counterparts of any of the Western notions of freedom, for in India freedom is generally conceived of as freedom from *karman.*

Reactions against the theories of *karman* of the Vedic ritualists characterize early Indian thought in the Upaniṣads and in Buddhism. In the Upaniṣads, the doctrine and efficacy of *karman* are challenged and often rejected, and the notion of *jñāna* "insight, knowledge" (plate 16) takes their place. The older notion of *svarga* "heaven," which parallels the notion of paradise in Western monotheism, is replaced by *mokṣa* "liberation." The *Muṇḍakopaniṣad* (1.2.7–10), for example, states that fools think they will attain the highest good by performing sacrifices; in fact, after a suitable period in heaven, they are reborn in this world or in a lower one (cf. Staal 1961b, p. 76). This criticism, too, is generalized. Later Hindu thought denied that any activity whatsoever can contribute to the emergence of *jñāna.*

The notion of *jñāna* developed in a great many ways, especially in the Vedānta, which also uses the term *vidyā,* and in Buddhism, where the corresponding term is *prajñā,* generally translated as "wisdom" (plate 8). In comparison with *karman,* which refers to physical activity, *jñāna* is a purely mental notion. In some of the systems of Indian philosophy, *jñāna* is regarded as a *vṛtti* "fluctuation" of the mind. As such it is one of the fluctuations which according to the Yoga have to be brought to a standstill. But in most Buddhist and Vedāntic thought, the concept of *jñāna* is divested of all traces of activity, mental as well as physical. It develops into what may be called a mystical concept. In order that this may be understood, I shall trace a few steps in the development of this notion, which illustrate a progression from ritualism to mysticism.

The Upaniṣadic reaction against ritualism took many different forms. Sometimes the ritual was interpreted symbolically; sometimes the ritual activity itself was "interiorized." It was also related to the ancient speculations on *prāṇa* "breath." As distinct from the *agnihotra,* a purely ritualistic sacrifice to the Vedic God Agni, mention is made of a more spiritual variant, the *agnihotra* of breath (*prāṇāgnihotra*). Then there developed the idea that it is not necessary to perform the ritual acts physically, but that it is sufficient to concentrate mentally on their sequence (this is called *upāsanā* "contemplation" or *vidyā* "knowledge"). We come across references to "mental cups" instead of the physical cups from which the Soma is drunk. In these practices we witness a transition from the Vedic ritual to the practice of meditation. In the final stages, the ritual is rejected outright (as in the above passage from the *Muṇḍakopaniṣad*), and the notion of *jñāna* takes its place.

In contemporary circles, where religion and irrationalism are regarded as inseparable, it is often emphasized that this *jñāna,* like the γνῶσις of the Gnostics and mystical knowledge in general, is altogether different from so-called "intellectual" knowledge. Such semantic demarcation may well be justified, but it is not very informative, and is mostly advocated only negatively as an expression of anti-intellectualism. In India, where there is no tradition of irrationalism, Śiva, the divine teacher (*dakṣiṇāmūrti*), who is the incorporation of *jñāna,* is represented with a book in his hand and expounding a commentary (as we have seen in chap. 11 and on plate 5). So let us look more closely.

The concept of *jñāna* may certainly be regarded as a "mystical" notion if only by definition or in the sense that such usage would in turn help to determine the meaning of the term "mystical" itself. At any rate, whether we deal with the Vedāntic *brahmajñāna* "knowledge of *brahman*" or with the Buddhist *prajñā* "wisdom," it is clear that the object of such knowledge is different from more mundane objects. Moreover, the object may coincide with the subject itself, as in the ordinary notion of "self-knowledge," or vanish altogether, as in *śūnyatā*. But we know already that all knowledge is not "intellectual" or taught in universities. There are many different kinds of knowledge, differing not only with regard to their object, but also with regard to the kind of object to which they are related, and with regard to the kind of relation to such an object. Since Ryle (1949, chap. 2), many philosophers, now supported by linguists, distinguish between "knowing that" and "knowing how." Knowing how to swim is different from knowing when to stop, knowing that the earth is round, knowing Mr. Nixon, or knowing mathematics (the Dutch mathematician G. Mannoury held that knowing mathematics is not a knowing that, but a knowing how). No wonder, then, that knowing *brahman* might again be different.

It is important to bear in mind that the Indian notion of *jñāna*, whether it is called mystical, intellectual, or anti-intellectual, is understood as objective and true. Śaṅkara is very explicit on this point. He distinguishes between subjective: *puruṣabuddhyapekṣa* "depending on man's notions" or *puruṣatantra* "depending on man," and objective: *vastutantra* "depending on things." That *jñāna* is objective is explained in the following passage, where it is contrasted with "option" (*vikalpa*):

> There is no option as to whether a thing is thus or thus, is or is not. Option depends on human notions. Knowledge of the nature of a thing does not depend on human notions. It depends only on the thing itself. To say with regard to a pillar "it is a pillar, or it is a man or it is something else" does not result from correct knowledge. To say that it is a man or something else does result from false knowledge. To say that it is a pillar results from correct knowledge, because it depends on the thing itself. Therefore the means of knowing objects, that are existent things, depend on the things themselves (*Brahmasūtrabhāṣya* 1.1.3, quoted in Staal 1962a, p. 62).

In Advaita Vedānta, *jñāna* is regarded as objective and often as descriptive, and it is conceived of as having for its object something that is *siddha* "established." This term is contrasted with the term *sādhya*, which denotes something that is "to be established." "To be established" are the objects not only of *vikalpa* "option" but also of *dharma* "duty," *karman* "activity," and *dhyāna* "meditation."

Concepts like the last four refer to entities which are related to what is subjective and which are often prescriptive. In elaborating on this contrast between *siddha* and *sādhya*, the Advaitins were undoubtedly thinking of their adversaries, the philosphers of the Mīmāṃsā. For in the Mīmāṃsā, which is a kind of hermeneutics of the Veda, each Vedic expression is interpreted as, or related to, a *vidhi* "injunction" which prompts to, or enjoins, *karman* "activity." Therefore the Mīmāṃsā is concerned with what is *sādhya* "to be established," not *siddha* "established."

Śaṅkara regards *dhyāna* "meditation" also as an activity, which is therefore dependent on man, subjective, and relates to what is *sādhya*. Meditation, unlike knowledge, therefore has "effects," which are generally referred to by the term *siddhi*, another derivative of the same root. (This term later acquired, as we have seen, like *prabhāva* or *vibhūti*, the more specific meaning of "supernatural power".) In thus subordinating *dhyāna*, Śaṅkara probably had the Yoga in mind. It is known that he was familiar with the *Yogasūtra*, and according to Hacker 1968, he was an adherent of the Yoga system before he converted to Advaita. Whatever his career may have been, Śaṅkara regarded meditation as subjective and not concerned with objective truth, even though he assigned it a definite place in the training of a mystic.

In Sanskrit there is another term derived from the same root as *siddha*, *siddhi*, and *sādhya*: namely, *sādhanā*, literally, "means of establishing," that is, "religious practice." In advocating knowledge which is confined to what is *siddha*, and in rejecting or subordinating all those other notions which pertain to what is *sādhya*, the Advaitins in fact undermined the foundations of religious practice. But unlike the Buddhists, they adhered to the Vedic tradition, and in practice adopted a kind of compromise. They could do this because they accepted the distinction of two levels, which originated with Nāgārjuna (see chap. 2). This distinction enabled Buddhists as well as Advaitins to justify in theory whatever practice they chose to adhere to.

Śaṅkara's pupil Sureśvara (second half of the eighth century), who according to the Indian tradition was first a proponent of the Mīmāṃsā, and was then converted to Advaita by Śaṅkara, refers to these notions, which he directly attaches to the Upaniṣadic tradition of reaction against the ritual. He says, for example, in the *Sambandhavārtika*, the introduction to his subcommentary on Śaṅkara's commentary on the *Bṛhadāraṇyakopaniṣad* (Mahadevan 1958, pp. 49–50; cf. Hacker 1950, pp. 1993–1995, and Van Boetzelaer 1971, pp. 10–16):

> Therefore, he who knows the truth of the Veda will realize the futility of rites, and seek the knowledge of the one self, purifying himself through austerity.
>
> Free from all desires on account of practice in a previous birth, he is eligible even in his first stage of life.[2] He does not need any more action.
>
> He who is detached and desires knowledge does not require anything other than knowledge. For action is required in respect of what is to be established (*sādhya*). In respect of the established (*siddha*) it is of no use.

In the earlier speculations on *karman* and in the extension of the notion of universal causality to the domain of the mind, we witness a concept of man which may be characterized as mechanistic. The term *sādhya* expresses man's urge to establish things in accordance with the causal mechanisms of *karman*, leading to merit and demerit. There is here a kind of principle of conservation: nothing is added and nothing is destroyed. Hara (1968–1969 and 1970) has compared these exchanges and transactions to the transfer of property or money. Though Hinduism did not develop any scientific theories to describe and explain the laws underlying these mechanisms, we read again and again that every activity leads to a result and that the sum total of these results, at the moment of death, determines a new birth. Mechanistic world views in the West developed quite differently. They were worked out in detail and subjected to experimentation and theory formation, but they remained largely confined to the physical world. Only during the last few centuries have there been attempts to deal with the science of man along mechanistic lines, attempts which on the whole have remained unsuccessful, as is shown, for example, in recent linguistics. It is tempting to conclude from ancient Indian and recent

2. This sentence refers to the four stages of life (*āśrama*) advocated in Hinduism: the first is that of the student (*brahmacārin*, litt., "who goes with *brahman*"); the second that of the householder (*gṛhastha*); the third that of the hermit (*vanaprastha*, litt., "forest-dweller"); and the fourth that of the wandering ascetic (*saṃnyāsin*).

Western experience that man cannot be explained along these lines.

In India, the experience of the mystic suggested something altogether different. His seemed to be a state which is unconditioned and unrelated to previous activity. It is experienced as *siddha*, not as *sādhya*. It is conceived of as *mokṣa* "liberation" and as *nirvāṇa* "extinction." It is *jñāna* "knowledge" because it does not through activity establish an object, but appears to reflect a situation which was already there and a condition already attained.

While the Yoga is concerned with the methods which lead to *samādhi*, the Upaniṣads begin to develop a notion of *mokṣa* which is beyond all methods. In the development of the Advaita Vedānta this notion is expressed in terms of the contrast between *siddha* and *sādhya*. These terms of course reflect interpretations, and belong to the superstructure. In Buddhism, the unconditionality of *nirvāṇa* is present in the superstructure almost from the beginning; but it is especially expounded by Nāgārjuna. In his philosophy, *nirvāṇa* is never attained because it is already there, and so there is no seeker of *nirvāṇa* and no process of liberation.

Gauḍapāda (*Māṇḍūkyakārikā* 2.32) described these notions in lines which use almost identical expressions:

> There is none in bondage, none aspiring for wisdom,
> No seeker of liberation, and none liberated.

Because of such similarities, several scholars have claimed that Gauḍapāda was not merely familiar with Nāgārjuna, but was himself a Buddhist. But Mahadevan (1960) maintains that he was an early Advaitin.

To the followers of a religion, doctrines like these are very hard to swallow. Philosophers can take them, since they don't commit anybody to anything, and anyway philosophers are not interested in *sādhanā* or religious practice. But most people turn to religion for guidance and comfort, and expect to be told what they should do or avoid. Here they are told that there is no path, and in the final resort they are not told anything at all. Such pristine ideas are therefore always mixed with others and tend to develop into new cults and disciplines. This happened in India and, when Buddhism disappeared from Indian soil, in Buddhist civilizations elsewhere in Asia. I shall give only one example, but it is striking.

Although Ch'an in China and Zen in Japan grew out of the Indian doctrines of "no effort," these Far Eastern traditions gave rise to schools which again preached that the seeker after enlightenment must undergo arduous training and be subjected to numerous tests. Zen is therefore noted for the stress on spontaneity which is present in its theory and expressed in its art, and for painful and military discipline which characterizes its practice. The two tendencies survive in somewhat modified form in the contemporary conflict between what Watts has called "Straight Zen" and "Beat Zen" (Watts 1967, pp. 77–110).

If we wish to eliminate superstructure as much as possible, what are we finally to make of these doctrines of "no effort"? Possibly we should reckon with a property of the mind, which is manifest in a mystical state or in mystical states, and which is independent of previous conditioning of any kind. It is in some respects similar to certain states of knowing. Such unconditionality is consistent with the fact that elsewhere in the superstructures of mystical religions and philosophies, we find many competing paths and methods advocated as leading to mystical states of mind. Such methods may be aids which in unexplained ways help to reach a point which is quite independent of each of them. Each of these methods is therefore dispensable. But just as certain mystical states can perhaps not be reached by any particular method to the exclusion of all others, they cannot perhaps be explored by any particular method to the exclusion of all others. For methods of mystic training, or methods of exploration, attach to themselves specific activities, observables, prescripts, and disciplines. The student of mysticism needs such support, and in my discussion of methods I need methods to discuss. Therefore the Yoga, with its amplification of methods and poverty of superstructure, provides excellent laboratories and testing grounds. But as a special challenge to the student of mysticism, it remains to be explored whether there are states of mind which are beyond all methods and paths. Such states as *jñāna* and *prajñā* would by definition be beyond methodical exploration, and so the student of mysticism could only be successful if at some point he happened to turn into a mystic. The available evidence suggests that he could still return to the "ordinary" state, and therefore be in a position to evolve a theory.

At this point a comparison with the study of dreamless sleep may again be made. Here we cannot easily explore the subjective experience of the person who is asleep: for he is not aware of the fact that he is asleep. The exploration of mystical experience is in a more favorable position: for the mystic is at least aware of his experiences. Even in the *Yogasūtra, asaṃprajñāta* "unaware" refers to external objects only.

So far I have described and discussed superstructures which are related to *bhakti* and to *jñāna*. Though *bhakti* appears late in the chronological development, it serves as a useful introduction to Indian forms of mysticism, especially for those who are raised in a Western monotheistic environment. The concept of *jñāna* introduces a notion which appears to be more basic to mysticism in general, and which may help us to understand some fundamental features of certain kinds of mystical experience. But *jñāna* itself appeared in a milieu of *karman*, and though I have often referred to this background, it has remained unexplained. Why should people advocate ritualism as the highest aim of life? In order to explore this idea, I shall move further back into Indian history. To pave the way, I shall first consider some efforts at synthesis.

In Indian philosophy there have been many attempts at a synthesis between the extreme view of "no-liberation," found in the Upaniṣads, in Buddhism, and in the Advaita Vedānta, and the tradition of ritual *karman* of the late Vedic period which culminated in the Mīmāṃsā. In the philosophical works, a particular combination was called *jñānakarmasamuccaya* "the combination of works and insight." This view was defended in some form or other by early philosophers of the Vedānta like Brahmadatta and Bhartṛprapañca, by the Advaitin Maṇḍanamiśra, and by the Mīmāṃsā philosopher Kumārila Bhaṭṭa (Hiriyanna 1925, pp. xxii–xxix; Kuppuswami Sastri 1937, pp. xlvi–xlix; and Dasgupta 1932, pp. 44, 100).

The popularity of the *Bhagavad Gītā* is partly due to the fact that it advocates another such synthesis. Combining Hindu conservatism with the revolutionary ideas of mystics, the *Gītā* insists that actions should be performed in accordance with one's prescribed duty, but it teaches that such actions should be taken without any attachment to the fruits of action (*karmaphalatyāga*). This restriction introduces renunciation and prevents activities from being regarded as methods or ways. The *Gītā* teaches many different things, but it is this doctrine which it propounds as its basic teaching:

> But these actions,
> Abandoning attachment and fruits,
> Must be performed, O Pārtha.
> This is my definite and highest doctrine.
> (*Bhagavad Gītā* 18.6)

This is not so very different from what Don Juan taught Castaneda: "We must know first that our acts are useless and yet we must proceed as if we didn't know it. That's a sorcerer's controlled folly" (Castaneda 1971, p. 97).

In the domain we are concerned with, there are other efforts at synthesis. We have seen that the effectiveness of drugs varies not only with the circumstances and with one's frame of mind, but also with the manner and extent to which one has prepared oneself. It is an illusion to imagine that drugs take effect with the inevitability of an avalanche. The effects are linked not only with the preceding state of the body, but also with that of the mind. Conscious volition may pave the way, and may also continue after the drug has taken effect. And so it is not surprising to find that drugs are also often combined with works.

A striking illustration of what might be called *oṣadhikarmasamuccaya*, or the combination of *karman* and drugs, was communicated by Slotkin (the investigator of the Peyote cult who joined the Native American Church) to Fischer, who describes and interprets it in the following terms:

> The greater the distance from the source of Peyote—the Rio Grande Valley—the scarcer is the supply; this appears to account for the fact that Indian tribes of the Northern Plains incorporate less Peyote during the ceremony than do Southern tribes. It is noteworthy, therefore, that it is in the Northern Plains that ceremonial cleansing precedes the rite; this takes the form of purges, sweatbaths and fasting (Slotkin, 1957). One is tempted to speculate about this trend. Do the Northern Plains tribes supplement the smaller quantities of Peyote available to them with stressful stimulation and thus produce an experience of similar intensity to that evoked solely by larger doses of Peyote? (Fischer 1958, p. 401)

We have already seen that the ceremony with which a drug is

dispensed contributes to its effect. Ritualistic circumstances must also account for the mild "contact high" observed by contemporary users of drugs: in a small group, more people get high than have actually taken a drug. There are ancient precursors. The *Ṛgveda* contains the solemn verse: "Soma unpressed has never intoxicated Indra, nor the pressed juices unaccompanied by sacred hymns" (*Ṛgveda* 7.26.1, quoted in Brough 1971, pp. 338–339). The term "intoxicated" is actually misleading, since the reference is not to alcohol: Soma was in all likelihood a hallucinogen, as we shall see. But the development of the Soma cult took unexpected turns. It offers a large-scale parallel in India to the Peyote phenomena observed by Slotkin. When the tribes of Indo-European speech who composed the Vedas, having entered the subcontinent from the northwest, moved deeper into India in eastern and southern directions, when the Soma cult moved further away from the mountains where the original Soma grew, when the plant became increasingly rare and substitutes were beginning to be used, there developed the Vedic ritual, in all likelihood the most elaborate ritual mankind has devised (plate 6).

To call the Soma ritual "stressful stimulation" would merely be casting a behavorist spell. But it would be correct to say that such ritual was partly a means to attain a certain state of mind, especially on the part of the main sacrificer (the *yajamāna*), who had undergone the consecration ceremonies (*dīkṣā*), but quite possibly also on the part of the priests, sixteen in number in the classical prototype, who drank small quantities of the Soma liquid.

That originally the real Soma produced an extraordinary high seems to be indicated in the *Ṛgveda* by descriptions of Indra and Rudra after they drank it. Later the quantities became symbolic (like wine in Christian churches or sake in Shinto shrines); moreover, substitutes were introduced. As in the case of peyote, the *karman* of ritual, which yielded the sacred *brahman* power, made up for these physical deficits. Finally, the ritual may have deteriorated into mere ceremonialism, and we come extremely close to the "distilled water, dispensed with appropriate ceremony," mentioned by Claridge. This entire development, which was spread out over many centuries, explains at least in part the extraordinary emphasis on the Soma ritual, and on ritual in general, which characterizes early Indian civilization. It constitutes the replacement of a hallucinogen by ritualism. But when ritualism lost, or was believed to have lost, its efficacy, it was replaced by more purely mental concepts, such as *dhyāna* "meditation" and *jñāna* "knowledge." This was in some ways a return to Vedic or even pre-Vedic experience, at least in that it produced direct access to a mental state. Hence the importance of the discussions of *karman* and *jñāna*, to some features of which I have drawn attention. With these discussions we enter the domain of Indian philosophy proper.

The possibility of attaining certain mental states by means of hallucinogens, of rituals, or combinations of both appears to be a basic feature of the mind that must be taken into account in the study of mysticism. The option between these alternatives suggests, for instance, that one could train oneself to obtain the same experience repeatedly, but by gradually decreasing the doses of a drug, just like people who jump from great heights using smaller and smaller parachutes. Whether or not the final result would be the same, such training would in effect be an exercise in a certain kind of meditation or jumping. In fact, what Castaneda learned with the help of drugs was to achieve certain results without the aid of drugs. In both cases there is an attempt to bring forces that first eluded us, under control. Conversely, people who are so inclined meditate easily under the influence of a drug.

Having surveyed some of the Indian superstructures, I shall now briefly discuss a few modern ones. The double fallacy, that drugs affect our body (*casu quo*, our brain) without having anything to do with our state of mind, and that their effects are completely determined and beyond our control, is committed by Zaehner. That his own single experiment with mescaline was "utterly trivial" throws light on the drug, but also on Zaehner, obviously (see also Smith 1964, pp. 523–524). Moreover, Zaehner's statement: "When Huxley came to take mescaline, his mind was permeated through and through with Vedāntin and Mahāyāna Buddhist ideas" (Zaehner 1961, pp. 2–3) may be a true statement (though Huxley 1946 contained a lot from Eckhart, St. John of the Cross, William Law, St. Teresa, Philo, Rūmī, Kabīr, Ruysbroeck, etc.), but it is not a valid argument against Huxley. On the other hand, that Zaehner's own mind "was penetrated through and through with Christian and ancient Iranian ideas" (as he does not say) goes a long way to explain the triviality of his own experience. For if Huxley is right, he says, "the conclusions . . . are alarming" (Zaehner 1961, p. 12); but they would be much less alarming within the perspective of less uptight religious traditions. Zaehner is, moreover, inconsistent, for he admits, at least half-seriously: "The fact that I am an assiduous reader of *Alice through the Looking-Glass* is probably not irrelevant to the nature of my experience" (Zaehner 1961, p. 226). Must we conclude that Zaehner was not prepared to take his mescaline experiment seriously, or that Alice's adventures made a deeper impression on him than the wide range of religious and mystical literature with which he is so familiar?

All of this shows that mysticism and drugs can certainly not be effectively studied or compared if the subjective aspects of experience are left out of consideration. It also indicates that different causes, physical as well as mental, and also combinations of these, may bring about particular states of the mind. That, of course, should not surprise anyone who has ever given the mind a thought. The specific character of the cases I have referred to reflects the specificity of these particular states of the mind. It would therefore not be surprising either, if it were found that these states constitute a separate domain of the mind, and that this domain is linked with a separate area of the brain. To Castaneda the separateness of this area of experience was sufficiently striking to adopt *A Separate Reality* as the title for his second book (1971).

Such a view also seems to be implicit in the words of Smythies (the same scholar who administered the drug to Zaehner), to the effect that the drug experiences are "the work of a highly differentiated mental compartment, without any apparent connection, emotional or volitional, with the aims, interests, or feelings of the person concerned" (quoted in Huxley 1963, p. 97). Though the first clause of this statement is probably correct, and the drift of the rest is not entirely unclear, the severance of connections which Smythies postulates is certainly presented in excessive terms. A person's will or feelings may well be affected by a drug, but they are by no means abolished and do not even seem restricted. They are surely different and differently oriented, and this may have something to do with the claim of many mystics that the ego can be and should be abolished: for the identity of the ego is largely felt to be determined by its own characteristic feelings and emotions. Smythies himself (1953, p. 344) quotes several accounts of changes that take place within the ego of a person who has taken a drug. But he was interested in the effects of mescalin precisely because, according to him, it is the only drug which leaves, in a normal subject, "his observational integrity intact and his critical judgment unclouded" (Smythies 1953, p. 339). Actually, this statement is far too monolithic and would require a great many qualifications.

Contemporary drug research has not, to my knowledge, taken into account the fact that even the drug-induced states are subject to efforts of the will. One can perceive, for example, nonordinary colors and movements when under the influence of mescalin by a volitional effort—something one can imagine, but not bring about, when in the normal state of consciousness. The awareness of the difference of such perceptions from imagined perceptions shows in turn that mystical visions are not imaginary in the ordinary sense (cf. chap. 1, n. 3).

It is not very clear what Smythies means by saying that there is no "apparent connection, emotional or volitional, with the aims, interests, or feelings of the person concerned." Are there such connections in my mind when I am watching a movie or playing chess? We are left with the unequivocal expression of a "highly differentiated mental compartment," which seems to describe very well what it is that is affected or produced by a drug or a mystical vision. It provides some justification for the talk of such brain states as "C" which I postulated in an earlier construction (page 170). But the connections of such an experience with the rest of the person are more aptly described by Huxley, who in this area has always been ahead of the professionals: "Almost never does the visionary see anything that reminds him of his own past. He is not remembering scenes, persons, or objects, and he is not inventing them; he is looking on at a new creation" (Huxley 1963, p. 97).

Though I find Huxley's speculations very often reasonable and certainly suggestive, and wish the experts took them more seriously (as Zaehner did), I am not convinced of the correctness of the Bergsonian theory that Huxley received via Broad and developed into the view that drugs give access to the "Mind at Large," that is, the total awareness of all that has happened and is happening to the individual, and from which everything that is not useful is under normal circumstances eliminated by the brain and nervous system. Instead of the hypothesis that drugs widen the mind, one could adopt the hypothesis that they narrow the mind—a theory which has actually been defended, through rather unconvincing criticisms of Huxley, by Cazeneuve (1959). Both theories are bold but exceedingly premature. Some information is beginning to become available about the filtering or screening of stimuli by brain mechanisms under the influence of certain drugs (Claridge 1972, chap. 8). Deikman's work, some of which points in an opposite direction, is also a contribution to our knowledge. But we need to know a great deal more about the world and about ourselves before we can come up with even a semblance of an argument in support of such grand theories as the "Mind at Large" or its opposite, which might be called the "Mind Reduced." It is not improbable that the truth lies somewhere in between, and that drugs in some respects widen, and in others narrow, the mind. This could mean at the same time that they give access to certain features or areas of reality, while obscuring others.

One might try to support the theory of the Mind at Large by showing that the information which that Mind possesses can also be obtained with the help of different and independent methods. Such knowledge need not be easily accessible; but it would be significant if it were found to be accessible in more than one way. The parallels from mysticism can be construed as suggesting this, but they have to be studied adequately first. In arguing for the rival theory of the Mind Reduced, it would not be enough to show that a drug-induced mind falls short in its experience of the ordinary world (and even this has not been done); one must also discover or at least postulate specific causes which can account for the fact that such a mind experiences what it experiences. Moreover, it is not the mere fact of experiencing something that is to be explained; it is rather the much more interesting fact that experience is influenced by the motivation (or lack of motivation) that lies behind it, so that certain perceptions, when sought, are also within reach, while others, when no longer sought, are also no longer within reach.

The moral and religious criticisms of the thesis that drugs and mysticism are related, and of the exploration of drugs and their effects on the mind in general, are not only similar to the age-old moral criticisms of religious movements that stress easy methods such as faith, but they also reflect the conservatism which characterizes all institutionalized religion. Watts is certainly justified in comparing the use of a drug to explore the mind to the use of a microscope or telescope to explore the universe (Watts 1962, p. 20: "mystical insight is no more in the chemical itself than biological knowledge is in the microscope"). He might have added in support of this analogy that Galilei was in fact criticized by Aristotelians among the clergy for inspecting God's work with the help of a diabolic device such as a telescope.

The analogy goes further. The excessive use of drugs might adversely affect the mind, just as the excessive looking through microscopes might adversely affect the eyes. In extreme cases, one loses one's mind, eyesight, or even life. But such risks are not generally censured. The evaluation of dangers and risks by society, or worse, by a government acting as a moral guardian, clearly reflect prejudices that happen to be prevalent in a certain area and during a certain period. It may be recalled that Muslim orthodoxy censured hashish, opium, contemplation of boys, and coffee. Nowadays we are warned by columnists, priests, and government agents that a person who uses a drug risks his mind or even his soul; and it is useful to bear in mind that this might very well be true. But the same agencies encourage us to admire people who explore new continents, climb Himalayan peaks, go to the moon, experiment with radiation, germs, new medicaments, and devices designed for destruction, or risk their lives in many other ways. In fact, the greatest adventures of science are considered great partly because of the risks they involve. The scientific exploration of drugs should be evaluated in the same spirit. While the taking of drugs is risky and can be dangerous, so that people who are looking for kicks should be advised to cool it or refrain, serious investigators will not make much real progress unless they subject themselves to experiments with drugs. At the same time it should be obvious, apart from the public search for truth, that no government should have the right to forbid adult citizens the freedom to explore their own inner consciousness in private.

This last phrase takes me to the Harvard experiments of Alpert and Leary (compare the evaluation of this alleged "academic debacle" in La Barre 1970, pp. 230–237). What Leary and Alpert might be criticized for is not that they experimented with drugs, but that they did not provide critical evaluations of their discoveries. They seemed to have lost their rational mind, and founded instead a religious sect. Alpert, in fact, has since turned to some kind of Yoga (Alpert 1971). This by itself is valuable in that it constitutes the latest evidence for the thesis that drug experience, when combined with the expectation of some sort of salvation, leads to religion. This thesis is further corroborated by the persecution (in the guise of American justice) of Leary as if he were a heretic, instead of the much more relevant rational evaluation of his claims. Students of mysticism should criticize Leary and Alpert for ceasing to be explorers and for turning into preachers. Unfortunately, the publicity surrounding these events has caused many sensible people to believe that the use of drugs permanently affects, or causes a person to lose, his mind. But this is clearly not always, and not even generally, the case. Many disastrous events we know about have undoubtedly been due less to drugs than to the persons taking them. Moreover, such a loss of mind may be apparent and similar to the state which Lao Tzu referred to when he wrote (see above, page 30):

> Mine is indeed the mind of a very idiot,
> So dull am I.

Christian critics may recall I Corinthians 1:19: "For it is written, I will destroy the wisdom of the wise, and will bring to nothing the understanding of the prudent."

We have surveyed some of the many religious and philosophical evaluations and interpretations of mystical experiences, and some of the discussions on methods which may lead to the attainment of these experiences. This immense variety is consistent with an equally immense variety of experiences, but it is also consistent with a very small number of basic experiences, or even with one kind of basic experience. Which description is the most accurate we cannot determine at present. But since we have seen that such variety is often due to psychological and cultural circumstances, it would be safe to assume that the experiences themselves are to some extent independent of their interpretations and evaluations. This suggests even more strongly than my earlier demonstrations that we can only make progress in the study of mysticism if we direct our attention away from the superstructures and back to the experiences themselves.

14

Mysticism and Religion

> As for the mind—when, how and from where it is obtained by those who share in that principle—it poses the greatest difficulties, which we must try to understand as best we can and as far as it is possible.
>
> ARISTOTLE, *De Generatione Animalium* II 3, 736 b 5–8

Whether or not there is a connection between mystical and drug-induced experiences, it is clear that drugs have little to do with religion as a social institution or as a belief in Gods or in God. This statement could be taken to suggest that the mystical experience itself, though it may lead to it, has also nothing to do with religion in that sense. This is precisely what I suspect to be the case. It seems likely that the belief in Gods is a special outcome of mystical experiences, interpreted as divine, and is in turn a device that facilitates the attainment of such experiences.

Such a view would be consistent with the following assumption, which would seem to be a reasonable working hypothesis. Let us assume that the various causes mentioned by Patañjali in the *Yogasūtra* and by Vasubandhu in the *Abhidharmakośa* are not merely causes of special supernatural powers, but are causes of various kinds of mystical experiences. That Patañjali's classification has a much wider application had earlier been suggested by Hubert and Mauss in their classical study of magic in Australian societies: "It is very remarkable that the Hindu classification of the different origins of magical power have almost identical application to Australian magic. One might say, with Patañjali, that it originates from birth, from the knowledge of formulas and substances, from ecstatic revelation" (Hubert and Mauss 1909, p. 140).

Pensa (1969, p. 202, n. 26) has objected to this extension: "It appears questionable however whether it is legitimate, from an historical point of view, to abstract and isolate a *sūtra* both from its particular context, i.e., the *Yogasūtra*, and from its general context, i.e., Indian religion, recurring in this way to an anti-historic comparativism." To me it seems obvious, on the contrary, that the "historicism" underlying Pensa's criticism is much more questionable, and that Hubert and Mauss' ahistorical and structural approach is to be adopted if we evere wish to gain an understanding of phenomena such as mysticism.

Patañjali's classification need not, of course, be taken as exhaustive. From Vasubandhu's list we may add *karman* "activity," which is certainly wider than *tapas*—in fact, which seems far too general. But if we take *karman* in the sense it generally had in late Vedic and in the earlier phases of Indian civilization, as "ritual activity," its inclusion is most appropriate. For the internalization of the ritual which took place in the Upaniṣads often assumed the form of a mental performance of or concentration upon the activities prescribed for the rituals. Such internalization conformed to the ritual in all its detail. As we have seen, a cup from which the Soma was drunk during an elaborate ceremony in the original ritual was replaced by a "mental" (*mānasa*) cup. The resulting "ritual meditations" are called *vidyā*, which is often synonymous with *jñāna*.

There are other specific methods used by mystics which seem to belong to the same category as the techniques and devices mentioned by Patañjali and Vasubandhu. They may all be described as *dhiyālamba* "support of contemplation." Foremost among these supports are the *yantras* or visual (and subsequently mental) aids, which parallel the mantras, which are auditory (and subsequently mental) aids. In Tantrism, Hindu as well as Buddhist, most *yantras* are line drawings or diagrams, consisting mainly of triangles, lotus petals, etc. A famous *yantra* is the *śrī yantra* (title page). Such *yantras,* also called *maṇḍala* (literally, "circle"), have acquired a certain fame through the depth-psychological speculations of C. G. Jung and his followers. Jung had observed that very similar images emerged in the dreams of his Western patients. From here it was only a step to his theory of archetypes, visual patterns, and structures which belong to the unconscious mind of mankind.

In Indian civilization, *yantras* or *maṇḍalas* are often constructed to initiate or consecrate a ritual or religious ceremony (plate 11b). The ground plans of many temples and religious monuments—e.g., Borobudur in Central Java (plate 11a)—are also *yantras or maṇḍalas.* Performing a circumambulation, clockwise oriented (*pradakṣiṇā*), around and then inside such a religious structure, is therefore tantamount to meditating with the aid of a *yantra.* The *yantras* are first objects of visual perception and concentration; then, just like *mantras,* they become objects of mental concentration (see, e.g., Zimmer 1926; Pott 1966). *Yantras* may also be combined with mantras by inscribing the syllables of the latter in specific locations inside the former, arranged in the same sequence in which the parts of the *yantra* have to be gone through.

Indian civilization has on the whole emphasized the ear more than Western civilization, which has stressed the eye. The preponderance of mantras in Indian religions is therefore not surprising. This implies that elsewhere mantras may not have the same significance they have in Indian forms of mysticism.

Among visual aids of contemplation in Buddhism the best-known is called *kasiṇa.* Different kinds of *kasiṇa* are mentioned in the Pāli texts, and others are added later. Heiler (1918, p. 24) mentions the following: The monk who wishes to meditate makes a circle or disk of clay or earth, sits down at a small distance, and concentrates his gaze upon it ("earth-*kasiṇa*"). Or he contemplates a small pond or bowl with water ("water-*kasiṇa*"). Or he lights a fire, makes a small opening in a mat or cloth, and looks through it into the fire ("fire-*kasiṇa*"). Or he gazes upon a treetop, moving in the wind ("wind-*kasiṇa*"). Or he concentrates upon a blue, yellow, white, or red piece of cloth (the four "color-*kasiṇas*"). Or he looks through an opening or small window into a house or cave ("space-*kasiṇa*"). Or else, the other way around, he looks from inside through an opening at the daylight, or through the branches and leaves of a tree ("light-*kasiṇa*").

In each of these exercises, a totalization or unification takes place. This is not just a matter of perception; it is partly the result of an effort of the will. The *Daśasāhasrikā* explains how these concentrations result from volitions (Lamotte 1970, pp. 1286–1287): "If one *wills* all the elements in the element earth, everything becomes one element, i.e., earth." The *kasiṇa*-meditation is still prevalent, among Buddhist monks in Ceylon (Gombrich 1971, p. 284), and very probably in Burma.

In Indian philosophy, the distinction is sometimes made between *brahmopāsana* "(direct) concentration on the absolute" and *pratīkopāsana* "(indirect) concentration on a symbol." The various objects mentioned so far are, within this perspective, to be regarded as *pratīka* "symbol." The most well-known and widespread of these are images of the deity, or "idols" (plates 1, 3, 4 and 5). That these are functionally similar to *yantras* has been clearly shown by Zimmer (1926). In both cases a ceremony called *prāṇapratiṣṭhā* takes place at the beginning of the act of worship: through it, the symbol is endowed with *prāṇa* "breath, life"; after that it stands in direct relationship with the worshiper, and is a fit object for meditation.

The act of "worshiping" an idol is often regarded as a ritualistic and rather formal ceremony. Actually, it often is a process of meditation on the part of the officiating priest. This holds for other rituals too, as is especially clear in Bali, the Indonesian island where remarkable forms of Hindu-Buddhist syncretism have developed. The priest, when performing such a ritual, includes *prāṇāyāma*, "breathing exercises." The Buddhist priest in Bali calls his worship *yoga*, and himself *yogīśvara* ("yogin-deity"), and the pavilion where he sits *balé pa-yoga-an* (Hooykaas 1966, p. 154). One remarkable feature of these forms is that two originally antagonistic trends, the ritual of the village caste society and the Yoga of the isolated hermit in the forest, are combined. A similar combination of meditation and ritual is found in Zen in flower arrangement and the tea ceremony.

That idols of deities, and rituals and ceremonies in general, are techniques or aids for meditation is not surprising in the context of Indian religion. In theistic religions, Gods come first. Idols are regarded as representations of a deity; rituals are dedicated to a deity. But in Indian religions, the situation is often the opposite: the Gods come last. While this is obvious in such atheistic religions as Buddhism and Jainism, where, despite a plethora of saints, that final point is not even included, it also holds for several forms of Hinduism. The most orthodox of the Hindu systems of philosophy, the Mīmāṃsā, is especially concerned with the interpretation of the Vedic ritual. This ritual is taken to be based upon Vedic injunctions such as: "The person who wishes to attain heaven should perform an Agniṣṭoma ritual *for Agni*" (*agniṣṭomayāgaṃ yajeta agnaye svargakāmaḥ*). The question arises, Who is that Agni, for whom the ritual is performed? The Mīmāṃsā answer is: He is an entity postulated as a referent to which the grammatical dative ("*agnaye*") refers.

This attitude toward deities characterizes much of Hinduism, and it is therefore not surprising to find it expressed in the Mīmāmsā, a system which maintains that the Veda is eternal (*ergo*, not created by a deity) and which assigns to Gods a subordinate place (like the lowest caste of the *śūdras*, for example, Gods are excluded from the sacrifice, not because they do not require it, but because they are not entitled or qualified to perform it). The appearance of Hinduism as a religion which swarms with Gods is on the whole misleading: Gods play often a subordinate part, and their interpretation as mental forces, which elsewhere smacks of excessive symbolism (as in the Alexandrian interpretations of the Homeric pantheon), is in Hinduism quite natural.

The religions of India provide the materials which one day may show that religion can be studied as a branch of psychology—a psychology, of course, which is an integrated science of the mind, the soul, and the spirit, not just a discipline that confines itself to experimentation with a small selection of mental phenomena. I know that critics of Indian religion will readily adopt such an evaluation. But the same approach can be applied to the study of all religions. That India should provide such materials more easily is due to a variety of circumstances: for example, the free and unhampered development of religion, and the importance of mental approaches (e.g., meditation) to the area of religion. Meditation is met with in almost all the domains of Indian civilization: it is practiced by kings (see illustration of King Jayavarman VII), by Gods (plate 1), by animals, and is frequently portrayed in the arts (plate 15). One feature of Indian thought in particular corroborates the hypothesis that religion may be studied as a branch of psychology: namely, the identification of the absolute *brahman* with the "self" (*ātman*). Though it is emphasized again and again that this self is not the empirical self (*jīvātman*) of our daily experience, it can undoubtedly be regarded as a psychological notion, albeit in a psychology which is suitably deepened and enlarged.

Among the causes of yogic powers enumerated by Patañjali, deities do not occur. (It is obvious that they are absent from the enumeration of the *Abhidharmakośa,* since Vasubandhu was a Buddhist.) But earlier in the *Yogasūtra,* Patañjali had stated that *samādhi* may also be gained through devotion to a deity (*īsvarapraṇidhāna*) (*Yogasūtra* 1.23; cf. 2.45). It does not matter whether such passages were inserted to bring the Yoga in line with theism. They show, supplementing our working hypothesis, that devotion to a deity may be regarded as another inducement producing a mystical state. This is only to be expected in theistic religion. Not surprisingly, successful meditation or prayer reinforces the belief in such a deity.

So far, the following causes may be assumed to be conducive to mystical experiences: birth, meditation, asceticism, drugs, mantras, *yantras,* special devices like *kasiṇa,* rituals, devotion to a deity. What is thereby obtained is access to a separate area of experience that is otherwise beyond reach, and that possesses characteristics and properties, and possibly connections with other areas of reality, about which little intelligible and reliable information is at present available.

The prevalent belief that mystical experiences (or at least the "real" ones) are divinely inspired is very similar to the age-old belief that dreams are divinely inspired. For countless millenia mankind has been puzzled by dreams, and people have therefore interpreted them as the signals of Gods, devils, or spirits. Presently we are beginning to suspect that most dreams, if not all, have very different origins. But humanity is still puzzled ("mystified" is the proper word) by mystical phenomena and mystical experiences. There are two simple hypotheses in the face of such a mystery: either deny that it exists at all, or else claim that it is a divine gift. With regard to mysticism, these are precisely the two prevalent views: the scientific view and the religious view. But since we have successfully abandoned both hypotheses with regard to dreams, it stands to reason that we may have to do the same with regard to mystical experiences.

The view that mysticism has nothing to do with Gods is not as revolutionary as it may sound, at least if we remember a well-known fact that is all too rarely taken into account: two of the great religions of the world, Theravāda Buddhism and Jainism, though replete with mysticism and "divine" personages, are atheistic. Buddhists and Jains have therefore never interpreted mystical experiences as divine gifts. The attitudes of Advaita Vedānta and of Taoism, though not identical, are in many respects similar. Advaita, moreover, adopted the Upaniṣadic view, that *mokṣa* and sleep are the same state, the difference being our awareness of the former and unawareness of the latter. Even if such awareness is believed to be divinely inspired, the state itself is not held to be caused by divine intervention. Just like awareness, the Gods may therefore be subjective, which does not mean imaginary. Such attitudes are certainly very different from the main currents of monotheistic religion in the West, which have colored the prevalent scholarly approaches to the exploration of mysticism.

If mystical experiences are removed from the realm of religion, their removal would in due course affect the notion and interpretation of religion itself. For it is not open to doubt that such experiences, when interpreted as divine inspirations, become the sources of many religious ideas and phenomena, if not of entire religions. Recent investigations have established that a similar role is played by drug-induced experiences—at least with reference to many so-called primitive religious cults and beliefs. The survey on "Hallucinogens of Plant Origin" that appeared in *Science* (Schultes 1969) is replete with references to the religion and magic of Asian, African, and especially (North, Central, and South) American Indian tribes. The same holds true for Heim's excellent monograph on hallucinogenic mushrooms (Heim 1963). We have seen that the case of Leary and Alpert adduces further evidence. In all these cases Marx's dictum: "religion . . . is the opium of the people" acquires special significance. But Wasson rightly stresses that this entire area is still largely unexplored: "Some are shocked that the key even to religion might be reduced to a mere drug. On the other hand, the drug is as mysterious as ever it was: 'like the wind it cometh we know not whence, nor why' " (Wasson 1972, p. 48).

It is the merit of Gordon Wasson to have defended the hypothesis that the experience of a hallucinogen constitutes an important source of one of the great religions of mankind, the Vedic religion, which, moreover, contains the origins of many later religious phenomena on the Indian subcontinent (Wasson 1968, 1970, 1971, 1972). Wasson's identification of the original Vedic Soma with the fly-agaric (*Amanita muscaria*) has been accepted or regarded as probable by some scholars (Kuiper 1970, Ingalls 1971), but it has been rejected by others (Brough 1971). However, this stronger thesis implies, but is not implied by, a weaker thesis, namely that the original Vedic Soma was a hallucinogenic plant. I regard this as the much more significant part of Wasson's hypothesis, which moreover has not to my knowledge been seriously challenged. I think in fact that the validity of this weaker hypothesis can be taken as established. A more detailed discussion of a few aspects of Wasson's theory will be taken up in an Appendix.

Even though this weaker thesis is probably correct, there are in the *Ṛgveda* not many detailed or specific descriptions of Soma-induced states of mind. But there is one hymn in the *Ṛgveda* which contains a fairly specific description of the effects of another hallucinogen, referred to as *viṣam*. This term, which is generally translated as "poison," cannot have that meaning in this context, where it is better rendered as "drug." This hymn of the *Ṛgveda* (10.136) is not only the earliest but one of the most impressive poetic descriptions of mystical experiences connected with the effects of a drug:

Long-hair holds fire, holds the drug, holds heaven and earth.
Long-hair opens everything under the sun. Long-hair declares it light.

These sages, swathed in wind, put dirty red tatters on.
When gods get in them, they ride with the rush of the wind.

"Crazy with wisdom, we have lifted ourselves to the wind.
Our bodies are all you merely mortals can see."

He sails through the air, seeing appearances spread out below.
The sage, this god and that his friend, friendly to all that's well-done.

The stallion of wind, companion of gales, and lashed on by gods—the sage.
He is home by two seas, the waters east and those of the west.

He moves in the motion of heavenly girls and youths, of beasts in the woods.
Long-hair, reading their minds, is their sweet and most pleasing companion.

The wind has stirred it, Kunaṃnamā prepared it for him.
Long-hair drinks from the cup, sharing the drug with Rudra.

This hymn contains a classical statement of the view I defended earlier: if we study mystics from the outside with behaviorist and physiological methods, all we can see is their bodies. I shall return to some other interesting issues raised by this hymn in the Appendix.

If my interpretation of these different facts is correct, we should conclude that a variety of mystical experiences (whether the effect of hidden mental processes, induced by drugs or other means, or combinations of these), which so far are unintelligible but need not have anything to do with a divine realm, tend to lead to religious beliefs or to the belief in Gods. At the present state of our knowledge that is still explaining *obscurum per obscurum*. But no longer, *per Obscurius*.

But let me return from speculation to the exploration of mysticism. Whatever else it may turn out to be in addition, the study of mysticism is at least in part the study of certain specific aspects of the mind. Mysticism and mystical experience cannot be understood in isolation from the more general problem of the nature of mind. Conversely, no theory of mind which cannot account for mystical experience can be adequate. Whether or not it is true that mysticism has little to do with religion, its study should not be left to philologists, historians, or phenomenologists of religion, for they have been singularly unsuccessful in formulating theories that offer adequate explanations. Such a study could be carried out by psychologists, if only we had the right kind of psychologists. But whoever undertakes it, he will have to put a stop to speculation and start a real investigation. Paradoxically, his first action may have to be contemplation under the guidance of a *guru*. No harm there, even if it yields, in addition to scholarly results, what Nāgārjuna called *dhyānasukham* "the joy of contemplation" (Lamotte 1949,

II, p. 1012: "joie de l'extase"). Without the joy of discovery the search for truth is incomplete. However, I don't think we shall find anything new unless we are convinced that what is lacking and needed most in the study of these aspects of the mind, is a combination of reason and an open mind.

Appendix

Hallucinogens in the *Ṛgveda*, and Other Matters

That Soma is not the only hallucinogen referred to in the *Ṛgveda* is clear from the long-hair hymn (above, pages 197–198). In each case the argument to establish that we are dealing with a hallucinogen would have to be along the lines adopted by Wasson in his theory about the Soma: (1) Soma was an inebriant; (2) Soma was not a fermented drink (see Wasson 1968, index, under "Soma and *súrā*").

Wasson laid great stress on the distinction between Soma, which is a hallucinogen and produces happiness (*mada*), and *surā*, which is an alcohol and produces evil intoxication (*durmada*) (Wasson 1968, p. 137). "Soma is truth, prosperity, light; and *surā*, untruth, misery, darkness" (*Śatapatha Brāhmaṇa* 5.1.2.10, quoted by Wasson, p. 95). The distinction continues to be made in India. Carstairs found in a village in Rajasthan that Rajputs drank *daru*, an alcoholic beverage, and felt guilty about it, while Brahmans took *bhang*, a hallucinogen, and approved of it. "Whereas the Rajput in his drinking bout knows that he is taking a holiday from his sober concerns, the Brahmin thinks of his intoxication with *bhang* as a flight not from but toward a more profound contact with reality" (Carstairs 1954, p. 235). Carstairs himself also came to regard *bhang* as superior to alcohol, but he considered *bhang* "so alien to his own cultural and personal pattern of ego defenses" that he didn't like it much (see also Carstairs 1957, p. 118).

The maintenance of a sharp distinction between an alcohol and a hallucinogen is not confined to India. Apart from the Siberian parallels, which Wasson refers to, Don Juan comments on peyote in the following terms: "Booze is what makes people crazy. It blurs the images. Mescalito, on the other hand, sharpens everything. It makes you see so very well. So very well!" (Castaneda 1971, p. 84).

If it is true that the Vedic Soma is a hallucinogen, it does not necessarily follow that some of the Soma hymns (e.g., *Rgveda* 10.119, which describes its effects to some extent) were composed under the influence of Soma. They "could easily have been composed by one without personal experience of the original *soma*" (Brough 1971, p. 341). A third possibility seems to be more likely, that the poet was himself familiar with the effects of the Soma, but was not under that influence when composing his poem. Similarly, battles described in the *Ṛgveda* and elsewhere were known to the poets from personal experience, but it does not follow that their poems were composed in battle.

While Brough's article (1971) contains valid criticisms of some of Wasson's statements, it should not be regarded as a decisive refutation of Wasson's theory. Moreover, Wasson has in a rejoinder (1972) pointed out inaccuracies, mistakes, and prejudices in Brough's paper, and has introduced several new themes into the discussion. Among the latter are further details about the preparation of the beverage from the plant: drying the plants, steeping them in water, and finally squeezing out the juice and consuming the juice mixed with other fluids (Wasson 1972, p. 42). If it is true that this method is the most effective one in bringing out the hallucinogenic properties of the fly-agaric, it certainly provides a strong argument for Wasson's theory, since the elaborate descriptions of the later Soma ritual are largely in agreement with such a procedure. But there are still elements that remain unexplained, such as the pounding of the plant. The only weakness that seems to be apparent in Wasson's theory is a certain unfalsifiability. A good theory should be liable to falsification. Theories which are true come what may and which can never be refuted by facts are uninformative, tautologous, or empty. In fact, apparent counterexamples to Wasson's theory can always be interpreted as consistent with the theory. When opponents point out, for example, that there are descriptions in the Veda which do not fit a mushroom, Wasson replies that the identity of the Soma was intentionally hidden by the Brahmans, or that these descriptions fit creepers and other substitutes. When the proponent of a theory is in a position to react in such a manner, the theory becomes unfalsifiable. Also, we have no means of determining whether Wasson's answers are correct, as they might well be. Although the theory has therefore not been refuted by such criticisms, the answers have not demonstrated its correctness either.

In general, criticisms of the kind made by Brough, and answers of the kind given by Wasson, are not going to be decisive in this matter.[1] Every theory has apparent flaws, and whether such flaws do constitute a refutation cannot be decided in isolation. The criticisms of Brough certainly raise problems. But none seems to be *incompatible* with the hypothesis that Soma was *Amanita muscaria*. *If* the Soma was a mushroom, special explanations would have to be given for these difficulties. On the other hand, Wasson's answers do not *establish* that the Soma was a mushroom.

Other tests of Wasson's theory, which would further determine its probability, are conceivable. The *Ṛgveda* mentions once where the best *SOMA* grew: on Mount Mūjavat (*Ṛgveda* 10.34.1). Other places are also mentioned explicitly: Śaryaṇāvat and the river Ārjīkīyā. If it were possible to identify these areas in the Hindu Kush region, it would be worthwhile to go and see what specific plants grow there at present. Archeological evidence of Soma implements in the same area is also not excluded: after all, green stone mortars and pestles, connected with the later *haoma* ceremony, were found by Schmidt in Persepolis. Though most of the Vedic ritual implements are now made of perishable materials (especially wood), reflecting their nomadic background, some of the Indo-European tribes might have settled temporarily in the Hindu Kush, where the Soma was so good, and there used more durable materials.

The only real test of Wasson's theory would be an alternative theory, offering another identification of the Soma plant. Theories are weakened, not refuted, by criticisms and objections; they are refuted only by other theories. Since there is at present no theory which offers another candidate for the identity of the Soma with the

1. With reference to *Ephedra*, one of the later substitutes for Soma, Brough (1971, p. 361) writes: "So far as I know, it has never been used as a substitute for Soma, and all the references to it in modern discussions of the Indian Soma appear to have been derived from Iranian information." However, the Nambudiri Brahmans of Kerala to the present day use *Ephedra vulgaris* for their Soma sacrifices. They obtain the plant from the territory of the former Raja of Kollangod in the Anaimalai Hills, where I accompanied them, found the creeper, and later had it identified (Staal 1964a).

same amount of seriousness and detail as does Wasson's theory, his identification stands in splendid isolation as the only, and therefore the best, theory.

The long-hair hymn, *Ṛgveda* 10.136—my translation was improved considerably by Leonard Nathan—requires further interpretation and raises further issues. (For textual problems in the hymn, see Renou 1967, pp. 170–171, and Renou 1966, p. 1.) The lady Kunamnamā (Hauer: *die bös sich Krümmende*: "badly turned") remains unidentified.

The wandering and moving of sages is characteristic of the *brahmacārins*, who were "going with *brahman*," and of the later *saṃnyāsins*, who were called, for example, *parivrājaka* "wandering person" or *paramahaṃsa* "highest goose." The wandering life of shepherds is also known to be conducive to mystic visions (Chadwick 1942, p. 59; plate 14a). The *Dhammapada* (13.9) speaks of geese going in the path of the sun and (hinting at levitation) of accomplished ascetics going through the sky. In Taoism, we find the same idea. The first chapter of Chuang Tzu's work is entitled "Free and Easy Wandering." Chuang Tzu used *yu* "to wander" to designate "the way in which the enlightened man wanders through all of creation, enjoying its delights without ever becoming attached to any one part of it" (Watson 1964, p. 6). These ideas may symbolize the journey of the soul, the shaman's heavenly ascent, and the mystic's rejection of conventional living. They may also be vestiges of the ancient nomadic life, viewed with nostalgia by a civilization that is beginning to become sedentary.

Wasson has drawn attention to a footnote in Caland and Henry (1906, p. 450): . . . *le sacrifice (fut) souvent métaphoriquement assimilé à une marche, un voyage, une expédition, et comportant d'ailleurs réellement un grand nombre d'évolutions processionelles* ("the sacrifice was often metaphorically assimilated to a march, a voyage, an expedition, and involved in fact a large number of procession-like movements"). Wasson comments, "In short, in that distant Aryan land Caland and Henry as early as 1906 gave us, in discussing Soma, a description of what today, in popular parlance, is called a 'trip.' The analogy with the Siberian tribesmen as well as with today's use of hallucinogens is manifest" (Wasson, 1972, p. 14).

The long hair of the Ṛgvedic sages symbolized their independence from the village civilization of the Vedic establishment. One of the ceremonies of the village ritual was the "first tonsure," to which all boys were subjected between the ages of three and five, depending on caste. This was followed by ritual shaving at the age of sixteen or later. At many larger rituals and sacrifices, the sacrificers had to have their hair and beard cut. There also was a ceremonial hair-cutting festival (*keśavapanīya*), which formed part of the ritual of royal consecration. The forest sages gave expression to their renouncement by letting their hair and beard grow; hence the term *keśin* (long-hair). Some famous sages adopted this description as their actual name, such as, Keśin Dārbhya, who was also a king. Among the Gods, Śiva the ascetic, successor to the Vedic Rudra mentioned in the last line of the poem, is always pictured with long hair (plates 3, 4 and 5). Kṛṣṇa, too, is called Keśava (Hare Krishna chanters shave their heads in spite of this).

Dandekar (1953), in an essay on the Vedic God Rudra, describes the main characteristics of the sages or *munis*, who looked upon Rudra as their leader: "These *munis* seem to have worn long hair and indulged in a sort of ecstasy-producing medicament. There are also indications that they attained certain miraculous or mystic powers which are comparable to the powers which are believed to be attained through *yoga*" (p. 99). Dandekar groups the *munis* together with other, similar kinds of wandering sages:

> The followers of the *vrātya*, the *brahmacārin*, and the *muni* cults did not adhere to the way of life and thought prescribed by the mechanised and ritualised religion of the Vedic poet-priests. For one thing, they were essentially *niragni*, that is to say, they had no faith in the efficacy of the Vedic ritual of which fire was the center. As against it, they had developed, on the one hand, peculiar practices of *yoga*, which helped them to attain magical and miraculous powers and, on the other, certain orgiastic practices, which facilitated what may be called religious ecstasy. Again, those *yogins* and *yatis* seem to have regarded isolation from normal social life as a *sine qua non* of truly spiritual life (Dandekar 1953, p. 137).

Arbman, who in his monograph on Rudra (1922) pays much attention to *Ṛgveda* 10.136, says that it depicts "the wild ecstatic roaming about of the god-possessed muni" (*das wild ekstatische Treiben des Götterbesessenen Muni*: Arbman 1922, p. 298), quotes

Oldenberg who had used similar expressions and also refers to the use of drugs by later ascetics, especially Śaivites. Gonda (1960, p. 85), also in a chapter on Rudra, refers to the *munis* as *Wildekstatikern* ("wild ecstatics"); Hauer (1958, pp. 29–30) offering a translation of hymn 10.136, relates the term for drug, *viṣam*, to Gaelic *whisge* (whence *whisky*; but Monier-Williams' Sanskrit dictionary relates *viṣam* to Greek *ἰός* and Latin *virus*), and refers in this connection to drug use (*Hanf, Opium, Stechapfel usw.*) among contemporary *yogins* "of the more common kind" *(der niederen Sorte)*. Hauer also emphasizes that the term "long-hair" was widely used (for Rudra himself; for Vāyu, the wind; for Durgā, the consort of Śiva; and for their followers; for others thus described, including a demon called *munikeśa*, see Renou 1967, p. 171). Eliade (1954, p. 13) rejects any special connection with Yoga, but attempts to relate some features of the description offered by the poet to shamanistic beliefs.

In later times, the term *viṣam* generally means "poison" (Geldner [1951] wrongly translates it thus in *Ṛgveda* 10.136: *Gifttrank*), and Śiva is called Nīlakaṇṭha ("blue-throat") because he drank the poison Halāhala or Kālakūṭa, which threatened to destroy the universe after the churning of the world ocean had taken place (see, e.g., Arbman 1922, p. 303). However, *halāhala* may also refer to a lizard, a snake, or a Jaina or Buddhist sage (though *halā* is used to address one's girlfriend); *kālakūṭa* is literally a darkish lump (like dried hemp); and Nīlakaṇṭha, in later Śaivite theology, is interpreted as "liberator" (cf. *vijayā* "victory," a later Sanskrit term for hemp, which occurs in the *Mahānirvāṇatantra*, for instance). The myth about Śiva's swallowing of poison, therefore, may be partly based upon misinterpretations of terms. But it could also be argued that the quantity administered determines the meaning of *viṣam*: what in small quantities is a hallucinogen, in large quantities becomes a poison.

This distinction is confirmed by later texts. The *Hevajratantra* contains several passages that may refer to hallucinogens which, when taken in large quantity, are poisonous. The Sanskrit term used in each case is *viṣam*: "With the very poison, a little of which would kill any other being, a man who understands poison would dispel another poison" (Snellgrove 1959, I, p. 93). "If he drinks strong poison, the simple man who does not understand it, falls senseless. But he who is free from delusion with his mind intent on the truth destroys it altogether" (p. 107).

Lastly, this tantric text introduces "the profoundest secret of the beauteous purifier of existence." This is likened to a gem, because "useless is a gem uncut, but once cut, it gives forth its brilliance. Likewise this gem of the *saṃsāra*, possessed of the properties of the five desires, becomes like poison in its unpurified state, but when purified it becomes ambrosia" (p. 117). The second of these statements is not only reminiscent of Śiva as Nīlakaṇṭha, but accords with the story of Alpert that he gave 915 micrograms of LSD to a yogin, who swallowed it without apparent effect (Alpert 1971, no page number).

Śiva's predecessor, the Vedic Rudra, who took drugs but not poison, was already described as *nīlagrīva* ("blue-neck") in such texts as *Taittirīyasaṃhitā* 4.5.1.8, though he was red all over the rest of his body (see, e.g., *Śatapatha-brāhmaṇa* 9.1.1.24, and Dandekar 1953, p. 97, and the references listed there).

For the hair-cutting ceremonies and their significance, see Hillebrandt 1897, p. 50, and especially Heesterman 1957, pp. 212–219. Heesterman (1957, pp. 106–107) also refers to a section of the royal unction ritual where a piece of lead or copper is kicked toward or thrown into the mouth of a long-haired person (*keśava*). The *Satapatha-brāhmaṇa* (5.4.1.2.) explains this as follows: "And as to why it is of a long-haired man—such a long-haired man is neither woman nor man; for being male, he is not a woman, and being long-haired, he is not a man. And copper is neither iron nor gold . . ." etc. (translated by Eggeling 1894, III, p. 90). In other, similar texts, the long-haired man is regarded as a eunuch (*klība, paṇḍaga*). It would be farfetched to read this meaning into the Ṛgvedic hymn, where only a certain impartiality with regard to girls, youths, and beasts may be observed.

About Keśin Dārbhya, see Heesterman 1962, p. 16; Tsuji 1966a, 1966b, 1971; and Sreekrishna Sarma 1968. The latter draws attention to a neglected passage in the *Jaiminīya-brāhmaṇa* (2.100–102), where King Keśin Dārbhya is worried about not being respected by his subjects: "even children used to call him *darbha*" (meaning "grass"). As a matter of fact, Keśin Dārbhya consecrated himself by sitting upon sacred *darbha* grass. There he was visited by Sutvā, the son of Yājñasena, who appeared in the form of a golden goose. King

Long-Hair addressed this resplendent visitor rather unexpectedly as *śunīti*, or "you bitch!"—as Caland and Keith, the foremost Western interpreters of this passage, correctly translated. Additional confirmation of this quite unoriental breach of hospitality comes from the continuation of the text, which describes King Keśin as immediately getting into a fit of anger. But Sreekrishna Sarma has now shown that the reading underlying this translation is based upon the wrong identification of a letter in the Grantha manuscript (reading *keśi śunīti* instead of *keśiȝnn iti*, the latter form with a lengthened "ī" lasting three time beats), so that the passage merely means that Sutvā loudly called the king by his name, Keśin. This naturally angered Keśin Dārbhya, for a consecrated person, let alone a king, should never be called by his name, and certainly not shouted at.

The ascetic features of the long-haired Śiva are well-known. In his manifestation as king of the dance (*naṭarāja*), Śiva's long flowing hair becomes the origin of India's rivers, especially the Ganges, which descends from his head (see above, pages 78–79). Also in his dances of destruction (like the killing and flaying of the elephant demon, *gajasaṃhāramūrti*: plate 4), Śiva's hair is long and it may be matted, as is the hair of yogins and ascetics. When Śiva is pictured as a wandering ascetic (*bhikṣāṭanamūrti*: plate 3), the matted hair is adorned with the same objects we find in the *Naṭarāja* manifestation: a skull, a cobra, a crescent moon, and the blossoms of the hallucinogenic datura plant (*dhurdhura*). It may be recalled how Don Juan taught Castaneda that the "third head" of datura is in the flowers, "and it is used to turn people crazy, or to make them obedient, or to kill them" (Castaneda 1968, p. 48).

As might be predicted, the Christian position on hair is irrational. I Corinthians 11:14 teaches that long hair is a shame to men and a glory to women. But actually, nuns' heads are shaved and their bridegroom Christ, like God himself, is invariably portrayed with hair of shoulder length.

Glossary

Terms not otherwise specified are in Sanskrit.

abhijñā, (1) recollection; (2) miraculous power
abhyāsa, repetition, practice
adhyāropa, superimposition
agni, fire
agnihotra, daily fire ritual
ahl (Arabic), people
ānanda, joy, bliss
anātmavāda, doctrine of the non-self
anirukta, unexpressed
aparavidyā, lower knowledge
araṇya, forest
artha, meaning, reference, thing
arthavāda, explanation (of purpose)
asaṃprajñāta, unconscious (of external objects)
asmi, "I am"
asmitā, awareness of the ego
āśrama, stage of life
aṣṭāṅga, eight-limbed
ātman, self
ātmavāda, doctrine of the self
āvaraṇa, obstruction
avasthā, state
āveśa, entry
avidyā, ignorance
āya (Arabic), sign, miracle, verse of the Koran
bandha, bond, fetter
bhakti, loving devotion (plate 9)
bhang (Hindi), *Cannabis sativa*
bhaṅga, (1) breaking, bursting; (2) hemp
bhāṣya, commentary
bhāva, state, mode of existence
bhāvanā, conception, thought, impression, meditation
bhikṣā, begging for alms (cf. plate 3)
bhikṣu (Pali: *bhikku*), monk
bhūmi, world, level
brahmacārin, (1) who goes with *brahman*; (2) student; (3) celibate
brahmacārya, (1) going with *brahman*; (2) study; (3) celibacy
brahman, absolute principle
cakra, (1) wheel; (2) nerve, center (plate 10b)
caturtha, fourth
catuṣkoṭi, tetralemma
citta, mind
dakṣiṇa, ***dakṣiṇā***, south
darbha, a kind of grass
darśana, viewpoint, (Hindu) school of philosophy
daru (Hindi), an alcoholic beverage
dhāraṇā, concentration

dharma, (1) duty, right, moral law; (2) (in Buddhism) element
dhikr (Arabic), repetition, recitation
dhīra, wise, experienced, gifted with vision
dhīti, vision
dhiyā(lamba), (support of) contemplation
dhurdhura, datura plant
dhyāna, meditation
dhyāyin, ecstatic
dīkṣā, initiation, consecration
dṛṣṭi, view
duḥkha, suffering, ill
durmada, intoxication
duścara, difficult to perform
dvandva, pair
ekāgra, one-pointed, concentrated
gaja, elephant (cf. plate 4)
gāna, chant
gandūz (Turkish), pupil, novice
gata, gone
gopura, (temple) gateway
granthi, knot, tie
gṛhastha, householder
guru, (1) heavy; (2) teacher (plate 5)
haṃsa, goose
haoma (Avestan) Soma
haṭhayoga, kind of Yoga emphasizing physical exercises
hetu, reason
*isrā*ʾ (Arabic), nocturnal journey (of Muhammad) (plate 12)
īśvara, God
iʿtikāf (Arabic), spiritual retreat
janma, birth, origin
jīvātman, empirical self
jñāna, knowledge, insight (plate 16)
jñānaniṣṭha, firmly established in knowledge
jñeya, object of knowledge
kaivalya, isolation
kāritra, activity
karman, (ritual) activity, action (plate 6)
karma-phala-tyāga, detachment from the fruits of action
kasiṇa (Pali), device for concentration
κατὰ τὸ αὐτό (Greek), in the same respect
keśa, hair
keśava, having (long) hair
keśavapanīya, hair-cutting festival
keśin, having (long) hair
kitāb (Arabic), book
kleśa, passion, attachment
klība, eunuch
kōan (Japanese), old saying; problem case
koṭi, ten million
kṣipta, scattered
kuṇḍalinī, (1) decorated with earrings (kuṇḍala); (2) a form of Yoga (plate 10b)
kung-an (Chinese), old saying; problem case
liṅga, (1) mark, sign; (2) penis
mada, inspiration; exhilaration
madya, wine
mahāvākya, great sentence, great statement (especially of the Upaniṣads)
maithuna, sexual intercourse
māṃsa, meat
manas, mind
mānasa, mental
maṇḍala, circle, mystic diagram (plates 11a–b)
mantra, sacred formula, spell, sacred syllable(s)
matsya, fish

māyā, appearance, magic, unreality
medhāvin, sensible, judicious
*mi*ʿ*raj* (Arabic), (1) ascension of Muhammad; (2) mystic ascent (plate 12)
moha, folly, delusion
mokṣa, liberation, freedom, release
mūḍha, confused
mudrā, (1) parched grain; (2) gesture; (3) the woman participating in Tantric ceremonies
muni, (1) silent person; (2) sage; (3) follower of a non-Vedic cult
murīd (Arabic), (1) desirous; (2) pupil, novice
murshid (Arabic), teacher
naṭarāja, king of the dance
nīlagrīva, (having a) blue neck (i.e., Śiva)
niragni, without fire
nirodha, cessation
nirvāṇa, liberation, extinction
nitya, permanent, eternal
oṣadhi, drug, herb
paṇḍaga, eunuch
paṇḍita, learned, scholar(ly)
paramārtha-satya, ultimate truth
pāramārthika, ultimate
paramparā, lineage
paraśarīrāveśa, entry of another body
paravidyā, higher knowledge
parivrājaka, wandering person
paryudāsa, negation of a term
phala, fruit, result
pir (Persian), teacher
prabhāva, manifestation, supernatural power
pradakṣiṇā, clockwise circumambulation
prahāṇa, vanishing
prajñā, wisdom, insight (plate 8)
prāṇa, breath
prāṇapratiṣṭhā, establishment of breath, infusion with breath
prāṇāyāma, breathing practice, breathing exercise
praṇidhāna, devotion (to God)
prapatti, surrender (to God) (plate 7)
prasajya-pratiṣedha, negation of a predicate
prasaṅga, reductio ad absurdum
pratibhāsa, error
prātibhāsika, erroneous, relating to error
pratijñā, proposition
pratīka, symbol
pratyāhāra, withdrawal (of the senses)
puruṣa, person, spirit
puruṣabuddhyapekṣa, depending on man's notions, subjective
puruṣatantra, depending on man, subjective
rahasya, secret
rājayoga, royal Yoga
retas, semen
ṛddhi, magical, supernatural power
ṛṣi, seer, composer of Vedic hymn
sādhanā, means of establishing; religious practice
sādhya, (1) to be established; (2) to be inferred, inferendum
samādhi, (1) attention; (2) state of yogic absorption
samāpatti, encounter, contemplation, a stage of meditation
sāṃkhya, (1) number, enumeration; (2) a system of philosophy
saṃnyāsa, renunciation
saṃnyāsin, renouncer
saṃprajñāta, conscious (of external objects)
saṃsāra, transmigration

saṃskāra, (1) perfection; (2) purification; (3) rite of passage; (4) mental impression
samuccaya, combination
saṃvṛti-satya, lower truth, empirical truth
saṃyama, stage of meditation
sandhābhāṣa, esoteric language (in Tantrism)
śastra, (1) weapon; (2) type of ritual recitation (of the *Ṛgveda*)
śāstra, scripture
satya, truth
shaikh (Arabic), teacher
shaṭḥ (Arabic), ecstatic exclamation
siddha, established
siddhi, achievement, miraculous power
silsila (Arabic), (spiritual) lineage
skandha, (1) shoulder; (2) (in Buddhism) constituent of human being
smṛti, (1) memory; (2) tradition
Soma, (1) a hallucinogenic plant, possibly the mushroom *Amanita muscaria*; (2) juice extracted from that plant; (3) the moon
śraddhā, confidence, trust
sthira, hard, firm
stobha, meaningless syllable inserted in a melody (in the *Sāmaveda*)
sudāruṇa, severe
śūdra, low caste
sukha, pleasant, joyful
śūnya, empty
śūnyatā, void, emptiness
surā, an alcoholic beverage
sūtra, (1) rule, formula, aphorism; (2) text consisting of such rules
svarga, heaven, paradise
tapas, heat; austerity (plate 2)
turīya, fourth; fourth state of consciousness
tyāga, detachment; abandon
uḍḍiyāna, a particular position of the fingers
upapattilābhika, inborn
upāsanā, contemplation
upāya, means
ūrdhva, straight
vairāgya, detachment
virāga, detachment
vanaprastha, forest-dweller, hermit
varṇa, caste
varnāśramadharma, duty in accordance with one's stage in life and caste
vaśa, will, wish
vāsanā, mental impression
vastutantra, depending on things, objective
veda, (1) knowledge; (2) one of the Vedas
vedānta, (1) end of knowledge; (2) the Upaniṣads; (3) a system of philosophy
vibhūti, miracle, miraculous power
vicāra, consideration, analysis
vidhi, injunction (especially of the Veda)
vidyā, knowledge
vijayā, (1) victory; (2) hemp
vikalpa, (1) option; (2) imagination
vikṣipta, distracted
virodhī, contradicting, contradictory
viruddha, contradicted
viṣam, poison, drug
vitarka, doubt, deliberation, uncertainty
vivarta, superimposition (especially of an effect upon a cause)
vrātya, follower of a non-Vedic cult

vṛtti, fluctuation
vyākaraṇa, grammar, analysis
vyākhyāna, commentary, gloss (cf. plate 5)
vyavahāra, ordinary reality
vyāvahārika, ordinary, empirical
yajamāna, sacrificer, patron of the sacrifice
yantra, diagram, instrument (title page; plates 11 a–b)
yati, sage, ascetic
Yoga, (1) method; (2) spiritual and physical discipline; (3) a system of philosophy
yogin, a person engaged in Yoga
yu (Chinese), to wander

Bibliography

Alpert, R. (1971), *Be Now Here*, San Cristóbal, Venezuela.

Anesaki, M. (1963), *History of Japanese Religion with Special Reference to the Social and Moral Life of the Nation*, Rutland, Vt., and Tokyo.

Arberry, A. J. (1962), "Bistamiana," *Bulletin of the School of Oriental and African Studies* 25.28–37.

Arbman, E. (1922), *Rudra: Untersuchungen zum altindischen Glauben und Kultus*, Uppsala.

Avalon, A. (1948), *Wave of Bliss: Ānandalaharī*, Madras.

Benoît, H. (1955), *The Supreme Doctrine: Psychological Studies in Zen Thought*, transl., Terence Gray, New York.

Benz, E. (1951), *Indische Einflüsse auf die früchristliche Theologie*, Wiesbaden.

Bergson, H. (1935), *The Two Sources of Morality and Religion*, transl. R. A. Audra and C. Brereton, London.

Berreman, G. D. (1972), *Hindus of the Himalayas: Ethnography and Change*, Berkeley, Los Angeles, London.

Bharatha Iyer, K. (1955), *Kathakali: the sacred dance-drama of Malabar*, London.

Bharati, A. (1965), "Śākta and Vajrayāna, their place in Indian thought," *Studies of Esoteric Buddhism and Tantrism*, Koyasan, pp. 73–99.

Bharati, A. (1970), *The Tantric Tradition*, New York.

Bhattacharya, K. (1971), "The dialectical method of Nāgārjuna," *Journal of Indian Philosophy*, 1.217–261.

Bloomfield, M. (1917), "On the art of entering another's body: a Hindu fiction motif," *Proceedings of the American Philosophical Society*, 56.1–43.

Bocheński, I. M. (1951), *Ancient Formal Logic*, Amsterdam.

Bodas, R. S. (ed.) (1892), *Pātañjalasūtrāṇi*, Bombay.

Boehtlingk, O. (1870), *Indische Sprüche*, I, St. Petersburg. (Reprint Osnabrück and Wiesbaden, 1966).

Boetzelaer, J. M. van (1971), Sureśvara's *Taittirīyopaniṣadbhāṣyavārtikam*, Leiden.

Bréhier, E. (ed. and transl.) (1924–1936), *Plotin: Ennéades*, I–VI, Paris.

Brosse, Th. (1963), *Etudes instrumentales des techniques du Yoga: Expérimentation psychosomatique*, Paris.

Brough, J. (1962), *The Gandhārī Dharmapada*, Oxford.

Brough, J. (1971), "Soma and *Amanita muscaria*," *Bulletin of the School of Oriental and African Studies*, 34.331–362.

Brunner, E. (1930), *Gott und Mensch: Vier Untersuchungen über das personhafte Sein*, Tübingen.

Brunschvicg, L. (ed.) (1957), *Pascal: Pensées*, Paris.

Burckhardt, T. (1971), *Alchemy: Science of the Cosmos—Science of the Soul*, Baltimore.

Cahill, J. (1972), *Scholar Painters of Japan: the Nanga School*, New York.

Caland, W., and V. Henry (1906), *L'Agniṣṭoma: description complète de la forme normale du sacrifice de soma dans le culte védique*, I–II, Paris.

Carroll, Lewis (1963), *Alice's Adventures in Wonderland* and *Through the Looking Glass*, Harmondsworth.

Carstairs, G. M. (1954), "Daru and bhang: cultural factors in the choice of intoxicant," *Quarterly Journal of Studies on Alcohol* 15.220–237.

Carstairs, G. M. (1957), *The Twice-born*, London.

Castaneda, C. (1968), *The Teachings of Don Juan: A Yaqui Way of Knowledge*, Berkeley and Los Angeles.

Castaneda, C. (1971), *A Separate Reality: Further Conversations with Don Juan*, New York.

Castaneda, C. (1972), *The Journey to Ixtlan*, New York.

Catalfomo, P., and C. H. Eugster (1970), "*Amanita muscaria*: present understanding of its chemistry," *Bulletin on Narcotics* 22:4.33–41.

Cazeneuve, J. (1959), "Le peyotisme au Nouveau-Mexique: notes sur une nouvelle religion," *Revue philosophique* 149.169–182.

Chadwick, N. K. (1942), *Poetry and Prophecy*, Cambridge.

Chihara, C. S., and J. A. Fodor (1965), "Operationalism and Ordinary Language: A Critique of Wittgenstein," *American Philosophical Quarterly* 2.281–295.

Chomsky, N. (1961), "On the Notion 'Rule of Grammar,'" *Proceedings of the Twelfth Symposium in Applied Mathematics* 12.6–24. Also published in Fodor and Katz (1964, pp. 119–136).

Chomsky, N. (1965), *Aspects of the Theory of Syntax*, Cambridge, Mass.

Claridge, G. (1972), *Drugs and Human Behaviour*, Harmondsworth.

Clausen, J. (1951), "Respiration movement in normal, neurotic, and psychotic subjects," *Journal of Mental Science* 97.189.

Coedès, G. (1967), *The making of South East Asia*, transl. H.M. Wright, Berkeley and Los Angeles.

Conze, E. (1951), *Buddhism: Its Essence and Development*, New York.

Conze, E. (1956), *Buddhist Meditation*, New York and Evanston, Ill.

Conze, E. (1962), *Buddhist Thought in India: Three Phases of Buddhist Philosophy*, London.

Corbin, H. (1969), *Creative Imagination in the Sūfism of Ibn ʿArabī*, Princeton.

Cornford, F. M. (1923), *Greek Religious Thought from Homer to the Age of Alexander*, London and Toronto.

Coster, G. (1934), *Yoga and Western Psychology: A Comparison*, London.

Cullman, O. (1948), *Christus und die Zeit: Die Urchristliche Zeit- und Geschichtsauffassung*, Zurich.

Dales, G. F. (1968), "Of dice and men," *Journal of the American Oriental Society* 88.14–23.

Dandekar, R. N. (1953), "Rudra in the Veda," *Journal of the University of Poona* 1.94–148.

Danielou, A. (1955), *Yoga: The Method of Re-integration*, New York.

Danto, A. C. (1972), *Mysticism and Morality: Oriental Thought and Moral Philosophy*, New York.

Dasgupta, S. C. (1922–1932), *A History of Indian Philosophy*, I–II, Cambridge.

Deikman, A. J. (1963), "Experimental meditation," *Journal of Nervous and Mental Disease* 136.329–343.

Deikman, A. J. (1966), "Implications of experimentally induced contemplative meditation," *Journal of Nervous and Mental Disease* 142.101–116.

de la Vallée Poussin, L. (ed.) (1903–1913), *Prasannapadā nāma mādhyamikavṛtti*, St. Petersburg (Leningrad).

de la Vallée Poussin, L. (transl.) (1923–1931), *L'Abhidharmakośa de Vasubandhu*, 6 vols., Paris.

Dodds, E. R. (1928), "The Parmenides and the Neoplatonic One," *Classical Quarterly* 22.129–143.

Dodds, E. R. (1957), *The Greeks and the Irrational*, Boston.

Dumont, L. (1953), "Définition structurale d'un dieu populaire tamoul: Aiya-Nār, le Maître," *Journal asiatique* 241.255–270.

Dumont, L. (1959), "Le renoncement dans les religions de l'Inde," *Archives de Sociologie des Religions* 7.45–69.

Dumont, L. (1960), "World renunciation in Indian religions," *Contributions to Indian Sociology* 4.33–62.

Dumont, L. (1966), *Homo Hierarchicus: essai sur le système des castes*, Paris.

Eggeling, J. (transl.) (1882–1900), *The Śatapatha-Brāhmaṇa According to the Text of the Mādhyandina School*, I–V, Oxford.

Eliade, M. (1951), *Le chamanisme et les techniques archaïques de l'extase*, Paris = (1964) *Shamanism: Archaic Techniques of Ecstasy*, transl. W. R. Trask, London.

Eliade, M. (1954), *Le Yoga: immortalité et liberté*, Paris = (1969) *Yoga: Immortality and Freedom*, transl. W. R. Trask, Princeton.

Eliot, C. (1954), *Hinduism and Buddhism: An Historical Sketch*, I–III, London.

Faddegon, B. (1906), *Çaṃkara's Gītābhāṣya, toegelicht en beoordeeld*, Amsterdam.

Filliozat, J. (1946), "Les origines d'une technique mystique indienne," *Revue philosophique* 136.208–220.

Filliozat, J. (1949), *La doctrine classique de la medicine indienne*, Paris.

Fischer, R. (1958), "Pharmacology and metabolism of mescalin," *Revue Canadienne de Biologie* 17.389–409.

Fodor, J. A., and J. J. Katz (1964), *The Structure of Language: Readings in the Philosophy of Language*, Englewood Cliffs, N. J.

Fontein, J., R. Soekmono, and S. Suleiman (1971), *Ancient Indonesian Art*, New York.

Frauwallner, E. (1953), *Geschichte der indischen Philosophie*, I, Salzburg.

Freud, S. (1953), *The Interpretation of Dreams*, transl. J. Strachey, I, London.

Freud, S. (1957), *Civilization and Its Discontents*, transl. J. Rivière, London.

Gauthier, L. (1948), *Ibn Rochd (Averroès)*, Paris.

Geertz, C. (1960), *The Religion of Java*, Glencoe, Ill.

Gelblum, T. (1962), Review of Zaehner (1960), *Bulletin of the School of Oriental and African Studies* 25.173–176.

Geldner, K. F. (transl.) (1951), *Der Rig-Veda*, I–III, Cambridge, Mass.

Gilson, E. (1952), *La philosophie au moyen âge*, Paris.

Gilson, E. (1955), *Christian Philosophy in the Middle Ages*, London.

Gombrich, R. F. (1971), *Precept and Practice: Traditional Buddhism in the Rural Highlands of Ceylon*, Oxford.

Gonda, J. (1959), *Four Studies in the Language of the Veda*, The Hague.

Gonda, J. (1960), *Die Religonen Indiens*, I, Stuttgart.

Gonda, J. (1963), *The Vision of the Vedic Poets*, The Hague.

Gonda, J. (1965), *Change and Continuity in Indian Religion*, The Hague.

Gonda, J. (1970), *Viṣṇuism and Śivaism: A Comparison*, London.

Gorton, B. E. (1962), "Current problems of physiological research in hypnosis," in G. H. Estabrooks (ed.), *Hypnosis: Current Problems*, New York and Evanston, Ill.

Graham, A. C. (1960), *The Book of Lieh-tzŭ*, London.

Graham, A. C. (1969), "Chuang Tzu's essay on seeing things as equal," *History of Religions*, 9.137–159.

Hacker, P. (1950), *Untersuchungen über Texte des frühen Advaitavāda, I: Die Schüler Śaṅkaras*, Wiesbaden.

Hacker, P. (1960), *Prahlāda. Werden und Wandlungen einer Idealgestalt*, *Beiträge zur Geschichte des Hinduismus*, I–II, Wiesbaden.

Hacker, P. (1965), "Relations of early Advaitins to Vaiṣṇavism," *Wiener Zeitschrift für die Kunde Süd- und Ostasiens und Archiv für indische Philosophie* 9.147–154.

Hacker, P. (1968), "Śaṅkara der Yogin und Śaṅkara der Advaitin," *Festschrift für Erich Frauwallner*, Vienna, pp. 119–148.

Hanson, A. S. (1970), "Buddhism and logic," *Middle Way* 45.70–72.

Hara, M. (1963–1964), "Note on two Sanskrit religious terms: *bhakti* and *śraddhā*," *Indo-Iranian Journal* 7.124–145.

Hara, M. (1968–1969), "Transfer of merit," *Adyar Library Bulletin* 31–32, 382–411.

Hara, M. (1970), "Tapo-dhana," *Acta Asiatica* 19.58–76.

Harle, J. C. (1963), *Temple Gateways of South India*, Oxford.

Hattori, M. (1968), *Dignāga, On Perception*, Cambridge, Mass.

Hauer, J. W. (1932, 1958), *Der Yoga: Ein indischer Weg zum Selbst*, Stuttgart.

Heesterman, J. C. (1957), *The Ancient Indian Royal Consecration*, The Hague.

Heesterman, J. C. (1962), "Vrātya and Sacrifice," *Indo-Iranian Journal* 6.1–37.

Heiler, F. (1918), *Die buddhistische Versenkung: eine religions-geschichtliche Untersuchung*, Munich.

Heim, R. (1963), *Les champignons toxiques et hallucinogènes*, Paris.

Hilgard, E. R. (1971), "Hypnotic phenomena: the struggle for scientific acceptance," *American Scientist* 59:5.567–577.

Hillebrandt, A. (1897), *Ritual-Literatur, Vedische Opfer und Zauber*, Strasbourg.

Hiriyanna, M. (ed.) (1925), *The Naiṣkarmya-siddhi of Sureśvarācārya*, Poona.

Hooykaas, C. (1966), *Sūrya-Sevana: The Way to God of a Balinese Śiva Priest*, Amsterdam.

Hopkins, E. W. (1901), "Yoga-technique in the great epic," *Journal of the American Oriental Society* 22.333–379.

Hubert, H., and M. Mauss (1909), "L'origine des pouvoirs magiques dans les sociétés australiennes," in *Mélanges d'histoire des religions*, Paris, pp. 131–187.

Huizinga, J. (1947), *Herfsttij der middeleeuwen*, Haarlem.

Huxley, A. (1946), *The Perennial Philosophy*, London.

Huxley, A. (1963), *The Doors of Perception* and *Heaven and Hell*, New York. (Combined edition.)

Ingalls, D. H. H. (1971), "Remarks on Mr. Wasson's *Soma*," *Journal of the American Oriental Society* 91.188–191.

Iyângâr, S. (transl.) (1893), *The Haṭha Yoga Pradīpikā*, Bombay.

Jacobs, H. (1961), *Western Psychotherapy and Hindu Sâdhanâ: A Contribution to Comparative Studies in Psychology and Metaphysics*, London.

Jaspers, K. (1948), *Der philosophische Glauben*, Zurich.

Jayatilleke, K. N. (1963), *Early Buddhist Theory of Knowledge*, London.

Jong, J. W. de (1949), *Cinq chapitres de la Prasannapadā*, Leiden.

Joos, M. (1947), *Theoretical Physics*, London and Glasgow.

Jung, C. G. (1944), *Psychologie und Alchemie*, Zurich.

Kajiyama, Y. (1957), "Bhāvaviveka and the Prāsaṅgika school," ("Introduction to the logic of the Svātantrika Mādhyamika philosophy"), *Nava-Nalanda Mahavihara Research Publication* 1.201–331.

Kajiyama, Y. (1973), "Three kinds of affirmation and two kinds of negation in Buddhist philosophy," *Wiener Zeitschrift für die Kunde Südasiens* 17.161–175.

Kaltenmark, M. (1969), *Lao Tzu and Taoism*, Stanford, Calif.

Kamiya, J. (1961), "Behavioral, subjective and physiological aspects of drowsiness and sleep," in D. W. Fiske and S. R. Maddi (eds.), *Functions of Varied Experience*, Homewood, Ill.

Kamiya, J. (1969), "Operant control of the EEG alpha rhythm and some of its reported effects on consciousness," in C. T. Tart (ed.) (1969), pp. 507–517.

Kasamatsu, A., and T. Hirai (1966), "An electroencephalographic study on the Zen meditation (Zazen)," *Folia Psychiatrica et Neurologica Japonica* 20.315–336.

Kosambi, D. D. (1965), *Ancient India: A History of Its Culture and Civilization*, New York.

Krishnaswami Aiyangar, S. (1917), "The Antiquities of Mahabalipur," *Indian Antiquary* 46.49–57 and 65–73.

Kuiper, F. B. J. (1970), Review of Wasson (1968), *Indo-Iranian Journal* 12.279–285.

Kuppuswami Sastri, S. (ed.) (1937), *Brahmasiddhi by Ācārya Maṇḍanamiśra*, Madras.

La Barre, W. (1970), *The Peyote Cult*, New York.

Labriolle, P. de (ed. and transl.) (1925), *Saint Augustin: Confessions*, I–II, Paris.

Lamotte, E. (1944–1970), *Le traité de la grande vertu de sagesse de Nāgārjuna*, Vol. I, 1944; Vol. II, 1949; Vol. III, 1970, Louvain.

Lamotte, E. (1958), *Histoire du bouddhisme indien*, Louvain.

Lancaster, L. R. (1975), "Samādhi Names in Buddhist Texts," *Malalasekara Memorial Volume*.

Leach, E. R. (1961), *Rethinking Anthropology*, London.

Leeuw, G. van der (1955), *La religion dans son essence et ses manifestations*, Paris.

Levenson, J. R., and F. Schurmann (1969), *China: An Interpretive History*, Berkeley and Los Angeles.

Levy, J., and J. F. Staal (1968), *The Four Vedas*, New York: Asch Mankind/Folkways (record album).

Lindquist, S. (1932), *Die Methoden des Yoga*, Lund.

Lindquist, S. (1935), *Siddhi und Abhiñña: Eine Studie über die klassischen Wunder des Yoga*, Uppsala.

Lucius, E. (1904), *Die Anfänge des Heiligenkults in der christlichen Kirche*, Tübingen.

Lüders, H. (1959), *Varuṇa*, II, Göttingen.

Mahadevan, T. M. P. (1957), *The Philosophy of Advaita with Special Reference to Bhāratītīrtha-Vidyāraṇya*, Madras.

Mahadevan, T. M. P. (1958), *The Saṁbandha-Vārtika of Sureśvarācārya*, Madras.

Mahadevan, T. M. P. (1960), *Gauḍapāda: A Study in Early Advaita*, Madras.

Maspero, H. (1950), *Le taoisme*, Paris.

Massignon, L. (1922), *La passion d'al-Hallâj, martyre mystique de l'Islam*, I–II, Paris.

Massignon, L. (1954), *Essai sur les origines du lexique technique de la mystique musulmane*, Paris.

Massignon, L. (1963), *Opera minora*, II, Beirut.

Matilal, B. K. (1971), *Epistemology, Logic, and Grammar in Indian Philosophical Analysis*, The Hague and Paris.

Maxwell, N. (1972), *India's China War*, Garden City, N.Y.

May, J. (1959), *Candrakīrti Prasannapadā Madhyamakavṛtti*, Paris.

Mehta, V. (1971), "Onward and upward with the arts: John is easy to please," *New Yorker*, May 8, pp. 44–87.

Merlan, P. (1953), *From Platonism to Neoplatonism*, The Hague.

Merleau-Ponty, M. (1962), *Phenomenology of Perception*, transl. C. Smith, London.

Meuli, K. (1935), "Scythica," *Hermes* 70.121–176.

Monchanin, J. (1956), "Yoga et Hésichasme," in *Entretiens 1955*, Pondicherry.

Murti, T. R. V. (1955), *The Central Philosophy of Buddhism: A Study of the Mādhyamika System*, London.

Nagao, G. M. (1954), "The interpretation of the term *saṁvṛti* (convention) in Buddhism," *Silver Jubilee Volume of the Zinbun-Kagaku-Kenkyusyo*, Kyoto, pp. 550–561.

Nakamura, H. (1954), "Kūgan no kigō-ronrigakuteki kaimei," *Journal of Indian and Buddhist Studies* 3.223–231.

Nakamura, H. (1958), "Buddhist logic expounded by means of symbolic logic," *Journal of Indian and Buddhist Studies* 7.375–395.

Nakamura, H. (1964), *Ways of Thinking of Eastern Peoples*, Honolulu.

Nakamura, H. (1967), *A History of the Development of Japanese Thought*, I–II, Tokyo.

Nakamura, H. (1973), "Faith and reason in early Buddhism and Christianity," *Journal of Ecumenical Studies* 10.30–50.

Needham, J. (1954–1965), *Science and Civilization in China*, I–IV, Cambridge.

Neumann, E. (1949), *Ursprungsgeschichte des Bewusstseins*, Zurich.

Nietzsche, F. (1954), *Werke*, I–III, Munich.

Nieuwenhuijze, C. A. O. van (1945), *Šamsu'l-Dīn van Pasai: Bijdrage tot de kennis der Sumatraansche mystiek*, Leiden.

Nilakanta Sastri, K. A. (1955), *A History of South India*, Oxford.

Niwa, Fumio (1966), *The Buddha Tree*, Rutland, Vt., and Tokyo.

Nölle, W. (n.d.), "Lehre und Kult der Kaulas," University of Tübingen, dissertation.

Oberhammer, G. (1965), "Meditation und Mystik im Yoga des Patañjali," *Wiener Zeitschrift für die Kunde Süd- und Ostasiens und Archiv für indische Philosophie* 9.98–118.

Ornstein, R. E. (1972), *The Psychology of Consciousness*, San Francisco.

Otto, R. (1916), *Dīpikā des Nivāsa: Eine indische Heilslehre*, Tübingen.

Otto, R. (1917), *Das Heilige: Über das Irrationale in der Idee des Göttlichen und sein Verhältnis zum Rationalen*, Breslau.

Otto, R. (1923a), *Vischnu-Narayana: Texte zum indischen Gottesmystik*, Jena. (Reprinted.)

Otto, R. (1923b), *Siddhānta des Rāmānuja: Ein Text zur indischen Gottesmystik*, Tübingen. (Reprinted.)

Otto. R. (1930), *Indiens Gnadenreligion und das Christentum*, Gotha.

Otto, R. (1959), *Mysticism East and West: A Comparative Analysis of the Nature of Mysticism*, New York. (First published in 1926.)

Panikkar, R. (1964a), *The Unknown Christ of Hinduism*, London.

Panikkar, R. (1964b), *Kultmysterium in Hinduismus und Christentum*, Munich.

Patris, R. (1948), *La guirlande de l'Iran*, Paris.

Pensa, C. (1969), "On the purification concept in Indian tradition, with special regard to Yoga," *East and West* 19.194–228.

Pines, S., and T. Gelblum (1966), "Al-Bīrūnī's Arabic version of Patañjali's *Yogasūtra*: a translation of his first chapter and a comparison with related Sanskrit texts," *Bulletin of the School of Oriental and African Studies* 29.302–325.

Pott, P. H. (1966), *Yoga and Yantra*, The Hague.

Puech, H. C. (1949), *Le manichéisme*, Paris.

Puech, H. C. (1951), "Temps, histoire et mythe dans le christianisme des premiers siècles," *Proceedings of the 7th Congress for the History of Religions*, Amsterdam, pp. 33–52.

Putnam, H. (1962), "Dreaming and 'depth grammar'" in R. J. Butler (ed.), *Analytical Philosophy*, Oxford, pp. 211–235.

Raju, P. T. (1954), "The principle of four-cornered negation in Indian philosophy," *Review of Metaphysics* 7.694–713.

Ranade, R. D. (1926), *A Constructive Survey of Upanisadic Philosophy*, Poona.

Rawson, P. (1973), *Tantra*, London.

Read, J. (1966), *Prelude to Chemistry: An Outline of Alchemy*, Cambridge and London.

Rele, V. G. (1932), *The Vedic Gods as Figures of Biology*, Bombay.

Renou, L. (1960), *Le destin du Veda dans l'Inde (Etudes védiques et pāṇinéennes, VI)*, Paris.

Renou, L. (1961), *Grammaire sanscrite*, Paris.

Renou, L. (1966–1967), *Etudes védiques et pāṇinéennes*, XV–XVI, Paris.

Rinkes, D. A. (1909), *Abdoerraoef van Singkel: Bijdrage tot de kennis van de mystiek op Sumatra en Java*, Heerenveen, Netherlands.

Robinson, R. H. (1957), "Some logical aspects of Nāgārjuna's system," *Philosophy East and West* 6.291–308.

Robinson, R. H. (1967), *Early Mādhyamika in India and China*, Madison, Milwaukee, and London.

Rösel, R. (1928), *Die psychologischen Grundlagen der Yogapraxis*, Stuttgart.

Ross, W. D. (ed.) (1924), *Aristotle's Metaphysics*, I–II, Oxford.

Ruben, W. (1940), "Schamanismus im alten Indien," *Acta Orientalia* 18.164–205.

Ruben, W. (1954), *Geschichte der indischen Philosophie*, Berlin.

Ruegg, D. S. (1971), "On the knowability and expressibility of absolute reality in Buddhism," *Journal of Indian and Buddhist Studies* 20.489–495.

Russell, B. (1953), *Mysticism and Logic*, London.

Ryle, G. (1949), *The Concept of Mind*, London.

Schär, H. (1946), *Religion und Seele in der Psychologie C. G. Jungs*, Zurich.

Schär, H. (1950), *Erlösungsvorstellungen und ihre psychologischen Aspekte*, Zurich.

Schayer, S. (1931), *Ausgewählte Kapitel aus der Prasannapadā*, Krakow.

Schayer, S. (1938), *Contributions to the Problem of Time in Indian Philosophy (Przyczynki do Zagadnienia Czasu w Filozofii Indyjskiej)*, Krakow.

Schomerus, H. W. (1936), *Meister Eckehart und Manikka-Vasgar: Mystik auf deutschen und indischen Boden*, Gütersloh, Germany.

Schultes, R. E. (1969), "Hallucinogens of plant origin," *Science* 163.245–254.

Schultz, J., and W. Luthe (1959), *Autogenic Training*, New York.

Schurmann, F. (1968), *Ideology and Organization in Communist China*, Berkeley and Los Angeles.

Senart, E. (1930), *Chāndogya-upaniṣad, traduite et annotée*, Paris.

Sivaramamurti, C. (1963), *South Indian Bronzes*, New Delhi.

Smith, H. (1964), "Do drugs have religious import?" *Journal of Philosophy* 61.517–530.

Smythies, J. R. (1953), "The Mescalin Phenomena," *British Journal for the Philosophy of Science* 3.339–347.

Snellgrove, D. L. (1959), *The Hevajra Tantra*, I–II, Oxford.

Snellgrove, D. (1961), *Himalayan Pilgrimage*, Oxford.

Sreekrishna Sarma, E. R. (1968), "Keśin Dārbhya and the legend of his Dīkṣā," *Annals of the Bhandarkar Oriental Research Institute* 48–49.241–245.

Srinivas, M. N. (1952), *Religion and Society Among the Coorgs of South India*, Oxford.

Staal, J. F. (1959), "Über die Idee der Toleranz im Hinduismus," *Kairos. Zeitschrift für Religionswissenschaft und Theologie* 1.215–218.

Staal, J. F. (1960), "Means of formalisation in Indian and Western logic," *Atti del XII Congresso Internazionale di Filosofia*, Firenze 10.221–227.

Staal, J. F. (1961a), *Nambudiri Veda Recitation*, The Hague.

Staal, J. F. (1961b), *Advaita and Neo-Platonism: A Critical Study in Comparative Philosophy*, Madras.

Staal, J. F. (1961c), Review of *Contributions to Indian Sociology*, 4, in *Journal of the American Oriental Society* 81.147–149.

Staal, J. F. (1962a), "Negation and the law of contradiction in Indian thought," *Bulletin of the School of Oriental and African Studies* 25.52–71.

Staal, J. F. (1962b), Review of Zaehner (1960), *Journal of the American Oriental Society* 82.96–98.

Staal, J. F. (1963), "Sanskrit and Sanskritization," *Journal of Asian Studies* 22.261–275.

Staal, J. F. (1964a), *Vedic Ritual in South India*, Utrecht (film).

Staal, J. F. (1964b), Review of Hacker (1960), *Journal of the American Oriental Society* 84.464–467.

Staal, J. F. (1965), "Euclid and Pāṇini," *Philosophy East and West*, 15.99–116.

Staal, J. F. (1967), *Word Order in Sanskrit and Universal Grammar*, Dordrecht.

Staal, J. F. (1970a), "De academicus als Nowhere Man," *De Gids* 133:7/8, 96–159.

Staal, J. F. (1970b), "Review of G. Cardona, Studies in Indian Grammarians, I: The method of description reflected in the Śivasūtras," *Language* 46.502–507.

Staal, J. F. (1970c), "Cambodia: Sanskrit Inscriptions," *New York Review of Books* 15:1.15.

Staal, J. F. (ed.) (1972), *A Reader on the Sanskrit Grammarians*, Cambridge.

Staal, J. F. (1973), "The concept of *pakṣa* in Indian logic," *Journal of Indian Philosophy* 2.156–166.

Staal, J. F. (1974), Review of Danto (1972), *Journal of Philosophy*, 71.174–181.

Staal, J. F. (unpublished), "The Academic Nowhere," 276 pp.; stencil.

Streng, F. J. (1971), "The Buddhist doctrine of two truths as religious philosophy," *Journal of Indian Philosophy* 1.262–271.

Suzuki, D. T. (1960), *Manual of Zen Buddhism*, New York.

Suzuki, D. T., E. Fromm, and R. de Martino (1960), *Zen Buddhism and Psychoanalysis*, New York.

Tart, C. T. (ed.) (1969), *Altered States of Consciousness: A Book of Readings*, New York.

Thibaut, G. (transl.) (1890), *The Vedānta-Sūtras with the Commentary by Śaṅkarācārya*, I–II, Oxford.

Timmons, B., and J. Kamiya (1970), "The psychology and physiology of meditation and related phenomena: a bibliography," *Journal of Transpersonal Psychology* 2.41–59.

Tsuji, N. (1966a), "Kēshin Dārubiya o megutte" ("Concerning Keśin Dārbhya"), Part I, *Kanakura Hakase kohi kinen: Indogaku bukkyōgaku ronshū (Festschrift Dr. Enshō Kanakura: Indological and Buddhist Studies)*, Tokyo.

Tsuji, N. (1966b), "Kēshin Dārubiya o megutte" ("Concerning Keśin Dārbhya"), Part II, *Suzuki gakujutsu zaidan nenpō (Annals of the Foundation Daisetusu Suzuki)* 3.29–34.

Tsuji, N. (1971), "Shiāba Ashuba monogatari" ("The Śyāvāśva legend"), *Kindaichi Hakase beiju kinen ronshū (Festschrift Kyōsuke Kindaichi)*, Tokyo.

Van Buitenen, J. A. B. (1968), *Rāmānuja on the Bhagavadgītā*, Delhi.

Van Buitenen, J. A. B. (transl.) (1973), *The Mahābhārata: I. The Book of the Beginning*, Chicago and London.

Von Grünebaum, E. (1961), *Medieval Islam*, Chicago and London.

Vos, F., and E. Zürcher (1964), *Spel zonder snaren: enige beschouwingen over Zen*, Deventer, Netherlands.

Waardenburg, J. D. J. (1961), *L'Islam dans le miroir de l'Occident*, The Hague.

Waley, A. (n.d.), *The Way and Its Power: A Study of the Tao Tê Ching and its Place in Chinese Thought*, New York.

Wallace, R. K. (1970a), *The Physiological Effects of Transcendental Meditation*, Los Angeles.

Wallace, R. K. (1970b), "Physiological effects of transcendental meditation," *Science* 167.1751–1754.

Wallace, R. K., and H. Benson (1972), "The physiology of meditation," *Scientific American* 226:2.85–90.

Warren, H. C. (1947), *Buddhism in Translations*, Cambridge.

Wasson, R. G. (1968), *Soma: Divine Mushroom of Immortality*, New York.

Wasson, R. G. (1970), "Soma: comments inspired by Professor Kuiper's review," *Indo-Iranian Journal* 12.286–298.

Wasson, R. G. (1971), "The Soma of the Rig-Veda: what was it?" *Journal of the American Oriental Society* 91.169–187.

Wasson, R. G. (1972), *Soma and the Fly-Agaric: Rejoinder to Professor Brough*, Cambridge, Mass.

Watson, B. (transl.) (1964), *Chuang Tzu: Basic Writings*, New York.

Watts, A. W. (1961), *Psychotherapy East and West*, New York.

Watts, A. W. (1962), *The Joyous Cosmology*, New York.

Watts, A. W. (1967), *This is IT and Other Essays on Zen and Spiritual Experience*, New York.

Welch, H. (1966), *Taoism: The Parting of the Way*, Boston.

Wensinck, A. J. (1940), *La pensée de Ghazzālī*, Paris.

Wensinck, A. J., and J. H. Kramers (1941), *Handwörterbuch des Islam*, Leiden.

Wertheim, W. F. (1974), *Evolution and Revolution: The Rising Waves of Emancipation*, Harmondsworth.

Whitehead, A. N. (1933), *Adventures of Ideas*, New York.

Wittgenstein, L. (1958), *Philosophical Investigations*, Oxford.

Woods, J. H. (transl.) (1927), *The Yoga-System of Patañjali*, Cambridge.

Zaehner, R. C. (1960), *Hindu and Muslim Mysticism*, London.

Zaehner, R. C. (1961), *Mysticism Sacred and Profane*, New York.

Zide, A. R. K., and K. V. Zvelebil (1970), reviews in *Language* 46.952–968.

Zimmer, H. (1926), *Kunstform und Yoga im indischen Kultbild*, Berlin.

Zimmer, H. (1946), *Myths and Symbols in Indian Art and Civilization*, New York.

Zimmer, H. (1944), *Der Weg zum Selbst: Lehre und Leben des indischen Heiligen Shri Ramana Maharshi aus Tiruvannamalai*, ed. C. G. Jung, Zurich.

Zimmer, H. (1951), *Philosophies of India*, London.

Zoete, B. de (1953), *The Other Mind: A Study of Dance in South India*, London.

Index